THE WINNING FORMULA

COLLINS

THE WINNING FORMULA

THE FOOTBALL ASSOCIATION

SOCCER SKILLS AND TACTICS

CHARLES HUGHES
F.A. Director of Coaching and Education

COLLINS

*Title Pages: (Top)
Holland's Ruud Gullit
rises to head the ball,
causing problems for the
USSR defence in a
1988 European
Championship match.
(Centre) Arsenal's
Michael Thomas
dribbles past Luton
Town's goalkeeper Andy
Dibble in the 1988
Littlewoods Cup final at
Wembley. (Bottom) In
pursuit of the ball,
Argentina's Diego
Maradona hurdles a
prone South Korean
defender during a 1986
World Cup match in
Mexico.*

William Collins Sons & Co Ltd

London   Glasgow   Sydney   Auckland
Toronto   Johannesburg

First published in 1990

© The Football Association 1990

A CIP catalogue record for this book is available
from the British Library

Editor: Rick Morris

Assistant editor: Ray Granger

Designers: Mander Gooch Callow

Computerized diagrams: Mandy Sherliker and Vanessa Wood

Illustrations: Michael Kirby

Photographs: Bob Thomas Sports Photography

Typeset by SX Composing Ltd, Rayleigh, Essex

Printed in Great Britain by William Collins Sons & Co Ltd

ISBN 0 00 191160 0   PB
ISBN 0 00 185354 6   HB

CONTENTS

R. H. Evans C.B.E.

**BRITISH AEROSPACE
PUBLIC LIMITED COMPANY**
11 STRAND
LONDON WC2N 5JT
Telephone: 01-930 1020
Facsimile: 01-839 4774
Telex: 919221

Direct Line: 01-389

R H EVANS C.B.E.
<u>Chief Executive</u>

It gives me great pleasure to introduce to you The Football Association's principal training and coaching book "The Winning Formula", which I am sure will not only become the basis for the future development of football here in the United Kingdom, but also make a substantial contribution to the game worldwide.

At the present time British Aerospace is leading several important initiatives for the expansion of British involvement in the fields of sport and youth welfare overseas, and clearly recognises the essential role and contribution of The Football Association. It has, therefore, invited The Association to play its part through the introduction of its educational schemes and services into these exciting international collaborative programmes.

All of us at British Aerospace recognise the tremendous achievements of The Football Association throughout its long and celebrated history, and look forward to working closely with it in the years to come for the success of these objectives and the expansion and development of sport as a whole.

[signature]

Registered in England & Wales No. 1470151   Registered Office 11 Strand London WC2N 5JT

Introduction

Association Football is the most popular game in the world. The reason for this is its appeal to both players and spectators, an appeal based on pure fun and enjoyment. Soccer is a very emotional game, full of joy and despair, triumph and tragedy; often it swings wildly between these extremes in the course of a single match, bringing drama and exhilaration into the lives of millions throughout the world.

It is hardly surprising that such a passionate game should arouse strong opinions, or that those opinions should vary greatly. From the first, soccer has always been long on opinions and short on facts; analysis has been rare or non-existent. Throughout the history of the game, coaches and managers have made claims and propounded theories based on opinions rather than facts.

One undeniable fact is that soccer has followed a basically negative and defensive trend for the last thirty or so years. One simple statistic illustrates this. In the 1954 World Cup finals 140 goals were scored in 26 matches, an average of 5.4 per game. In the 1986 finals exactly twice as many games produced 132 goals, an average of 2.5 per game. Measured in these terms, it can be seen that football is not as good as it was.

What makes soccer exciting both to play and to watch is the ebb and flow of the game: end to end play. It is goals, shots at goal, spectacular saves, near misses and other goalmouth incidents; it is players crossing the ball in full flight or completing skilful dribbles. Few players or spectators enjoy bouts of prolonged midfield play. However, the fact that fewer goals are scored also means fewer shots at goal, fewer crosses, fewer goalmouth incidents. In other words, modern football has less of everything that produces excitement.

The reason for this lies not in new, efficient defensive strategies so much as a misguided attacking strategy, that of possession football. Those who believe in possession play argue that a team without the ball cannot score and that therefore a team which keeps the ball for long periods is more likely to score.

The overwhelming evidence is that the proponents of possession play are mistaken. The fact is that the longer a team takes to build an attack when it has possession of the ball, expressed in the number of consecutive passes in a move, the more time the defending team has to recover, regroup and reorganize. As a general rule, in soccer time is always on the side of the defenders. The logical result of possession play is a succession of goalless draws.

To point out this flaw in the theory of possession play is not an endorsement of kick and rush tactics, with the ball being punted forward in the general direction of the opponents' penalty area at every opportunity.

Success comes as might be expected, in a balance between the extremes of possession play and kick and rush. Direct play involves moving the ball forward in a controlled way. The amount of possession, expressed in terms of the number of consecutive passes in a move, should be just enough to achieve the objective of creating a chance of a shot at goal.

All of the facts point to the conclusion that when the number of consecutive passes in a move exceeds five, the chances of creating a scoring opportunity at the end of the move decrease. The more the ball is passed around, the more remote become the chances of a shot at goal. Of course, the chances of scoring a goal are never zero, even if there are ten or more passes in the move, but the odds get longer with every extra pass. No more than 3% of goals (less than one goal in thirty) is scored from a move involving ten or more consecutive passes.

Some coaches have argued that the value of possession play is to manoeuvre opposing players out of position or to break their concentration with a series of crossfield passes that repeatedly change the direction of play. This idea is unsupported by analysis.

The simple fact is that teams are at their most vulnerable at the moment they lose possession of the ball. It is then that players are most likely to lose concentration and fail to defend correctly, giving their opponents a chance to play the ball forward. Failure to play the ball forward in these circumstances gives defenders time to recover their concentration and their position. The team with the ball will retain possession but lose the initiative.

The Winning Formula, developed as a result of analyzing live matches and films of top-class football matches, is concerned with seizing the initiative and then retaining it by playing – both as individuals and a team – to a system which gives the best percentage chance of winning matches. That it also increases the number of goals, shots and excitement in a match is a welcome bonus for players and spectators alike.

The purpose of this book, and the video tapes which have been produced in conjunction with it, is to illustrate the various elements involved in direct play and show how these elements link together to make a Winning Formula. No-one should expect players, and still less coaches and managers, to change their beliefs and methods without persuasion. All that can be asked is that they look at the evidence presented here with an open and inquiring mind. If they do this, then they will surely come to one inevitable conclusion; controlled direct play will give any team at any level of skill the best chance of winning football matches.

Although direct play is the best strategy, it is not all that is required for success. It is certainly not a substitute for physical fitness. Indeed, sustaining direct play through a 90-minute game requires higher levels of fitness than other ways of playing. Because of this we have conducted research into the fitness levels required, working with both the F.A.'s Human Performance Department at Lilleshall and the Sports Science Department at Loughborough University. The series of which this book is a part will also include a book and a video tape on the specific subject of fitness for football.

Nor is The Winning Formula a substitute for good technique.

It is a fact, at every level of soccer, that approximately 85% of goals – more than four out of every five – are scored from five consecutive passes or less. **The analysis of the number of consecutive passes involved in scoring shows diminishing returns for moves involving high numbers of consecutive passes.**

PASSING MOVEMENTS PRIOR TO GOALS

Number of Passes	0	1	2	3	4	5	6	7	8	9	10	11	12	13	14	15	16
Total Goals 202	53	29	35	26	17	16	7	7	1	5	2	2	2	–	–	–	–

◄——— 87% ———► ◄——— 13% ———►

More than a quarter of the goals in our sample of 109 top-flight matches are recorded as being the result of no passes ('0' passes). These are goals scored directly from set plays, from defensive rebounds, or when an attacker dispossesses a defender or intercepts a pass and goes through to score. Could it be that moves involving a high number of consecutive passes end with a rebound or set play? We have analyzed the passing movements immediately prior to the '0' pass goals. **Goals from '0' pass movements were preceded by moves of six or more passes in just 11% of cases.**

PASSING MOVEMENTS IMMEDIATELY PRIOR TO THE '0' PASS GOALS

Number of Passes	0	1	2	3	4	5	6	7	8	9	10	11	12	13	14
Total '0' Pass Goals 53	12	13	11	5	5	1	2	1	1	1	–	–	–	–	1

◄——— 89% ———► ◄——— 11% ———►

Some people – and none more so than soccer coaches and tacticians – are suspicious of statistics. Few, however, would ignore the evidence of this research and these statistics, and the inescapable conclusion to be drawn from them. World soccer has been moving in the wrong strategic direction for the better part of 30 years.

Further statistics that indicate the benefits of direct play are included in the section *Direct Play – the Analysis,* at the end of the book.

Successfully using The Winning Formula requires good technical ability and skilful application of a number of key techniques. These techniques are identified and highlighted in this book. Some very basic elements of these techniques, designed specifically for children aged 7-13 years, form the basis of the Football Association's new *Soccer Star* scheme, for which a book and video tape were released in September 1988 as part of this overall series. The tests in this scheme have been very carefully researched for reliability and validity by the Social Statistics Department of Southampton University. Most of all the *Soccer Star* tests are designed to encourage young children to practice essential techniques in an enjoyable way.

Some people see advocates of direct

play as people who wish to sacrifice the fine skills and beauty of the game in order to win. Critics of direct play say that it is all about playing long balls forward to the exclusion of all else. This is simply untrue. Certainly, the ability to hit long, accurate forward passes is an essential weapon in the armoury of outstanding players, but so is the ability to control the ball, to turn with it, run with it, dribble with it and cross it; just as important is the ability to head or shoot for goal with accuracy, to say nothing of a wide range of defensive techniques. An outstanding player, in direct play as in any other system, is one who has mastered all these techniques and who has the skill to know which technique to use in any and every situation.

Successful players also need to develop the right mental attitude. Assertiveness and self-confidence are essential to the total performance. Assertiveness is needed to gain and retain the initiative, and confidence allows a player to use his skill and accept responsibility. When the right attitude is combined with high levels of physical fitness and technical expertise, the right method – direct play – truly becomes a Winning Formula.

The author's background

My experience of match analysis began in January 1964 when I joined the staff of The Football Association as Assistant Director of Coaching, and Manager of the England Amateur team and the Great Britain Olympic team. At the F.A. headquarters at Lancaster Gate was a library of 16mm films of F.A. Cup finals and International matches. Between 1964 and 1967 I watched all these matches and extracted all the goals. These goals were then analyzed more closely to establish what were the key factors in scoring goals and winning matches.

The results of this analysis were used in the playing method of all the International teams I managed between 1964 and 1974 – 77 matches in all. The essence of this work was published in 1973 in a book entitled *Tactics and Teamwork* and a series of 11 films under the same title.

The work of analyzing football matches has continued ever since. In the early part of 1982 I had the pleasure of meeting a wonderful man named Charles Reep, who had been analyzing football matches for 30 years, successfully advising a number of Football League clubs. As a result of this meeting I persuaded my Personal Assistant at The F.A., Mandy Primus, to use her shorthand skills to help me in further analysis of football matches. Her method of notation is different from that of Charles Reep, but the principle is the same. The method of analysis itself, which I devised around 25 years ago, is actually different from Charles Reep's.

Charles Reep has probably analyzed more matches than any other person. He and I have, despite our different methods, reached broadly similar conclusions. At our first meeting, he told me that he had analyzed one of our Amateur International matches and had been impressed by the effective direct play of the England team. He assumed that I had heard of him and his methods while I assumed he had read my book *Tactics and Teamwork*!

Although Charles Reep and I had come by our strategic philosophy by different routes, there was no disagreement on the major conclusion; the strategy of direct play is far preferable to that of possession football. The facts are irrefutable and the evidence overwhelming.

The author, Charles Hughes, who is Director of Coaching and Education at The Football Association, with his Personal Assistant, Mandy Primus.

PASSING
AND SUPPORT PLAY

The two techniques most often used in soccer are controlling the ball and passing it. On most occasions when a player has the ball he will pass to a team-mate; on other occasions he will either run with the ball, dribble or shoot. Passing, therefore, is a vital technique. To be more precise, it is vital that a player should have a good range of techniques for passing the ball. **There is no substitute for good technique in passing and there is no strategy which caters for inaccurate passing.**

Good passing, though, is not entirely a matter of good technique. It depends in the first place on understanding; understanding what is required and what will bring the best results, and understanding what one is capable of technically.

FORWARD PASSING

The first requirement is that players and coaches alike should understand that soccer is a forward thinking, forward passing and forward moving game. This produces not only the best chance of success but also the greatest enjoyment both for players and spectators.

Attitude plays an important part in both success and failure. Negative attitudes breed failure, positive attitudes lead to success. Analysis shows that possession play – movements with high numbers of consecutive passes – produces negative results. This strategy is the result of negative, defensive thinking – of not losing possession of the ball. Direct play, on the other hand, embodies a positive attitude. It is about playing to win, rather than playing to avoid defeat; it is not conditioned by a fear of losing the ball but by a desire to score.

Upon receiving the ball a player should instantly ask himself one question: can I play the ball forward? If the answer is 'yes', then he must choose from four possible actions; a shot, a dribble, a run with the ball or a pass. The first three choices are dealt with elsewhere in the book. Should he decide to pass the ball forward, the next step is to select the appropriate passing technique.

THE PASSING CHECK LIST

A good pass is an important attacking weapon. The types of pass listed below are dealt with in order of priority from an attacker's point of view – the most lethal comes first. Broadly, there are five possible types of pass.

1. A pass into space behind the defence.

2. A pass to the feet of the most advanced attacker.

3. A pass beyond at least one defender.

4. A crossfield pass to switch the line of attack.

5. A pass backwards to a supporting player.

1. Passes into space behind the defence

A pass into space behind the opposing defence causes defenders more problems than any other. Having decided to pass the ball forward, all players, including the goalkeeper, should look to see if a pass to the back of the defence is possible before deciding on a less ambitious route.

The ball can either be played between defenders on the ground or over their heads with a chip or lofted drive, depending on the distance to be covered. Of course, players should only make passes to the back of the defence if they can see a team-mate positioned to take advantage of the pass.

Defenders are especially vulnerable to passes behind them immediately after their side loses possession. They may have 'pushed up' too far in support of an attack, leaving more space behind them than usual and one or more of them may have lost concentration. It is often possible to expose defenders with a well aimed pass behind them before they have corrected their positions and gathered their concentration. If the ball is won in the defending or middle third of the field this may involve a pass of between 30 and 60 yards. The three principal channels to look for are shown on the next two pages.

Previous page: Bryan Robson, captain of England, showing good balance and technique as he plays the ball forward. His non-kicking foot is alongside the ball, his head is still and his eyes are on the ball.

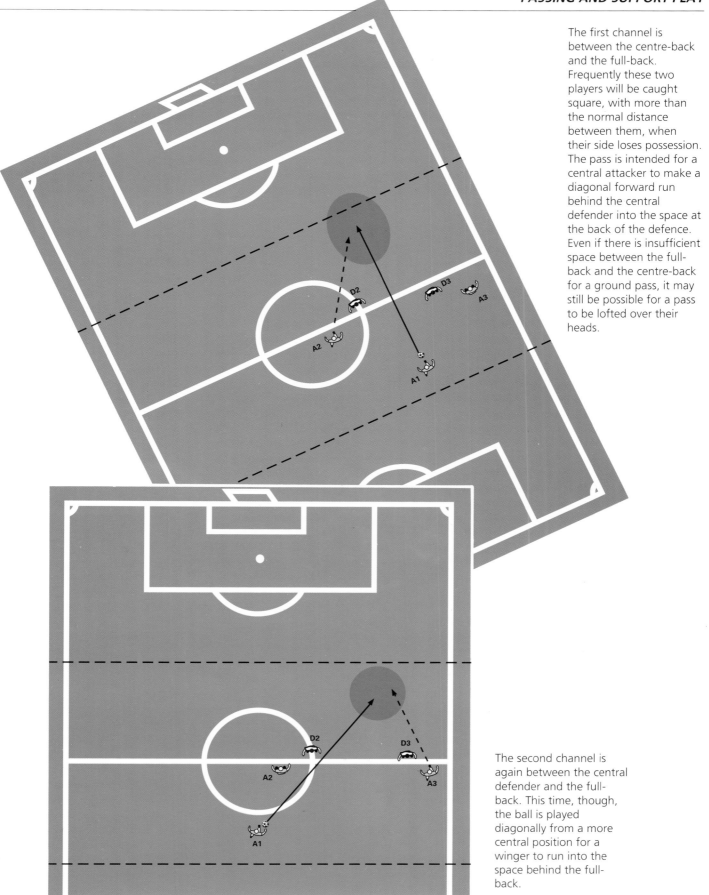

The first channel is between the centre-back and the full-back. Frequently these two players will be caught square, with more than the normal distance between them, when their side loses possession. The pass is intended for a central attacker to make a diagonal forward run behind the central defender into the space at the back of the defence. Even if there is insufficient space between the full-back and the centre-back for a ground pass, it may still be possible for a pass to be lofted over their heads.

The second channel is again between the central defender and the full-back. This time, though, the ball is played diagonally from a more central position for a winger to run into the space behind the full-back.

The third channel offers two possibilities.

(1) A diagonal pass over the heads of the central defenders into the space behind them. This pass is intended for a central attacker making a forward run to receive the ball in space behind the defence.

(2) A longer diagonal pass over the heads of the central defenders into the space behind the full-back on the opposite flank. This pass is intended for a winger running into the space behind the full-back.

A well-placed pass to the back of the defence takes defenders out of the game. Sergei Aleinikov of the USSR tries to recover as Holland's Ronald Koeman runs on to a through ball.

Purists may argue that such passing opportunities should not occur at the highest level. No doubt that is true. Despite this, the fact is that they do occur at the highest level and especially so at the moment when one team gains possession from the other.

The diagonal pass to the back of the defence is possibly the most lethal pass of all. Every player should develop a good understanding and appreciation of this. The technique for passing the ball over long distances will be dealt with later in this chapter. At the moment it is enough to know that the ability to make long, accurate forward passes is an essential weapon in the armoury of attacking players and an essential part of effective direct play.

Analysis shows that long forward passing is a factor in 27% of all goals scored. Long diagonal passes are an element in 12% of goals, and long direct passes are an element in 15% of goals.

2. Passing to feet

If a forward pass to the back of the defence is not possible, then the next best option is to play the ball to the feet of the most advanced attacking player. Apart from the pass to the back of the defence, this pass is the most penetrative; it is played behind most of the opponents, causing them to turn and retreat.

The quality of the pass is important. It must give the attacker the chance either to screen the ball and turn his opponent or to screen and hold the ball until support is available. Pass (1) is not good because the defender D2 would have a good chance of winning the ball. Pass (2) is much better because it gives A2 an excellent chance of successfully screening the ball.

3. Other forward passes

If a pass cannot be made to the most forward attacking player, the next best option is to play the ball past as many opponents as possible. Even playing the ball past one opponent will cause some problems, not only for the player who is beaten but also for the other defenders who will have to adjust their positions as a consequence.

4. Switching the attack

If there is no space to play the ball forward, the attacker should next check to see if he can switch the direction of the attack. A player on the right side of the field should look left, and vice versa. Very often if play is tight on one side of the field, there will be space on the other, with attacking players unmarked and ready to exploit it. If this is the case, switch the play as quickly as possible with a cross-field ball and allow a team-mate to use the space to initiate direct play.

5. Passing back – the last resort

If it is not possible to switch play, then, and only then, the ball should be played back to a supporting player who should have the time, space and field of vision to play the ball forward and initiate direct play.

This check list is meant to encourage players to look for the best attacking possibility first and settle for the lowest priority pass last. The better that players become at making these decisions, the more often direct play will be the result. The more possession play is emphasized, the more likely it is that the lowest priority pass will be selected.

SUPPORT IN ATTACK

Defenders will attempt to pressurize the man with the ball and prevent him passing the ball forward. The purpose of support in attack is to release that pressure. This is done by a player getting into position to receive a ball played back to him and then doing what his pressurized team-mate could not – play it forward.

The better a team pressurizes, the more important it is for their opponents to support each other. It is very difficult to build successful attacks consistently without good support. It is important that supporting players move into position early so that closely marked team-mates have the option of passing the ball with their first touch.

The supporting player has two main decisions to make; he must find the right distance from the man with the ball, and the right angle.

Supporting distance

How far away a supporting player should be from the man with the ball depends whereabouts they are on the pitch. In the attacking third of the field it will almost certainly be necessary to support at a closer distance, perhaps five or six yards, as opposed to the middle and defending third, when the distance could increase to between 10 and 25 yards.

In the attacking third it will usually be necessary to play in a confined space and at times at maximum speed – one-touch soccer. This is not to say that such considerations will never apply in the middle third or, on occasions, in the defending third, but it is far less likely.

Ground conditions, too, affect supporting positions. On bumpy pitches players need a little more time to control the ball and the supporting players should stand further away. The pace of pitches varies according to weather conditions and it is not unusual for parts of the same pitch to vary in pace. On slow, wet pitches, the support needs to be closer than on fast, dry pitches.

The angle of support

The supporting player should take up a position where he has a wide field of forward vision and can receive the ball.

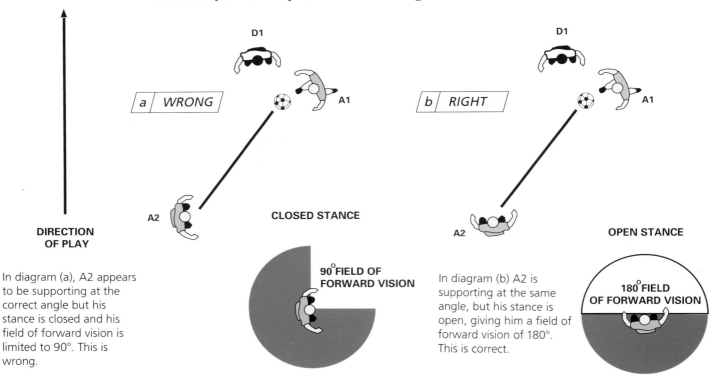

DIRECTION OF PLAY

a | WRONG

D1

A1

A2

CLOSED STANCE

90° FIELD OF FORWARD VISION

b | RIGHT

D1

A1

A2

OPEN STANCE

180° FIELD OF FORWARD VISION

In diagram (a), A2 appears to be supporting at the correct angle but his stance is closed and his field of forward vision is limited to 90°. This is wrong.

In diagram (b) A2 is supporting at the same angle, but his stance is open, giving him a field of forward vision of 180°. This is correct.

The widest possible range of forward vision is particularly important as it is likely that the supporting player will want to change the direction of play. He should certainly be considering the possibilities of a diagonal forward pass. It is not possible for him to do this properly unless he is facing forward.

There is, of course, no point in a player taking up a supporting position affording a wide range of forward vision if he cannot receive the ball there.

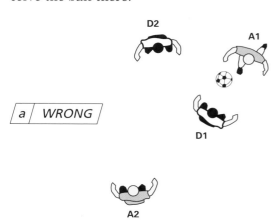

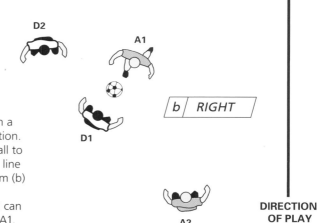

In diagram (a) A2 is in a poor supporting position. A1 cannot play the ball to him since D1 is in the line of the pass. In diagram (b) A2 is at a good supporting angle and can receive the ball from A1.

DIRECTION OF PLAY

The point has already been made that the supporting player will look to change the point of the attack.

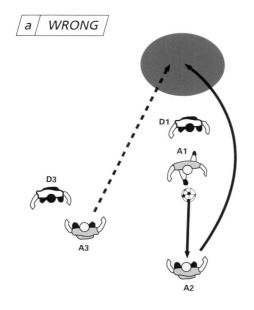

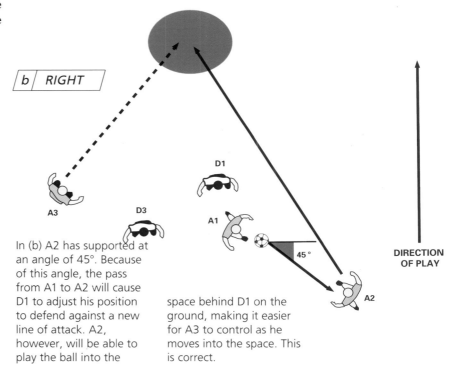

In (b) A2 has supported at an angle of 45°. Because of this angle, the pass from A1 to A2 will cause D1 to adjust his position to defend against a new line of attack. A2, however, will be able to play the ball into the space behind D1 on the ground, making it easier for A3 to control as he moves into the space. This is correct.

DIRECTION OF PLAY

In (a) A2 has taken up a supporting position in line with A1 and D1. The pass back from A1 to A2 is not likely to cause D1 to adjust his position. Also, in order to exploit the space behind D1, A2 must make a difficult chip over his head, and A3, running into the space to receive the pass, will have to control a bouncing ball. This is incorrect.

The correct distance and angle of support, then, is important to achieve the following.

⚽ A full field of forward vision.

⚽ A position in which to receive the ball comfortably.

⚽ A position which changes the line of the attack.

⚽ A position with time and space to play the ball forward.

The importance of support in one-touch play

One-touch play is of the utmost importance in exploiting space – especially restricted space – in the attacking third of the field. Playing the ball and moving quickly into a close supporting position, at the correct angle, is an essential skill if shooting opportunities are to be created in tight situations.

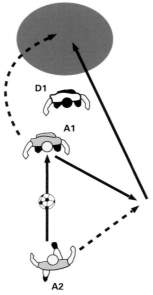

A2 has played the ball to A1. As the ball is travelling, A2 is moving into a close supporting position at a wide angle to receive a one-touch pass from A1, who spins away in the opposite direction to the pass and attacks the space behind D1. This presents D1 with a dilemma. The ball has been played to his immediate opponent and away again without him being able to challenge for the ball. Worse, the ball has gone one way and his opponent has moved in the opposite direction. Does he follow the ball? Does he turn and follow his opponent? Does he retreat into the space? Whatever decision he makes, one thing is certain; he had better do it quickly, or A2 will play the ball with one touch into the space behind D1 for A1 to run on to.

One-touch football is important and it is impossible to achieve without good support. Played well, at the right time in the correct circumstances, it is a joy to watch and a joy for the attackers to play. It epitomizes the art of playing football – doing the simple things quickly and well.

When not to support

Part of the skill in being a good supporting player is in knowing when to support and when to move into positions ahead of the ball. There is one simple rule; players should stop supporting when the player in possession no longer needs support, when he has turned and achieved the space in which to play the ball forward. If there is any doubt, the supporting player should hold his position. If there is no doubt, however, the supporting player should move forward, with one of two aims in view.

1. To create an extra possibility for a forward pass.

2. To act as a decoy in order to draw defenders out of key positions.

Both these possibilities are considered in full in the chapter on *Forward Runs*.

The importance of turning with the ball

Techniques of turning with the ball are dealt with in the chapter on *Creating Space*. However, it is appropriate to refer to turning at this point. Frequently players pass the ball backwards when they have room to turn and pass forward. This is wrong for two reasons: it slows down the momentum of the attack and allows defenders to recover; and the opportunity to send an extra player into an advanced attacking position is lost. Players can help their team-mates to turn more often simply by giving an early call of "Turn" when they see adequate space is available. Remember: anything which contributes to increasing the speed and momentum of an attack will also contribute to the increased discomfiture of defenders.

South American sides tend to build attacks with many short passes rather than using incisive long balls. Here, Uruguay's Herrera plays a push pass inside his Argentinian opponent.

THE SKILL OF PASSING

There are five basic skills involved in passing.

1 Disguise.

2 Pass selection.

3 Timing of the release of the ball.

4 Weighting, or pacing, the ball.

5 Accuracy.

1. Disguise

Defenders will always try to make the play predictable. Attackers, therefore, must try to do the opposite, to make it more difficult for defenders to read the game. The best way to do this is for attackers to pretend to make one movement and then make another – to disguise their intentions. Players who can disguise their intentions and make the play unpredictable are very difficult to play against.

There are many simple ways of disguising:

pretending to play the ball and then holding it; pretending to stop the ball then letting it run; pretending to pass in one direction then passing in another direction. In every case the pretence, or false movement, must be exaggerated. It is important that the opponent should get a very clear view and indication of what the attacker is not going to do!

The purpose of disguise is twofold; to create space and passing angles which did not exist before and to deceive defenders into adopting false or poor defending positions.

2. Pass selection

The type of pass one selects should depend on what one wants to achieve. If a long diagonal ball to the back of the defence is possible, but there are defenders in the way, then a lofted pass will reach its target and a ground ball will probably be intercepted. Alternatively, if the ground route is clear, then a lofted pass would be the wrong choice, as the player receiving the pass will have a control problem he should not have had.

The skill in passing is largely a matter of selecting the right technique to do the job at the right time.

3. Timing the pass

A correctly timed pass puts the passer's team-mate in a position of maximum advantage while making the defenders' jobs as difficult as possible.

If the ball is released before the space is available or before there is a team-mate positioned and ready to take advantage of it, then it is being released too early. On most occasions, though, a mistimed pass is too late.

Sometimes the player with the ball does not notice that the pass is on; sometimes he hesitates and gives the defenders time to cut down space and seal off passing angles; sometimes the player for whom the pass is intended runs offside or into a poor position. Whatever the problem, the primary cause is the passer playing with his head down and failing to look up and observe play unfolding in front of him.

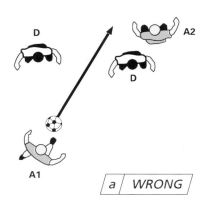

In diagram (a) A1 has allowed A2 to run into an offside position before releasing the ball; the pass, therefore, is too late. In (b) the timing of the pass is correct; A1 has released the ball when A2 is just onside.

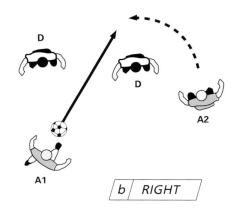

a | WRONG

b | RIGHT

4. The weight or pace of the pass

Ideally defenders would rather win the ball by intercepting a pass than making a tackle. They can only do this, though, if the pass is weighted incorrectly or is inaccurate.

Passes that are too slow – underweighted – will be intercepted. Passes that are too fast – overweighted – may go out of play, or to an opponent; or they will present control problems for the receiver; at the very least they will give him insufficient time in which to create space.

A good pass is one weighted to reach its target at a pace which creates or maintains necessary space and gives the receiver the minimum of control problems.

In diagram (a), A1 has passed the ball with insufficient pace to beat the defenders and it is intercepted.

In diagram (b), A1 has played the pass with too much pace and it has gone over the goal-line before A2 can reach it.

In (c), the pass is correctly weighted; it has beaten both defenders and A2 has reached it in space behind the defence.

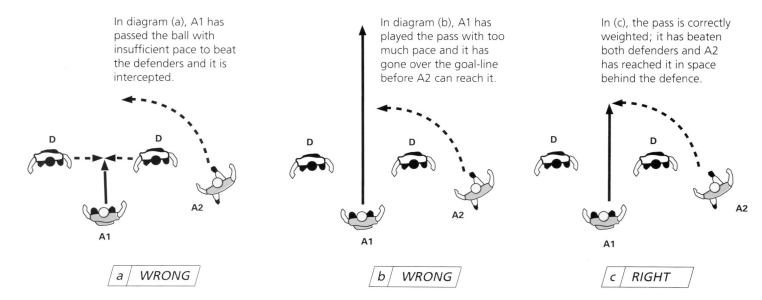

a | WRONG

b | WRONG

c | RIGHT

5. Accuracy

Accuracy is not everything in passing, but everything else counts for nothing if the pass is inaccurate. Accuracy depends on good technique. The technique required differs according to the situation, however, so it is necessary to master a wide range of passing techniques. Types of pass and the techniques involved are now considered in detail.

PASSING TECHNIQUES

Many of the following passing techniques can be used in shooting situations, where accurate placement or power are required. These situations are dealt with more thoroughly in the chapter on *Shooting*. No matter what type of pass (or shot) is played, the head should always be steady and the eyes should be looking down at the ball to ensure a firm, clean contact.

THE PUSH PASS

This pass, made with the inside of the foot, is the most reliable technique for short, accurate passes.

The kicking foot is turned outward so that the side of the boot makes contact with the ball at a right angle to the line of the pass.

The ankle must be firm. In order to keep the pass low, the boot should make contact through the middle of the ball.

1. The push pass – the part of the foot used to make contact with the ball.

Advantage

⚽ *The push pass offers the best guarantee of accuracy because of the large surface of the boot presented to the ball.*

Disadvantages

⚽ *The pass is easy for defenders to predict.*

⚽ *It is difficult to generate power with this technique, so it is unsuitable for long passing.*

⚽ *It is a difficult pass to make on the run as it is not possible to position correctly without interrupting the stride pattern.*

2. **The non-kicking foot** should be placed far enough to the side of the ball to allow the kicking leg to swing freely.

3. Playing the push pass – the kicking foot at right angles to the line of the pass, with the head looking down.

THE INSTEP PASS

This is a more difficult technique than the push pass and takes more practice to master.

The kicking foot makes contact through the horizontal mid-line of the ball. The toe must be pointing down towards the ground. If the toe is not kept pointing down, the instep is likely to make contact with the ball through the bottom half, causing it to rise. The foot should make contact with the ball through the vertical line, too, if the pass is to go straight. The approach to the ball is from an angle and the boot almost always goes through the vertical line at an angle.

The non-kicking foot should be alongside the ball and few inches away from it, otherwise the kicking foot will probably make contact through the bottom half of the ball, causing it to rise.

Advantages

⚽ *It is easy for the passer to disguise his intentions, making it difficult for defenders to predict the pass.*

⚽ *It is possible to add power and pace, making it a valuable technique both for long passing and shooting.*

⚽ *Instep passes can be made while running at speed without interrupting the stride pattern.*

Disadvantage

⚽ *The instep pass is a difficult technique to perform; a relatively small part of the boot strikes the ball and a relatively small area of the ball has to be hit for the pass to be accurate.*

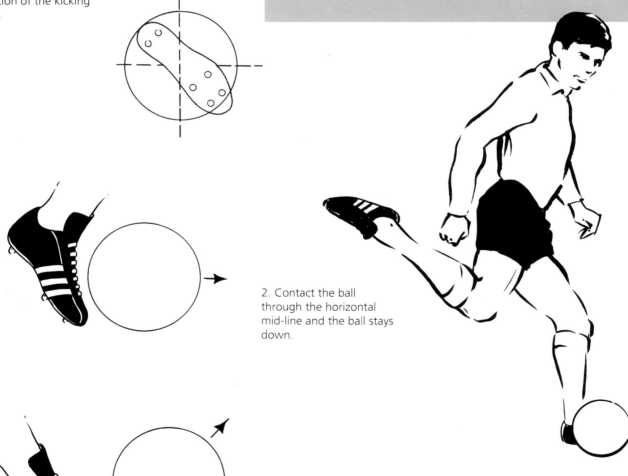

1. The instep pass — position of the kicking foot.

2. Contact the ball through the horizontal mid-line and the ball stays down.

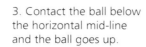

3. Contact the ball below the horizontal mid-line and the ball goes up.

PASSING WITH THE OUTSIDE OF THE FOOT

Passing the ball with the outside of the foot is an essential technique for those who wish to play at a high level. Over short distances and in tight situations it can be used to flick the ball through quite wide angles with heavy disguise. Over long distances it can be used to swerve the ball past opponents.

The flick pass

The kicking foot is placed inside the ball, which is flicked with an outward rotation of the foot. To keep the ball down, contact with the ball should be made through the horizontal mid-line.

The non-kicking foot should be placed a little behind and to the side of the ball. This position makes for easier movement of the kicking foot.

1. The flick pass allows heavy disguise but can only be played over short distances.

The flick pass is a particularly useful technique when tightly marked from behind.

2. Preparing to receive the ball – the knee of the kicking leg is bent.

3. Playing the ball – the kicking leg is extended and rotated outwards.

4. Having played the ball, spin off and move away from the marker, usually in the opposite direction to the pass.

Advantage
⚽ The pass can be made with the minimum of foot movement and the maximum of disguise.

Disadvantage
⚽ The technique can only be used over short distances.

The swerve pass

The kicking foot comes across the body and across the ball from outside to inside, contacting the ball just inside the vertical mid-line, thus imparting spin and swerve from inside to out. The foot should make contact with the horizontal mid-line to keep the ball low.

The non-kicking foot, as with the flick pass, should be placed a little behind and to the side of the ball. This position makes for easier movement of the kicking foot.

1. The swerve pass using the outside of the foot. The foot comes across the ball – from right to left for a right-footed kick.

2. Contact is made with the outside of the foot just inside the centre of the ball – the left side for a right-footed kick.

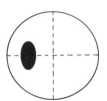

3. The kicking foot follows through across the body – this movement is helped by the non-kicking foot being behind the ball.

Advantages

⚽ It can be used to bend the ball round an opponent.

⚽ It can be used over long distances and is therefore also a valuable shooting technique.

⚽ It can be used when running at speed without breaking the stride pattern.

⚽ It can be used to draw the ball away from the goalkeeper when crossed from a flank.

Disadvantage

⚽ The more swerve required, the more difficult it is to support the kick.

PASSING WITH THE INSIDE OF THE FOOT

Spin and swerve can also be imparted to the ball with the inside of the foot. This technique can be used over both short and long distances.

The kicking foot comes across the ball from inside to outside. There is an outward rotation of the kicking leg. Contact is made with the forward part of the inside of the kicking foot, in the region where the big toe joins the foot. The ball is struck just outside the vertical mid-line, imparting spin and swerve from outside to in, and through the horizontal mid-line, to keep the pass low.

1. The kicking foot comes across the ball from inside to outside – from left to right with the right foot.

2. The ball is struck with the inside of the foot just outside the centre – right of centre with the right foot.

Advantages

⚽ *The ball can be bent around an opponent.*

⚽ *The pass can be used over short and long distances and is therefore also a valuable shooting technique.*

⚽ *If contact is made slightly below the horizontal mid-line, the ball can easily be lifted a few inches over a defender's outstretched legs.*

⚽ *A great deal of swerve can be imparted to the ball, and the swerve is easier to control than that imparted with the outside of the foot.*

⚽ *The ball can be drawn away from the goalkeeper when crossed from the flank.*

Disadvantage

⚽ *The ball will never go straight and will always be spinning, possibly making control more difficult.*

3. **The non-kicking foot** is positioned 8 to 12 inches to the side of the ball and slightly behind it, to allow the kicking foot to move freely across the ball.

4. The follow-through is away from the body.

LOFTED PASSES

The techniques for lifting the ball over defenders' heads are essential in order fully to exploit the space behind them. This is not to say that this space cannot be exploited with ground passes. Of course, it can. The longer the range, however, the more likely it is that the pass will have to be lofted over the defenders. If there is any doubt about getting the ball through on the ground, an attacker should always select the aerial route.

Some 'experts' claim that playing passes in the air is not good soccer. In fact, playing ground balls that are duly intercepted is bad soccer. There is a time and a place for everything; if the ground route is blocked, the ball has to be played over the heads of defenders.

There are three basic techniques for playing passes in the air; the lofted drive, the chip and the volley. Within these broad groups there are four ways of playing the lofted drive and two ways of playing the volley. One factor links all these techniques; contact is made through the bottom half of the ball, below the horizontal mid-line. No other contact will make the ball rise.

1. To loft the ball, contact must be made below the horizontal mid-line.

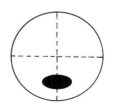

Which technique is selected will depend on three considerations: the length of the pass; the space available in front of the nearest defender whom the ball must clear; and the space behind the defender where the ball will pitch. There is a pass for each situation.

LOFTED DRIVES WITH THE INSTEP

From a slightly angled approach

The kicking foot should make contact with the ball below the horizontal mid-line and through the vertical mid-line. The ankle should be extended and firm.

The non-kicking foot should be slightly to the side of the ball and behind it.

1. Lofted drive with the instep from a slightly angled approach – the non-kicking foot is slightly behind the ball.

2. Contact on the ball is through the bottom half.

3. The body leans back slightly.

Advantages

⚽ *The ball can be played over distances of more than 40 yards.*

⚽ *The ball can be played with considerable pace, giving defenders little chance to recover.*

Disadvantage

⚽ *The ball will not rise steeply, and it is difficult to clear defenders less than 10 or 12 yards away.*

From a wide-angled approach

The kicking foot should be pointed outwards and the ankle kept firm and extended. The foot should sweep through the bottom half of the ball.

The non-kicking foot should be 12 to 18 inches to the side of the ball and behind it.

Advantages

⚽ *The pass can be played over distances of more than 40 yards.*

⚽ *It is not difficult to control.*

⚽ *It is possible to put a certain amount of backspin on the ball, slowing it down when it pitches so it is ready for a team-mate to run on to.*

⚽ *A steeper trajectory can be achieved than with the approach from a slight angle.*

Disadvantage

⚽ *The ball cannot be hit with as much pace as some other methods. Defenders therefore have a little more time to adjust their position when the ball is in flight.*

1. The wide-angled approach, front view – the kicking leg should be extended and the non-kicking foot positioned to the side of the ball.

2. The wide-angled approach, rear view – the kicking foot sweeps through the bottom half of the ball.

LOFTED DRIVES WITH THE OUTSIDE OF THE FOOT

The kicking foot should come across the ball and across the body from outside to inside, imparting swerve and spin to the ball. The foot makes contact with the ball just below the horizontal mid-line and just inside the vertical mid-line.

1. Contact is made through the bottom half of the ball on the inside — the left side for a right-footed pass.

The non-kicking foot should be positioned to the side of the ball and slightly behind it.

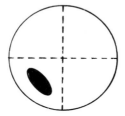

Advantages

⚽ *It can be played over distances of more than 40 yards.*

⚽ *It can be played with pace.*

⚽ *The ball can be swerved away from defenders, making interceptions more difficult.*

⚽ *The ball can be swerved into the path of an attacking player.*

Disadvantages

⚽ *It is difficult to control the ball over long distances.*

⚽ *The ball will not rise steeply.*

⚽ *The ball will continue to roll away after pitching, making it difficult to judge the pace of the pass into space.*

England striker Alan Smith sets himself to play a lofted drive forward in a friendly international against Greece.

LOFTED DRIVES WITH THE INSIDE OF THE FOOT

The kicking foot should come across the ball from inside to outside with an outward rotation of the kicking leg. The forward part of the inside of the foot makes contact with the ball below the horizontal mid-line and slightly outside the vertical mid-line.

1. Contact is made through the bottom half of the ball on the outside – right of centre for a right-footed player.
The non-kicking foot should be positioned to the side of the ball and behind it.

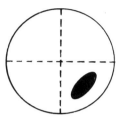

Advantages

⚽ *The pass can be played over distances of more than 40 yards.*

⚽ *The ball can be played with pace.*

⚽ *The ball can be swerved away from defenders, making interception more difficult.*

⚽ *The ball can be swerved into the path of an attacking player.*

⚽ *It is relatively easy to control.*

⚽ *The ball can be made to rise reasonably steeply.*

Disadvantage

⚽ *The ball will continue to roll after pitching, making it difficult to judge the pace of the pass into space.*

INSTEP VOLLEY FROM A STRAIGHT APPROACH

The kicking foot should contact the ball through the vertical mid-line and through the bottom half of the ball, not underneath it. The ankle should be extended.

More elements of this technique are shown on the next two pages.

1. Volley with the instep from a straight approach – preparing to volley.

2. Ankle extended as the knee is raised.

29

INSTEP VOLLEY FROM A STRAIGHT APPROACH continued

The non-kicking foot should always be behind the ball. If it is played early in flight it will be further behind the ball than if it is played late in its flight.

3. Contact with the instep (laces) through the vertical mid-line.

4. Body balanced and head still after contact has been made.

5. Playing the ball early in flight – the non-kicking foot is well back.

6. Playing the ball late in flight – the non-kicking foot is much nearer to the ball.

Advantages

⚽ The ball can be played over the heads of opponents who are only a few yards from the ball.

⚽ The ball can be played early.

⚽ The ball can be played over long distances.

⚽ The ball can be played with considerable pace.

⚽ The ball can be 'dipped' by imparting topspin to the ball.

Disadvantages

⚽ The accuracy of the pass is difficult to control.

⚽ The pace of the pass is difficult to control.

The Welsh striker, Mark Hughes, is famed for his volleying skills; here he has just played a flick volley to an unmarked colleague on his right.

31

INSTEP VOLLEY FROM A SIDEWAYS APPROACH

This type of kick is often referred to as a 'hook volley'. The essential feature is that the body is positioned sideways-on to the line of the ball. The leading shoulder should fall away to allow the kicking leg to swing through smoothly.

The kicking foot should point outwards and the kicking leg should swing forward and across the body. Contact with the ball is made just below the horizontal mid-line.

1. The hook volley – adopt a sideways stance early.

2. The ankle is extended as the knee is brought through in advance of the foot.

Ireland's John Aldridge attempts to volley the ball forward under challenge from a Maltese defender in a World Cup qualifying match in Dublin.

The non-kicking foot should be well to the side of the ball in order to allow the swing and follow-through of the kicking leg. The body rotates on the standing leg.

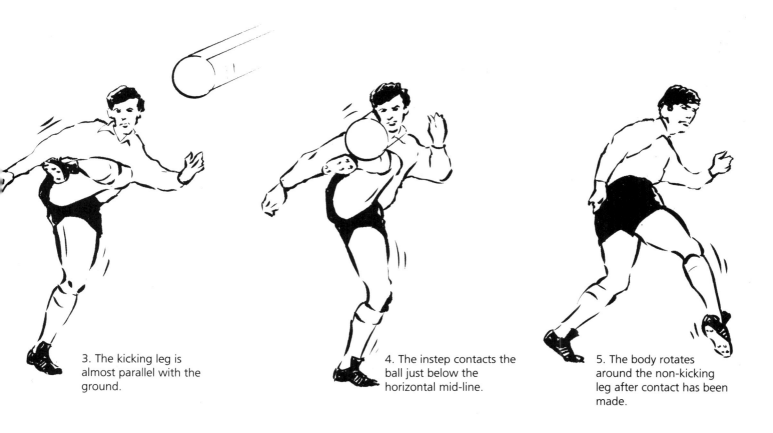

3. The kicking leg is almost parallel with the ground.

4. The instep contacts the ball just below the horizontal mid-line.

5. The body rotates around the non-kicking leg after contact has been made.

Advantages

⚽ *The ball can be played over the heads of opponents only a few yards from the ball.*

⚽ *The ball can be played over long distances.*

⚽ *Considerable pace can be achieved.*

⚽ *The ball can be played early.*

Disadvantages

⚽ *The accuracy of this type of volley is even more difficult to control than the previous one.*

⚽ *The pace of the pass is difficult to control.*

THE CHIP PASS

The kicking foot should contact the ball at the point where it touches the ground. This is done with a stabbing movement, or downward thrust of the kicking leg, with no follow-through. This imparts strong backspin to the ball.

The non-kicking foot should be no more than three or four inches to the side of the ball.

1. The chip pass – the approach is straight.

2. The kicking foot stabs downward at the bottom of the ball, imparting strong backspin.

Advantages

⚽ *Because of the backspin on the ball it rises very steeply, making it possible to clear the heads of opponents only five or six yards from the ball.*

⚽ *Again because of the backspin, it is possible to stop the ball in a small space.*

Disadvantages

⚽ *The pass can only be played over distances of 20 to 25 yards.*

⚽ *Players running on to the pass may find the ball difficult to control as they would be moving against the spin.*

Good technique, the combined skills of players in supporting each other, positive thinking and an assertive approach in seizing every chance of direct play combine to constitute the first, essential requirement of The Winning Formula.

FORWARD RUNS

FORWARD RUNS
WITH AND WITHOUT THE BALL

What a player does when he has not got the ball is of critical importance in soccer. Analysis shows that on average the ball will only be in play for 60 minutes of a 90-minute game. In an even game, therefore, each team will have possession for about 30 minutes and, when the time the ball is actually in flight is subtracted from the total, this means that each player will, on average, have the ball only for around two minutes per match.

Good teamwork depends very much on what players do without the ball. The harder individual players are prepared to work in terms of the quality and quantity of their running, and the more they can combine, integrate and time their movements, the more problems the team as a whole will pose for their opponents.

Running in soccer is essentially about repeated sprinting. Players will have to run at sprinting speed over distances of anything from 5 to 50 yards and repeat this at frequent but irregular intervals throughout the game.

If a team consists of players of very different physical capacities, it will prove difficult, even impossible, effectively to combine and integrate their movements. Certainly the team will not be able to maintain the high tempo that is required for effective direct play. Keeping up a high tempo of play for the full 90 minutes demands high levels of speed endurance from all the outfield players in the team.

Possession soccer does not make the same demands, and the importance of speed endurance is greatly reduced. This is no reason, however, for advocating possession soccer — quite the opposite. A team with a superior strategy should be fit enough and skilful enough to impose that strategy on their opponents. Remember that a swift attack is harder to defend against than one with a slow build-up. Time usually works in the defenders' favour.

Essential though it is, good speed endurance is not everything. To be a truly effective runner, with or without the ball, a player also needs to understand when, how and why he should make a run.

RUNNING WITH THE BALL

When not to run with the ball

Do not run when there are team-mates available to take a pass in a more threatening position. If there is space behind the opposing defence and a player poised to exploit it, the most direct play is a pass into that space. Running with the ball, delaying its release, would be foolish, as it gives the defence time to recover. If there is any doubt about whether to pass or run, pass, working on the theory that the ball can be moved forward quicker with a pass than a run.

Do not run when there is not enough space to run into. This may seem obvious, but sometimes players set off on a run without assessing the space available. As a result they either run into trouble with their opponents and lose the ball, or they are forced to turn away from the defence and play it back to a supporting player. When this happens, not only is the attack less direct than it should be, but time is lost and the advantage shifts to the opposition.

Do not run when it is muddy. Muddy conditions hold up the ball and the runner alike. Players quite literally get stuck and get themselves into a position where they cannot make a quality shot, pass or dribble. It is very rare, however, for such conditions to engulf the whole pitch. Quite often the centre of the pitch is a quagmire while the flanks are firm and ideal for running with the ball. If this is the case, the best route for direct play will be down the flanks.

Do not run when it is frosty or the pitch dry and bumpy. Such conditions present unnecessary problems with ball control, making it more difficult to make a quality shot, pass or dribble at the end of the run. Besides, if it is frosty, defenders are more vulnerable to the ball being played past them for attackers to run on to. Defenders turn more slowly, and are more likely to lose their footing in frosty conditions than any others.

When to run with the ball

Players should run with the ball only when there is space available and no better alternative play. It may be, for instance, that in a central position in the attacking third the best option will be a shot. In a flank position in the attacking third, the best option may be an early cross, rather than a run with the ball toward the goal-line. In the middle third or defending third of the pitch, the best option may be to pass.

Running with the ball means running **forward**. Players should run only when there is space in front of them and no defender ready to close down that space. The amount of space varies, of course, but there should be at least 15 yards. If the defending side are in retreat, however, it is justifiable to run with the ball when there is less space available.

The main thing for players to avoid – and the most common fault of players running with the ball – is running without purpose or direction. Often, players do this because the situation they see in front of them is not very clear and they run with the ball simply to get away from opponents. There is never any real directional drive to such runs, and their course is generally across the field, with the result that momentum – and often possession – is lost.

Before deciding to run with the ball, a player should ask himself three questions.

● Is there a better alternative play?

● Is there enough space ahead to run into?

● Where is the run going and what should happen at the end of it?

How to run with the ball

Running with the ball is very different from dribbling. There are four important elements.

The first touch. This should be with the in-step (laces) of the front foot, in order to maintain a balanced running stride. The ball should be played well forward; how far will depend on the amount of space. If the ball is played too far forward, defenders will be encouraged to challenge for it. If it is not played far enough, too many touches will be required and it will take longer to cover the ground. Besides, the more touches taken, the more time will be spent looking at the ball rather than looking up to assess play.

As a rough guide, if a player were running with the ball over a distance of 40 yards, he should not require more than three touches.

The fewer the touches, the better the technical performance will be.

It is important in direct play that the forward run should be directed like an arrow. If it is directed at a particular defender, the runner should run straight at him without veering to either side by even half a yard. If it is directed at the heart of the defence, the runner should go straight for it.

Looking up to assess play. A common fault of players running with the ball is keeping their head down, concentrating on the ball rather than the movements of players ahead. Without looking up to assess the situation, the runner cannot make the best decision about what to do next.

Decision. When running with the ball, a player should make a decision before each touch on the ball. The decision may be to play the ball forward again, but ultimately a successful run will lead to a pass, a dribble, a cross or a shot.

> *If the run takes a player into the attacking third of the field, these general guidelines should apply.*
>
> ⚽ *If there is an opportunity to shoot, shoot.*
>
> ⚽ *If the choice is between passing and dribbling, choose to dribble.*
>
> ⚽ *If the run is down a flank, and there is space to cross the ball, do so early and preferably to the back of the defence.*
>
> ⚽ *If there is any doubt at all, shoot.*

Whatever the decision, it is best made as quickly as possible, allowing the maximum amount of time for execution.

Execution. The performance must be positive. There should be no question of changing the decision. Indecision causes a loss of attacking momentum, and the second that momentum is lost the initiative begins to shift to the defending players.

Timing and accuracy are prime considerations in a calm, unhurried performance.

> **Analysis of twenty years of goals reveals that forward runs with the ball are an element in more than one of every seven goals scored.**

FORWARD RUNS WITHOUT THE BALL

There are two types of forward runs which players will make without the ball: runs to create space and runs to exploit space. These can be further sub-divided according to whether the run starts from behind the ball or in front of it.

Before considering the types of forward runs which attacking players may make, it is worth considering how defenders may react. If in doubt, defenders will retreat towards their own goal. If they elect to give up space it will be in one of two places, either in front of the defence or down the wings.

The one thing a defence in retreat dislikes most is for attackers to run straight at them with the ball or, worse, to pass the ball into the space behind them, while at the same time players without the ball make diagonal runs across them. If these diagonal runs take them behind the defence the defenders' discomfiture is complete. As far as flank attacks are concerned, defenders have good cause to be fearful of early crosses played at pace behind the defence.

The message for attackers therefore, is to attack on as wide a front as possible and to try to take defenders wide and out of their normal lines of retreat.

CREATING SPACE

Running from in front of the ball

Defenders will always react to the movement of attacking players, but they will be much less worried about opponents who run up and down the field than those who move across it.

In diagram (a), the attackers' paths are not likely to trouble the defenders, who will be able to mark players and space as well as support one another.

a | WRONG

The alternative paths in diagram (b) present far more problems. If a defender chooses to mark a player, he will be pulled out of position. If he marks the space he will run the risk of an attacker getting free in a dangerous position. Whatever option he chooses, he will find it more difficult to support his team-mates.

b | RIGHT

Diagonal runs are therefore of great importance in the creation of space. There are two types of diagonal run.

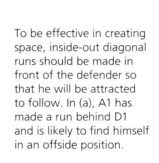

Inside-out diagonal runs are runs made from the centre of the field diagonally towards a flank.

To be effective in creating space, inside-out diagonal runs should be made in front of the defender so that he will be attracted to follow. In (a), A1 has made a run behind D1 and is likely to find himself in an offside position.

a | WRONG

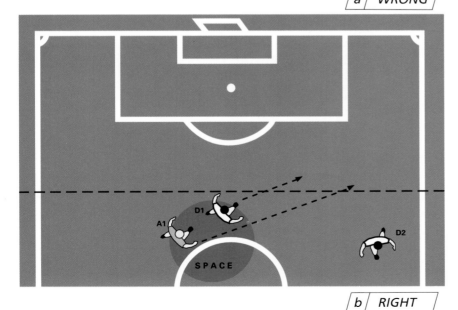

SPACE

b | RIGHT

In (b), A1 has made a run in front of D1, but behind D2. D1 is likely to track this run and this will create space in a central position.

The main problem for markers is deciding how far to follow an attacker making an inside-out diagonal run.

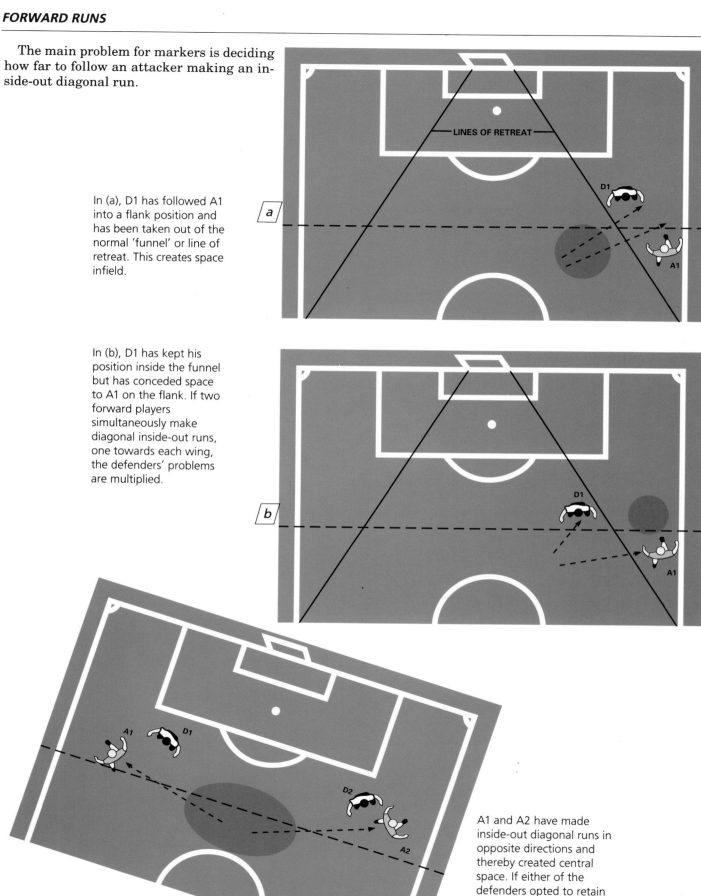

LINES OF RETREAT

In (a), D1 has followed A1 into a flank position and has been taken out of the normal 'funnel' or line of retreat. This creates space infield.

In (b), D1 has kept his position inside the funnel but has conceded space to A1 on the flank. If two forward players simultaneously make diagonal inside-out runs, one towards each wing, the defenders' problems are multiplied.

A1 and A2 have made inside-out diagonal runs in opposite directions and thereby created central space. If either of the defenders opted to retain a central position, he would concede space to the player he was marking.

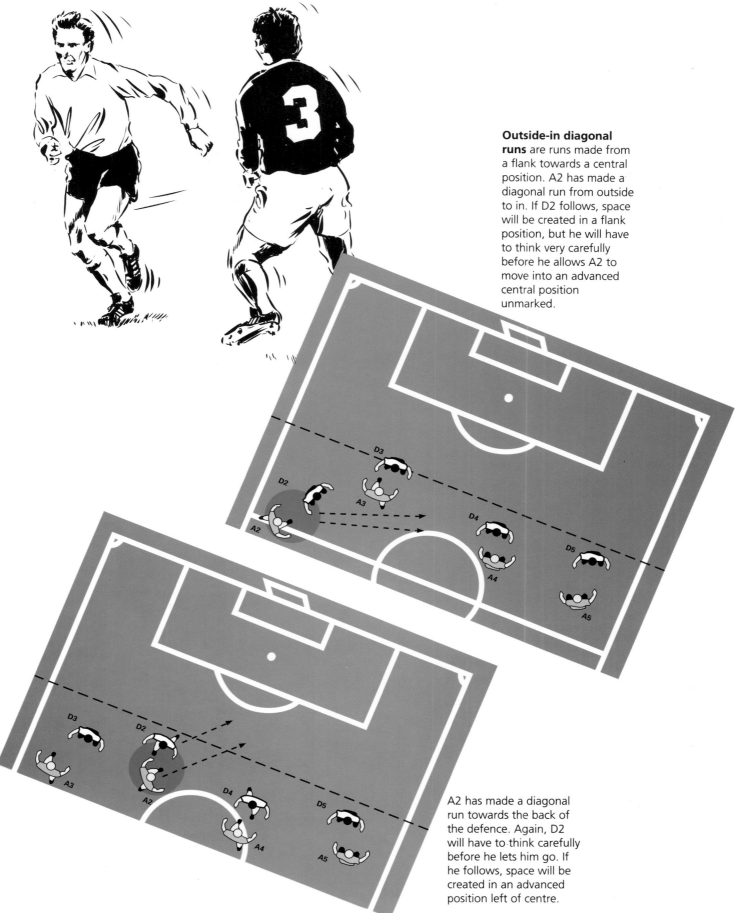

Outside-in diagonal runs are runs made from a flank towards a central position. A2 has made a diagonal run from outside to in. If D2 follows, space will be created in a flank position, but he will have to think very carefully before he allows A2 to move into an advanced central position unmarked.

A2 has made a diagonal run towards the back of the defence. Again, D2 will have to think carefully before he lets him go. If he follows, space will be created in an advanced position left of centre.

Running from behind the ball

Runs made from behind the ball can create space by drawing defenders out of central defending positions and especially out of defensive support positions. There are basically two types of run.

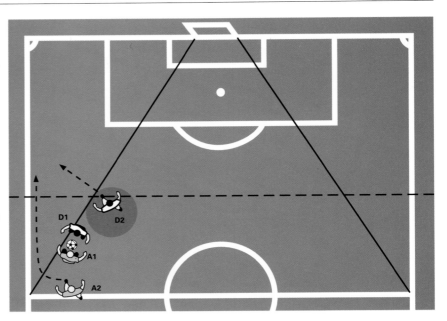

Overlap runs. Here, A1 is in possession of the ball. A2 has made a run outside A1 into a position well in advance of the ball. The effect of this is to draw D2 out of a central position inside the 'funnel', thereby creating space. If D2 does not cover A2's run, A1 can give A2 the ball in space.

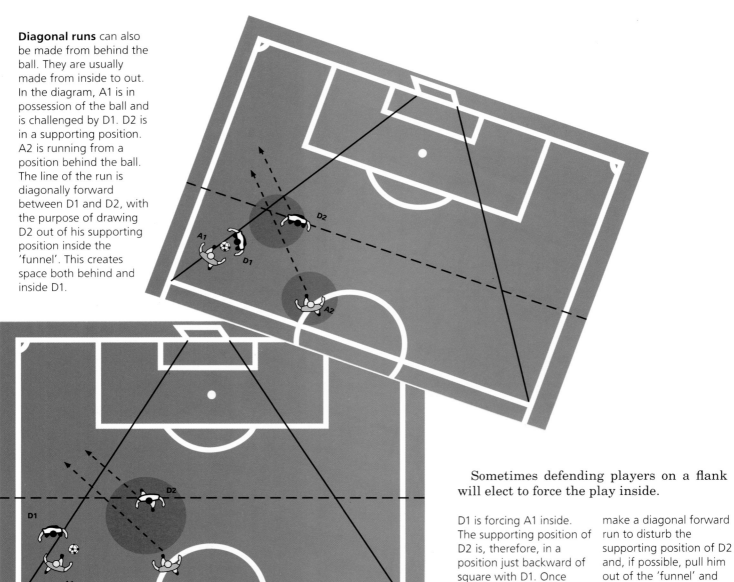

Diagonal runs can also be made from behind the ball. They are usually made from inside to out. In the diagram, A1 is in possession of the ball and is challenged by D1. D2 is in a supporting position. A2 is running from a position behind the ball. The line of the run is diagonally forward between D1 and D2, with the purpose of drawing D2 out of his supporting position inside the 'funnel'. This creates space both behind and inside D1.

Sometimes defending players on a flank will elect to force the play inside.

D1 is forcing A1 inside. The supporting position of D2 is, therefore, in a position just backward of square with D1. Once again, the task of A2 is to make a diagonal forward run to disturb the supporting position of D2 and, if possible, pull him out of the 'funnel' and create space inside D1.

EXPLOITING SPACE

Running from in front of the ball

Forward runs from in front of the ball designed to exploit space will invariably be runs to the back of the defence and will almost always be diagonal runs. The ideal circumstance is where a defender has been drawn towards the ball, thus increasing the space behind him.

A1 is in possession of the ball. A3 has moved towards A1 and drawn D3 with him. This movement creates space behind D3. A2 makes a diagonal forward run into the space to receive a through ball from A1. This is a typical example of A1 running forward with the ball and correctly timing the release of the pass.

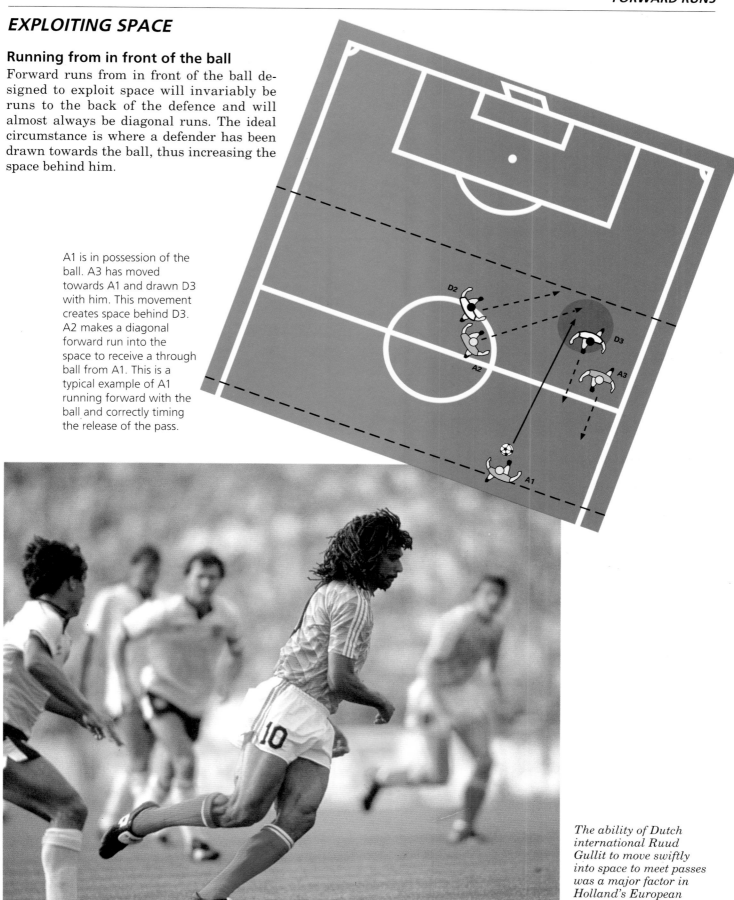

The ability of Dutch international Ruud Gullit to move swiftly into space to meet passes was a major factor in Holland's European Championship victory in 1988 in West Germany.

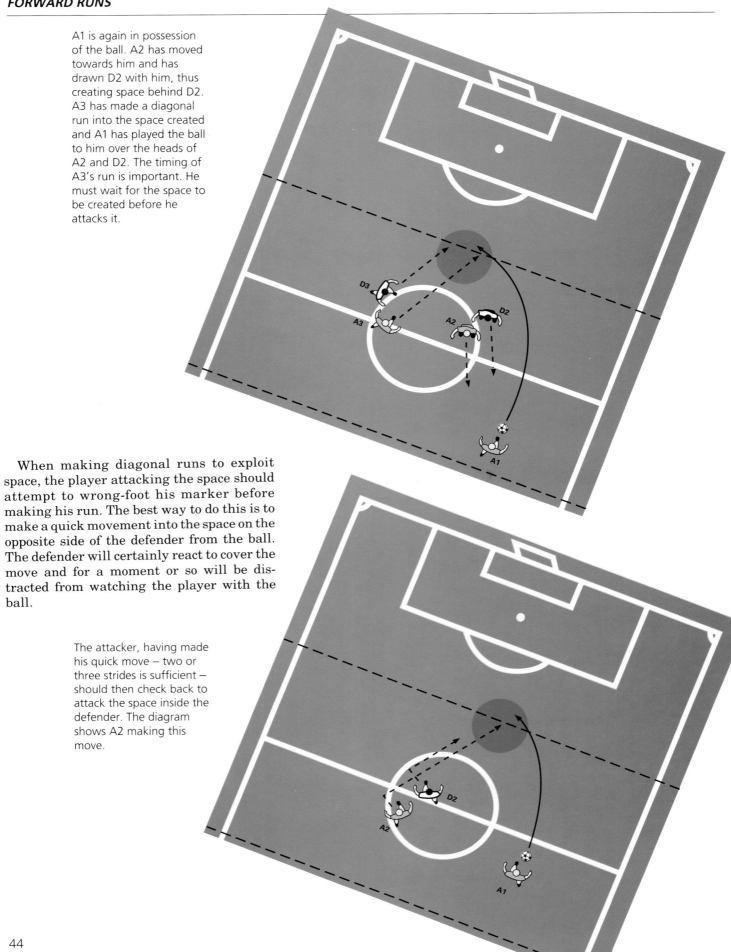

A1 is again in possession of the ball. A2 has moved towards him and has drawn D2 with him, thus creating space behind D2. A3 has made a diagonal run into the space created and A1 has played the ball to him over the heads of A2 and D2. The timing of A3's run is important. He must wait for the space to be created before he attacks it.

When making diagonal runs to exploit space, the player attacking the space should attempt to wrong-foot his marker before making his run. The best way to do this is to make a quick movement into the space on the opposite side of the defender from the ball. The defender will certainly react to cover the move and for a moment or so will be distracted from watching the player with the ball.

The attacker, having made his quick move – two or three strides is sufficient – should then check back to attack the space inside the defender. The diagram shows A2 making this move.

Attackers should remember that defenders will try to retain a position on the goal-side of their opponent in a triangle drawn between the ball, the person they are marking and the centre of the goal.

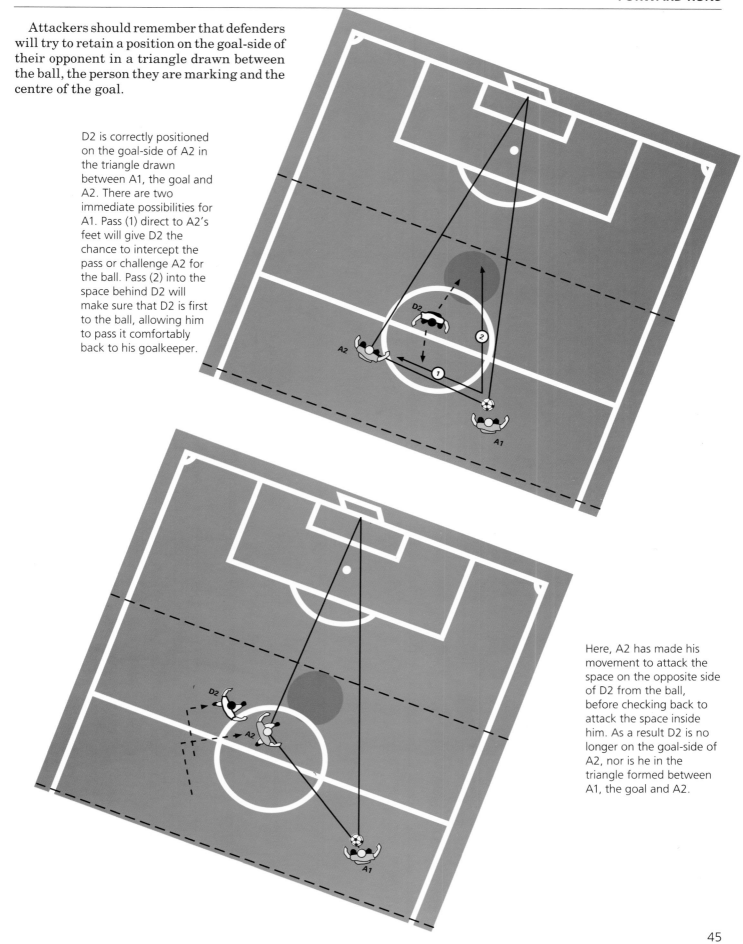

D2 is correctly positioned on the goal-side of A2 in the triangle drawn between A1, the goal and A2. There are two immediate possibilities for A1. Pass (1) direct to A2's feet will give D2 the chance to intercept the pass or challenge A2 for the ball. Pass (2) into the space behind D2 will make sure that D2 is first to the ball, allowing him to pass it comfortably back to his goalkeeper.

Here, A2 has made his movement to attack the space on the opposite side of D2 from the ball, before checking back to attack the space inside him. As a result D2 is no longer on the goal-side of A2, nor is he in the triangle formed between A1, the goal and A2.

Central attackers can sometimes make split runs to create central space for exploitation by an attacker moving from a deeper position. Players on the opposite side of the field from the ball should be constantly aware of this possibility.

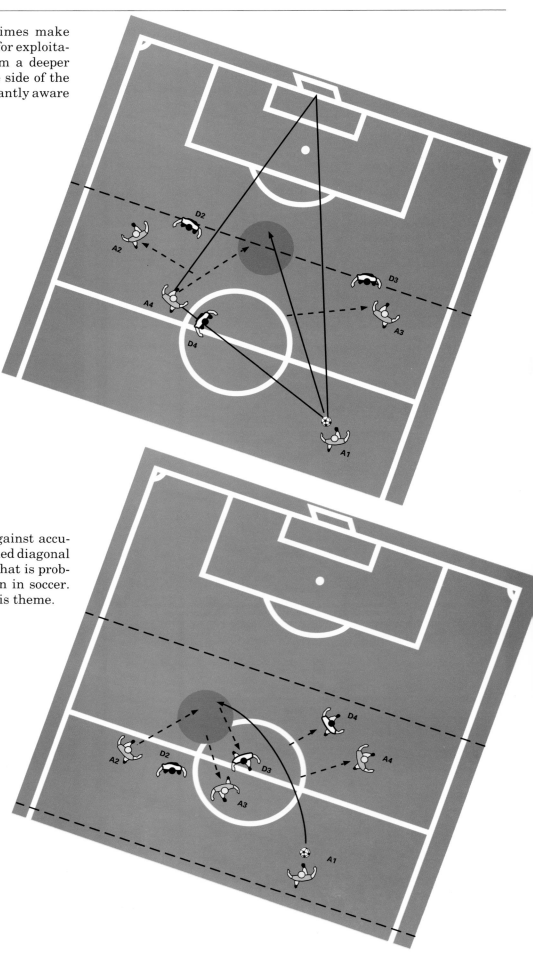

A2 and A3 have made split diagonal runs, with A2 going left and A3 going right. As a result space has been created in the centre. A4 exploits the space by making a forward diagonal run to receive a pass from A1. Defenders frequently defend badly on the side of the field opposite to the ball. The main reason for this is that they do not position correctly on the goal-side of their opponent and are frequently caught outside the triangle formed by the ball, the goal and their immediate opponent, allowing opponents to get into space behind them. Here, A4 has found space behind D4.

It is very difficult to defend against accurate diagonal passes and well-timed diagonal runs. Together, they add up to what is probably the most lethal combination in soccer. There are many variations on this theme.

A1 is in possession of the ball. A4 has made a diagonal run to the right, taking D4 with him. A3 is moving towards A1 and is marked by D3. Space has therefore been created behind D3 in a central position. A2 has made a diagonal forward run into the space and receives a diagonal forward pass from A1.

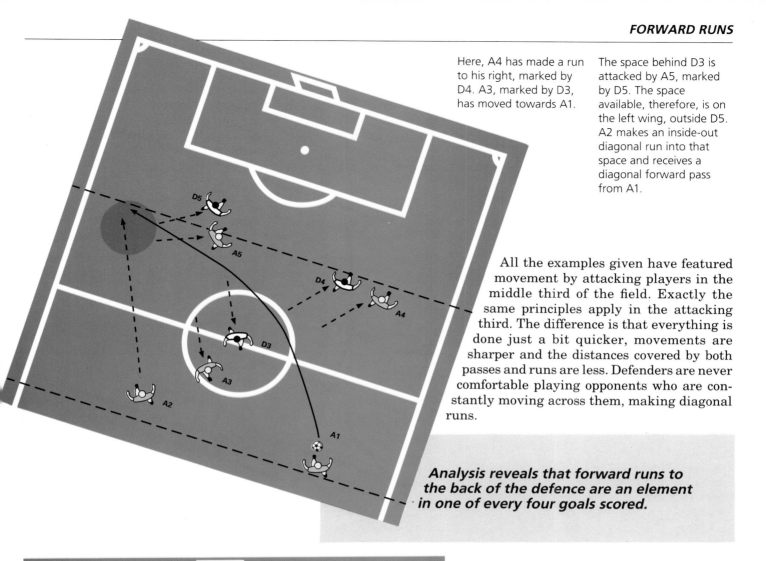

Here, A4 has made a run to his right, marked by D4. A3, marked by D3, has moved towards A1.

The space behind D3 is attacked by A5, marked by D5. The space available, therefore, is on the left wing, outside D5. A2 makes an inside-out diagonal run into that space and receives a diagonal forward pass from A1.

All the examples given have featured movement by attacking players in the middle third of the field. Exactly the same principles apply in the attacking third. The difference is that everything is done just a bit quicker, movements are sharper and the distances covered by both passes and runs are less. Defenders are never comfortable playing opponents who are constantly moving across them, making diagonal runs.

Analysis reveals that forward runs to the back of the defence are an element in one of every four goals scored.

Running from behind the ball

Probably the best example of a forward run from behind the ball to exploit space is an overlap run in a situation where the challenging player is not supported.

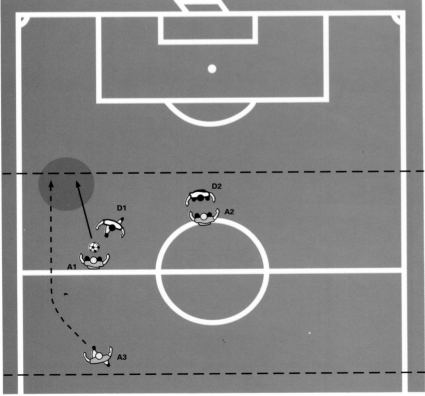

A1 is in possession of the ball and is challenged by D1. D2 is marking A2 and is both too far away and at the wrong angle to support D1. Space is therefore available on the flank behind D1. A3 exploits that space by making a forward run outside A1 to receive the ball in space.

This situation occurs frequently in the attacking third, because defenders are very reluctant to be drawn out of central defending positions. If central attackers were to move out to exploit the space on the flanks, their markers would usually follow them, so the best player to exploit the space on the flanks is one running forward from a position behind the ball. Once in space on the flanks, in the attacking third of the field, the most important technique is crossing the ball on the run.

This movement, finished off with a good cross on the run, should not be underestimated. One goal in four is scored from a cross.

In modern football, it is essential that players should be prepared to move forward from behind the ball and that they should have the necessary technical ability to deal with the situation when they get the ball in an advanced position.

A1 is in possession of the ball. A2 has made an inside-out diagonal run to destroy the support for D1, who is challenging A1. Space is, therefore, created inside D1. A3 moves forward into the space to receive the ball from A1.

A3 must now think and play as an attacker. First he must look for a forward pass to the back of the defence. It will probably be necessary for him to have the technical ability to run with the ball. At the end of that run he must be able to produce a pass or a cross, to dribble or to shoot.

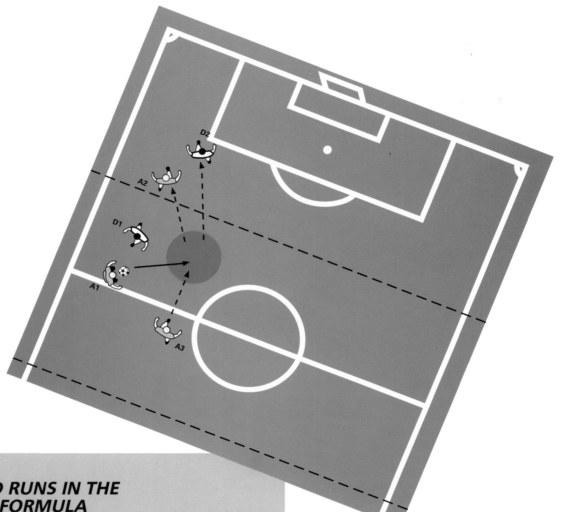

FORWARD RUNS IN THE WINNING FORMULA

The whole strategic emphasis of direct attacking play is embodied in these three objectives.

⚽ *Making forward progress as directly and quickly as possible.*

⚽ *Gaining entry into the attacking third of the field with each attack.*

⚽ *Retaining the momentum of the attack in the attacking third, whether by passing, crossing, dribbling or shooting.*

All these are more easily and more often achieved if a team is capable of attacking opponents by making forward runs with and without the ball.

DRIBBLING

DRIBBLING

Dribbling is one of the most exciting aspects of attacking play. Players who have a good dribbling technique are invaluable to a team; all the best teams have three or four. It is no coincidence that most of the best players are good dribblers of the ball.

Two things make dribbling an invaluable technique.

⚽ It creates space for a pass or a shot.

⚽ In beating opponents and taking them out of the game it creates a numerical advantage.

Three things are necessary to become a good dribbler.

⚽ The right attitude and understanding.

⚽ Good technique.

⚽ The right application.

ATTITUDE AND UNDERSTANDING

Understanding a few basic factors will affect the attitude of players.

Direct play
Dribbling is an essential part of the strategy for direct play. Without it, players will sometimes be forced to select a less direct option and so hold up the attack, allowing defenders to recover their positions.

Suppose a winger is opposed by a defender on the flanks in the attacking third of the field. If he can dribble he will pass the defender and cross the ball, creating the chance for a shot; if not, he will need support and may have to pass the ball backwards, slowing down the attack.

Momentum
It is essential that the momentum of an attack should be kept up, and if possible increased, when entering the attacking third of

Previous page: The art of beating a man with close ball control and trickery is not only a crowd-pleasing manoeuvre, but a vital attacking weapon. Here, Italy's Fernando de Napoli has just beaten Holland's Peter Huistra and is looking up to find a target for a cross.

the field. Once an attack has been slowed down, it is likely that it will get bogged down and fail.

One of the main ways that an attack loses momentum is through the hesitation of the player with the ball. Some players hesitate and lose a chance to shoot, some hesitate and lose a chance to pass, but most hesitate when they have a chance to dribble.

Positive action
It is vital to seize the initiative, to be positive and self-assertive. Positive action is the essence of direct play. If a team is to apply The Winning Formula, every player should take his chance for direct play whenever the opportunity arises. The ability to make the correct decision quickly has to be developed alongside technique.

Safety and risk
It is part of any player's football education to learn how to balance safety and risk, to weigh up the chances – and the consequences – of success and failure. In relation to dribbling, it is a matter of knowing in which areas of the field dribbling is safe, and which areas present an unacceptable risk. In the defending third of the field dribbling is usually too risky; losing the ball could prove disastrous. It is in the attacking third of the field that dribbling will pay the highest dividends. In the middle of the field it is very much a matter of careful judgement.

It is important that players should understand risk and failure in percentage terms. A 90% success rate in dribbling clear from defence represents failure, as the one occasion in ten when the ball is lost may lead to a goal being conceded. A 25% success rate in dribbling in attack is a risk worth taking, as a goal may be scored as a result.

If a player expects 100% success he will be disappointed and end up never dribbling at all. Dribbling is a risky technique and no-one can guarantee 100% success. Spectators may not see it this way; they are either thrilled to see a successful dribble or disgusted at a failure. They never show their pleasure in

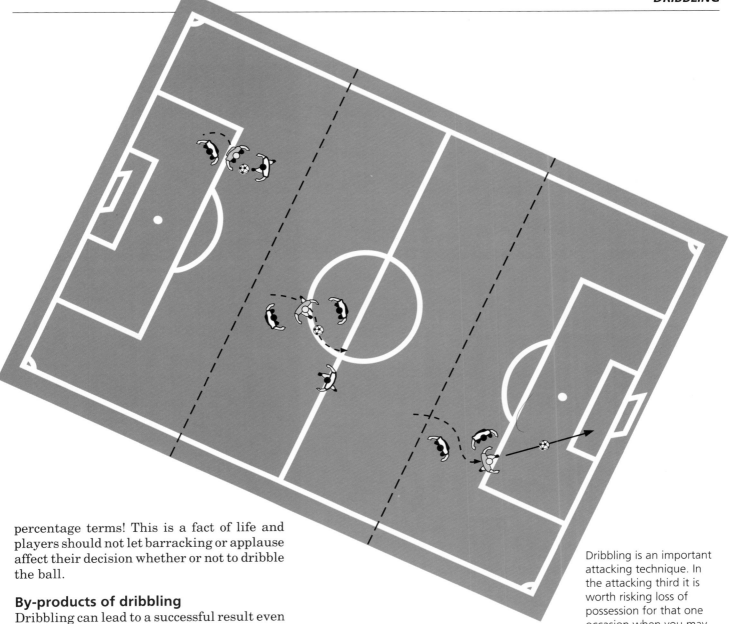

percentage terms! This is a fact of life and players should not let barracking or applause affect their decision whether or not to dribble the ball.

By-products of dribbling

Dribbling can lead to a successful result even when the dribble has failed to take the player free of opponents. Around half of all goals scored come from set plays, either directly or through regaining a ball that has been cleared from a set play. Dribbling plays a major part in winning set plays. Either the dribbler will be tripped, winning a free kick or penalty, or he will be tackled so that the ball goes off for a corner or a throw-in.

TECHNIQUE

There are four important elements to a good dribbling technique.

1. Close control.

2. Tricking and unbalancing an opponent.

3. Change of direction.

4. Change of pace.

Close control

There is a considerable difference between running with the ball and dribbling. Running with the ball involves covering the ground as quickly as possible without beating any opponents. The ball is played well ahead of playing distance so that the runner can watch play unfolding in front of him and does not have to keep playing the ball every stride or two. Dribbling, however, involves beating an opponent who is marking tightly. Close control is important and the first touch is vital. The first touch should do two things:

1. It should bring the ball under control in such a way that the marking defender cannot make a successful tackle.

2. It should position the ball to attack the defender without delay. There is more on this in the section about applying technique.

Dribbling is an important attacking technique. In the attacking third it is worth risking loss of possession for that one occasion when you may break through and be in a position to score or to set up a goal. Dribbling in the defending third is a risk not worth taking because, sooner or later, you will lose possession and perhaps present your opponents with a goal-scoring opportunity.

Tricking and unbalancing an opponent

Sometimes it is possible to beat an opponent by pace alone. This is only possible, however, when there is space to run into behind the defender. If the attacker receives the ball in a congested area, or the defender is supported, it will be necessary to put him off balance or on to the wrong foot with a piece of trickery, while keeping close control over the ball. It is helpful, therefore, for a dribbling player to have two or three different movements designed to throw an opponent on to the wrong foot so he can be passed.

We suggest players master the technique of the following three moves, each of them with three parts. All the moves can be made using either foot; to play with the other foot simply read left for right and vice versa throughout.

The Matthews Move

This movement is named after Sir Stanley Matthews, an England international who used it to such great effect in his long and illustrious career that he came to be known as the Wizard of the Dribble.

1. Move the ball with the inside of your right foot to your left side. Lean to your left, dropping the left shoulder, and pretend to go left. This move should be exaggerated as this is the part of the technique that is designed to unbalance your opponent.

2. Move your right foot quickly behind the ball so that the outside of your right foot is behind the ball.

3. Play the ball forward and past your opponent with the outside of your right foot. As you play the ball, accelerate away.

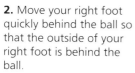

1.

2.

3.

The Scissors Move

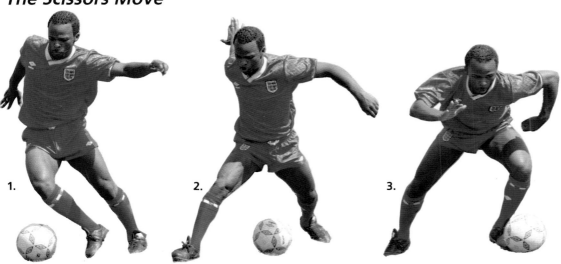

1.   2.   3.

1. Play the ball out in front of you to your right side.

2. Pretend to play the ball with the outside of the right foot but instead step over it. This puts the defender on the wrong foot.

3. Play the ball forward and past your opponent with the outside of the left foot, accelerating away as you do so.

The Double Touch Move

1.   2.   3.

1. Pretend that you are going to pass the ball to your right with the inside of your right foot (note that this move will not necessarily fool a defender if there is no-one to your right to pass to).

2. Draw the ball across your body with the inside of your right foot.

3. Take the ball away on your left side by playing it forward and past your opponent with the inside of your left foot, accelerating away as you do so.

Change of direction

Two of the tricks above involve a change of direction as a part of the process of wrong-footing an opponent. It is important that players master at least one dribbling technique which involves a change of direction, because good defenders will watch the ball and only react to movement of the ball.

The Scissors Move does not change the direction of the ball and is less likely to un-balance a good defender than the Matthews Move or the Double Touch Move. However, if the defender is retreating and the attacker is running at him at speed, the Scissors Move will often prove the most effective. It will cer-tainly be easier to perform technically.

Part of the skill of dribbling is in selecting the most appropriate technique for each situation. Practise against several defenders; you'll soon learn when to use each move.

Change of pace

Having wrong-footed the opponent with a trick, the most important thing is to acceler-ate past him and away. The time taken by the defender to recover his balance should be used by the attacker to get away from him and put him out of the game.

Attackers should realize that it is not pos-sible to be an effective dribbler of the ball without the ability to change pace and accel-erate away rapidly. Sometimes, defenders can be deceived by change of pace alone. If a player cannot change pace, tricks alone will not compensate for it. However, that said, lack of ability to change pace, to step up a gear, often results from indecision and a lack of mental aggression.

The dribbler should master at least one move involving change of direction as well as one that can be performed at speed.

APPLYING TECHNIQUE

There are three phases in the application of dribbling technique: approaching an opponent, tricking him, and eliminating him from play.

Once a player has beaten an opponent in a dribble, it is essential that he plays the ball away from him and prevents him getting in a second tackle.

The approach
The approach should be full of controlled aggression. The most important factors are the line of approach and its speed.

The line of approach should be as direct as possible. Run straight at your opponent with the ball or, if he is incorrectly positioned, run at the vital space in line to goal. Doing this gives you the best chance of maintaining momentum and direct play and makes it more difficult for opponents to defend.

The speed of approach should be quick, but at less than maximum speed. There are two things to remember. First, at the end of the approach you will have to trick and wrong-foot your opponent. This will be more difficult at maximum speed. Second, after tricking the defender a change of pace will be necessary to take you past him. Obviously, this will not be possible if you are already moving at top speed.

Sometimes you will receive the ball with a defender so close that the approach phase simply does not exist. To dribble past him you will almost certainly have to use a technique that involves a change of direction of the ball followed by a change of pace.

Tricking an opponent
Some techniques for tricking an opponent have already been described. Applying them is a matter of timing, depending on the speed at which you are going and how far away the defender is.

The faster your approach, the further away from the defender you should be when you perform your trick. The ideal distance, however, is just outside tackling range, some four or five feet from your opponent.

Ideally, the trick should take the defender out of the line he is defending and open up to the attacker the most direct route to goal. If the trick is performed effectively, the next phase should be relatively easy.

Eliminating the defender
The last phase of a dribble is to eliminate the defender. This is done by playing the ball past him and accelerating at maximum speed. The ball has to be played *past* the defender rather than to his side. Two problems arise when the ball is played to the side. First, the attack is not as direct as it should be and momentum may be lost. Second, it gives the defender the chance to recover and get goal-side of the ball again.

Dribbling well requires good technique in all three phases of the dribble. A trick on its own is worthless. It also requires a positive, aggressive attitude. Some people think that aggression is a quality only to be expected in defenders. This is not so.

Dribbling is a vital technique in direct play and is very often an unseen and unrecorded factor behind a number of elements in The Winning Formula.

DRIBBLING AS PART OF THE WINNING FORMULA
Analysis of goals scored over the last 20 years shows that dribbling is a factor in more than one of every six goals scored.

CROSSES

When a team funnels back into its own defending third, the majority of the players will be concentrated in a central area, a little less than the width of the penalty area. This is in order to deflect attacks toward the flanks, away from the danger area. It is essential, therefore, for teams to be able to attack effectively down the flanks, where more space will be available.

The main thing to remember about crosses from the flank is that they are passes, and the principles of effective passing remain paramount. **The first requirement is to pass the ball to the back of the defence**.

THE PRIME TARGET AREA

The first objective in crossing the ball should be getting the ball to the back of the defence and into the prime target area.

The prime target area extends out eight yards, from two yards inside the six-yard box to the penalty spot, and across 20 yards, the width of the six-yard box. It is where, ideally, the ball should be crossed to, if at all possible arriving before any defending players. The cross will be too far out for the goalkeeper to deal with and will fall invitingly for incoming attacking players.

The situation that attacking players should try to create is one in which the ball has been crossed into the prime target area, forcing the defenders to attempt a clearance from a position where they are under challenge and facing their own goal. Under these circumstances attackers are often first to the ball and get a clear strike at goal.

Previous page: An accurate cross, delivered early, is one of the deadliest weapons in soccer. England's central defender Mark Wright looks on aghast as Colombia's Carlos Valderrama plays an early ball into the England area.

Our analysis has shown that balls played into the prime target area behind the defence are the most successful type of crosses. About four goals in every five scored from crosses are hit from the prime target area.

56

RELEASING THE BALL

The traditional role of a winger, or flank player, has been to get to the goal-line, in a position either just inside or just outside the penalty area, and only then to cross the ball.

There is no doubt that this is a particularly dangerous position. However three points must be made.

1. It is not an easy position to get into if the defenders are concentrating.

2. Most successful crosses do not originate from this area.

3. It is rarely possible to play the ball to the back of the defence from this position, as the defence will have regrouped and repositioned in and around the six-yard box.

It should be appreciated, therefore, that if flank players become obsessed with getting to the goal-line before releasing the ball then the number of goals scored from crosses will decrease. Flank players should instead look to release the ball early, if necessary from fairly deep, wide positions.

A wide position could be within a yard or so of the touch-line (position 1). A deep position could be just inside the attacking third of the field (position 2). Often these crosses will be made on the run, with the winger playing the ball in full flight without halting his stride.

It is not always necessary for the winger to dribble past a defender before crossing. Often, in fact, it is not only unnecessary but undesirable. The time taken to beat a defender is often all the time his team-mates need to take up defensive positions in the prime target area.

CROSSING THE BALL

There are three phases to crossing the ball; observing the situation, deciding what to do and making the cross.

Observation

The best players constantly observe the unfolding situation, particularly in regard to the amount of space available to them, the positions of their opponents and the position of their team-mates.

The available space to concentrate on is that in the prime target area. If it is free of defenders, then the sooner the ball is crossed into it the better.

If the prime target area is free of defenders, then there are only two defenders whose positions are of interest, the immediate opponent and the goalkeeper. The whereabouts of the immediate opponent will affect the timing and technique of the cross, while the whereabouts of the goalkeeper will affect its placement.

Since the goalkeeper has the enormous advantage of being able to use his hands, it is essential that the cross is played into that part of the prime target area which makes it most difficult for him to get to the ball. The ball should be crossed into the front half of the prime target area if the goalkeeper is covering the rear half of the goal and vice versa.

In practice, the right decision can only be made by observing the goalkeeper's position. However, it helps to know where to expect a good goalkeeper to be in relation to the position of the ball.

The nearer the ball is to the touch-line, the more likely it is that the goalkeeper will be covering the back half of his goal. The cross should be aimed for the near half of the prime target area.

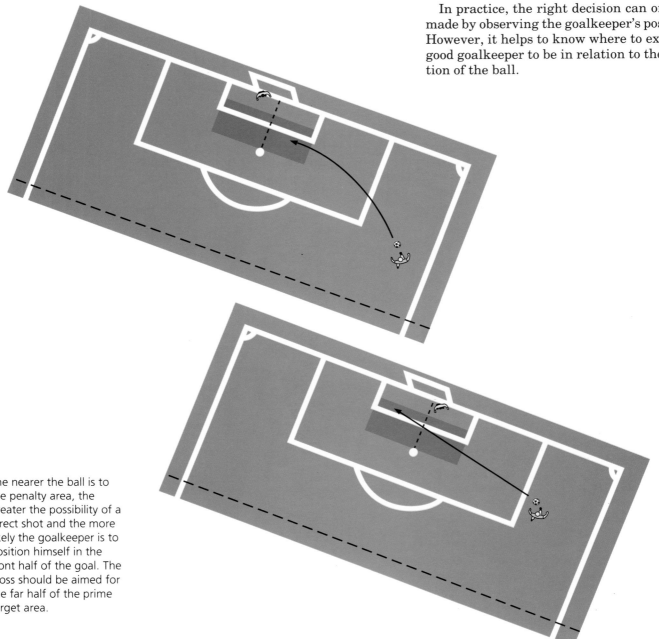

The nearer the ball is to the penalty area, the greater the possibility of a direct shot and the more likely the goalkeeper is to position himself in the front half of the goal. The cross should be aimed for the far half of the prime target area.

Of course, before crossing the ball a player also has to see where his team-mates are. There is no point in playing a cross in to any area if there are not attacking players to take advantage of it. The most likely situation, though, is that there will be one or two attackers, marked by two or three defenders, on or around the edge of the penalty area. The job of the player crossing the ball is then to deliver it into the target area at the correct time and with the correct pace to give the attacking players the best possible chance of producing a strike at goal.

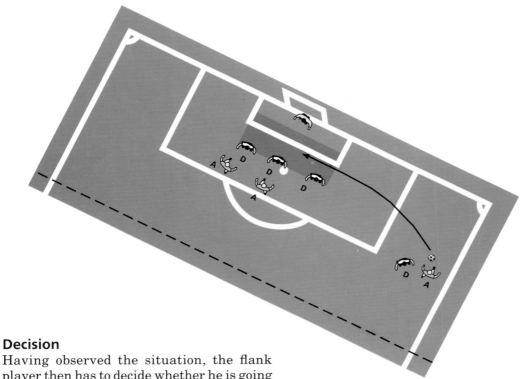

Space is available in the prime target area and the situation strongly favours the attacking players, even though they are outnumbered. Here, the earlier the ball is played into the prime target area, the better. Any pass made behind defenders, with attackers available to challenge for the ball, is to the attacking team's advantage. Defenders dislike being put under pressure in the prime target area even less than they like it anywhere else on the field.

Decision

Having observed the situation, the flank player then has to decide whether he is going to cross the ball. If there is space available into which to aim a cross, and a team-mate on hand to take advantage of it, he should always cross the ball, and as early as possible.

If he is challenged, he has to decide whether to dribble past the challenging player before crossing the ball. If it is at all possible to cross the ball without first dribbling, he should do so. It is less risky, and it gets the ball into the prime target area earlier.

The whole philosophy of direct play is based on quick, positive thinking and assertive action, where every chance of taking the initiative is seized upon. Putting in an early cross is just one more occasion where this approach bears fruit.

Execution

The best crosses are those which give defenders as little time as possible in which to recover and make it as difficult as possible for them to play the ball. In practice this means crosses hit to the back of the defence, low and with pace.

Low means below head height, but preferably not along the ground. This height is ideal for attackers running in to volley or to take diving headers at goal, and is particularly difficult for defenders to clear to any distance.

The cross should be hit with pace to give the defenders as little time as possible in which to recover and to make sure that any deflection off an incoming player, attacker or defender, will still have sufficient pace to score.

Two things are needed to put in this kind of cross; space and the correct technique. If there is sufficient space, either because the defender is badly positioned or the attacker has dribbled past him, all that is required is a good contact on the ball. If, however, the defender is in a good position, the attacker will have to create space in which to play, otherwise the cross will be blocked.

The best technique is a swerve kick with the inside of the foot (see the chapter on *Passing and Support Play* for details of this technique). This bends the ball around the retreating defence and into the prime target area, where the swerve will tend to take the ball away from the goalkeeper. It also lets the player put considerable pace on the ball without sacrificing accuracy.

MOVING INTO THE PRIME TARGET AREA

The point has already been made that there is little profit in crossing balls into the prime target area if there are no attacking players there to convert the cross into an attempt on goal. This section is about how to arrive in the prime target area and what to do once there.

Movement before the cross

Defenders have a natural tendency to move towards the ball. Attacking players should therefore develop a tendency to move away from the ball. This immediately hands the defender a problem – how to keep the ball and his immediate opponent in view. Attackers should move away from their markers on the opposite side to the ball, going as far forward as possible without being caught offside.

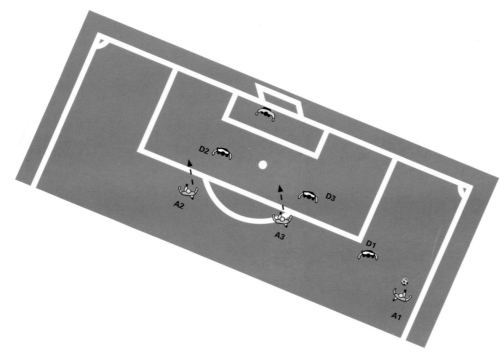

A1 has the ball on the right flank. A2 and A3 have moved away from their markers, as far forward as possible without moving offside. D2 and D3 will have to drop back and open their stance to keep both their immediate opponents and the ball in view.

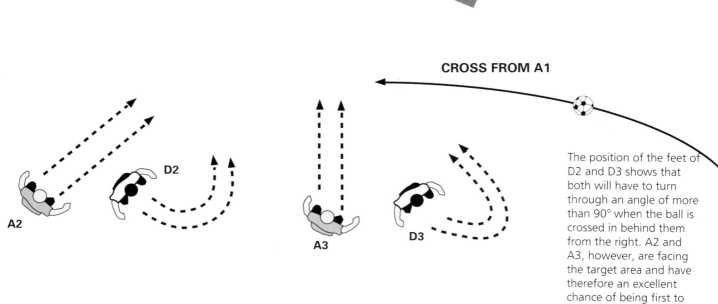

CROSS FROM A1

The position of the feet of D2 and D3 shows that both will have to turn through an angle of more than 90° when the ball is crossed in behind them from the right. A2 and A3, however, are facing the target area and have therefore an excellent chance of being first to the ball.

If the defenders are marking tightly man to man, they will probably move with the attacker on his initial movement away from the ball. If so, the attacker should feint one way then cut back to attack the ball as it is delivered.

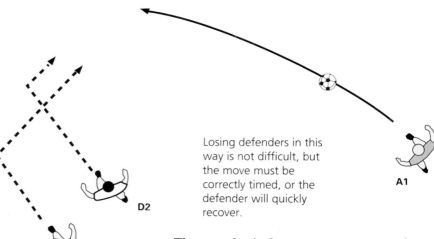

A2 has moved to get behind D2, who has covered the movement. As D2 moves back to cover, however, A2 changes direction to cut across him, giving himself an excellent chance of being first to the ball when it is crossed in.

Losing defenders in this way is not difficult, but the move must be correctly timed, or the defender will quickly recover.

The attacker's first movement away from the ball is critical; it makes the run into the prime target area much easier to accomplish successfully and makes the job of the defenders that much more difficult.

Timing a run to meet a cross

Runs into the prime target area should be made late – as late as possible – and at top speed. Inexperienced players make the run too soon and find that they are either caught offside or standing in the space waiting for the ball to arrive. One of the few certainties in football is that if there is an attacker hanging around waiting for the ball to arrive, it never will – even the most hapless defender will see to that.

Ideally the attacker should arrive in the prime target area at the same moment as the ball. Attackers arriving fast and late may well have to make a diving header at the end of their run. This is a positive advantage, for even if a defender has tracked the attacker's run into the prime target area, he has no chance of stopping him making a diving header. Very few defenders are going to risk diving at the ball while running toward their own goal.

Angling a run to meet a cross

The more a run can be angled to take the attacker into the line of the ball, rather than across it, the better the chance of a successful contact on the ball.

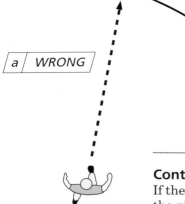

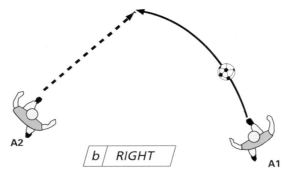

a WRONG

b RIGHT

The angle of the run in (a) is across the line of the ball, making it difficult for the attacker to make a strong contact. The angle in (b) brings the attacker into the line of the ball, enabling him to make a strong contact.

Contacting the ball

If the run to attack the ball has been made at the right time and the right angle, then all that is needed to beat the goalkeeper is a good contact on the ball. The momentum of the run added to the pace of the ball will generate all the power required, so the attacker should concentrate on making accurate contact.

Contact should be through the top half of the ball, to make sure it stays down. If the ball is in the air, even a foot or two off the ground, contact is best made with the head. This provides better control than with the feet and requires little or no adjustment to the running action.

ATTACKING DIFFERENT PARTS OF THE PRIME TARGET AREA

If two or more attackers are positioned to go for a cross, the most important thing is that they should attack different parts of the prime target area. If there are two attackers, one should attack the front half of the prime target area and the other the back half. If there is a third attacker, he should attack the mid-goal area.

This is not only important because it means players avoid getting in each other's way, but also because it means they will be well positioned to pick up any deflections or rebounds. Not every cross can produce a direct shot at goal. Sometimes the player at the near post will flick the ball on towards the far post; sometimes he will feint to play, so as to commit the goalkeeper, then let the ball run across the face of the goal.

CROSSING FROM THE GOAL-LINE

The goal-line used to be regarded as the main, sometimes the only, place from which to cross the ball. We now know this is not so, but there are still occasions when it is correct to take the ball to the goal-line before crossing it.

Basically there are three possibilities from this position; a drive across the face of the goal, a pull-back towards the penalty spot, or a lofted cross to the far post.

England's Neil Webb whips in a cross behind the retreating Albanian defence in a World Cup qualifying match in Tirana.

The driven cross

A driven cross pays the highest dividends when a flank player has outpaced the defence and reached the goal-line while the defenders are recovering at speed but have yet to reach the six-yard line.

A1 is on the goal-line with the ball, and the goalkeeper is positioned at the near post. The rest of the defenders are running toward the six-yard box, while A2, A3 and A4 are moving to attack the near-post, mid-goal and far-post areas respectively. A1 drives the ball low and hard across the face of the goal, and about four yards out, in order to eliminate the goalkeeper. All the attacking players will have to do is steer the ball into an unguarded net. The recovering defenders will find it difficult to avoid doing the same!

The pull-back
The best time to use the pull-back is when defenders have recovered into the six-yard box but there is space available between the six-yard line and the edge of the penalty area.

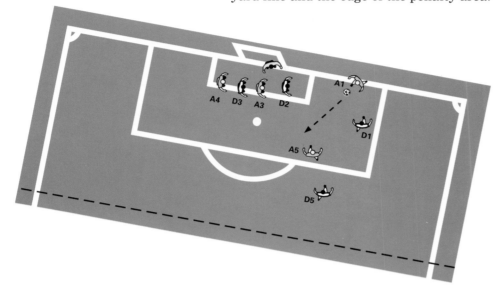

A1 is confronted with a congested six-yard box, and a low drive would be blocked. Space is available, though, between the six-yard box and the edge of the penalty area, and so A1 has pulled the ball back for A5 to move in and shoot from around 15 yards. In this situation the pull-back gives the best chance of a shot at goal. The pass should be weighted so that a first-time shot can be taken.

The point should be made that although this move is often called a pull-back to the penalty spot, the pass is in fact usually to a position several yards to the near side of the penalty spot.

The lofted cross
A lofted cross, like all crosses, must eliminate the goalkeeper. It is essential to look up and check the goalkeeper's position, but when an attacker has reached the goal-line with the ball the goalkeeper will almost always be positioned at or close to the near post. To beat him, the ball must be lifted over his head.

The target area is the far post, about two or three yards out, making for a relatively easy header at goal. The cross must be 'clipped', i.e. lofted with pace, so as not to allow the goalkeeper time to recover his ground. A high, looping cross might well give him just enough time to arrive at his far post to gather the ball.

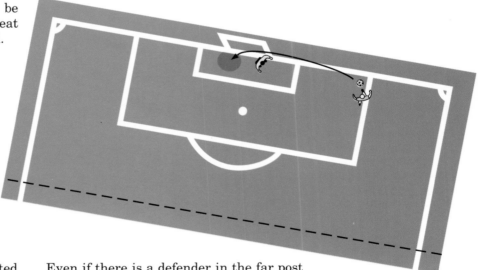

The clipped cross is similar to the lofted drive with wide-angled approach (see the chapter on *Passing and Support Play* for illustrations of this technique) except that the ball is kicked with a stabbing action and little or no follow-through. This gives the ball a steep trajectory and fast delivery.

Even if there is a defender in the far post target area, he will be placed under considerable pressure if there is an attacker running in to head the ball. The attacker will have the advantage of gaining extra height if he leaps at the end of his run, while the defender will have to make a standing jump.

CROSSES BEYOND THE FAR POST

Sometimes it is necessary to cross the ball beyond the far post. This will happen with crosses from wide positions and positions near to the goal-line when the prime target area is full of defenders and the goalkeeper is covering the back half of his goal. The best technique for this type of cross is a lofted drive with a wide-angled approach (see the chapter on *Passing and Support Play* for illustrations of this technique).

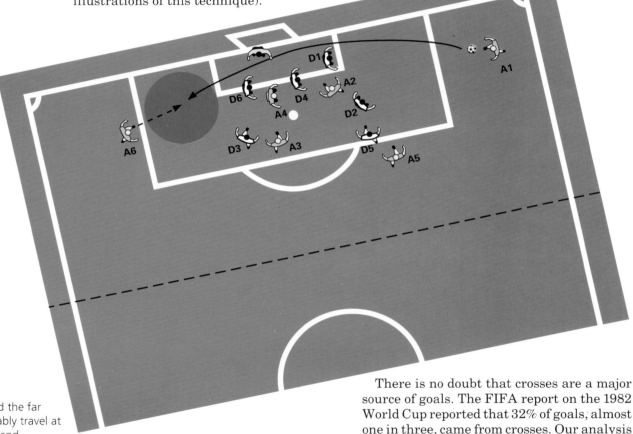

A cross beyond the far post will probably travel at least 40 yards and perhaps as much as 50 yards. Attackers, such as A6, who intend to get on the end of a long cross should take up a position at the side of the penalty area so as to be able to move in and attack the ball. A defender is unlikely to be drawn into such a wide position on the opposite side of the pitch to the ball, so he will find himself moving backwards to try to deal with the cross.

A6 is unlikely to score from such a wide position, and has two alternatives. He can either head the ball back across goal in the direction from which it came, to what is for him the far post, or simply play it back across the face of the goal. Which alternative he chooses depends entirely on the positions of his team-mates and opponents.

There is no doubt that crosses are a major source of goals. The FIFA report on the 1982 World Cup reported that 32% of goals, almost one in three, came from crosses. Our analysis of a larger sample of games gives the lower (but still substantial) figure of 26%, just over one in four. Neither of these statistics, of course, takes into account goals scored directly or indirectly from set plays won as a result of the pressure and confusion which good crosses spread through a defence.

The majority of attacks enter the attacking third down the flank, and crosses in from the flanks are an essential part of direct play. If the crosses are made early and into the prime target area they will inevitably lead to more goals being scored.

HEADING FOR GOAL

HEADING FOR GOAL

About one goal in every five overall is scored with a header. The ability to make powerful, accurate attacking headers is, therefore, a considerable asset in any player, in any team.

COURAGE

Without courage, it is simply impossible to be a good header of the ball. Very young players often fear being hurt when their heads make contact with the ball. This can usually be resolved by learning the correct technique.

In matches, courage is required to use the head to make contact with the ball in situations where it is not unreasonable to expect defenders to use a boot. This type of courage is more to do with character than technique. Good attacking players must look to get into the danger areas. Their desire to score must outweigh any considerations they have for their personal safety.

No amount of technique will adequately compensate for a lack of personal courage. Only courage can motivate a player to throw himself into situations in a match where his heading technique can be used to best effect. Such players are always immensely difficult to play against and always likely to win a match out of nothing. That likelihood increases where their team employs direct play to increase the number of shooting opportunities.

ATTACKING THE BALL

Young players who are afraid of heading the ball show their fear in two ways. First, they close their eyes before making contact with the ball. Second, they hunch their shoulders and turn their head on impact. They react, in fact, as if they were being attacked by the ball.

Exactly the opposite attitude is necessary

When learning to head the ball young players often make two common mistakes. They either **1.** close their eyes well before impact or **2.** they hunch their shoulders and turn their head away. These reactions make a powerful, accurate header impossible. The first rule of heading is to attack the ball – strike it with the head, rather than let it strike your head.

Previous page: Frank Stapleton of the Republic of Ireland, here seen in Manchester United's colours, demonstrates excellent heading technique, with his eyes on the ball, a good jump, and the upper half of his body jack-knifing forwards to add power to the header.

if they are to develop a good heading technique. The basic rule is to strike the ball with the head, rather than let it strike the head. Four basic aspects of technique need to be perfected in order to head the ball accurately, powerfully and painlessly.

Accurate contact
Contact with the ball should be made by the forehead, with the eyes open and looking through the ball. It is normal for the eyes to close involuntarily on contact with the ball, but they should be kept open until that point. To direct the ball downwards, the head must make contact with the top half of the ball.

Jumping to attack the ball
Additional power can be given to a header by running and jumping to meet the ball in flight. The greater the running speed, the greater the force imparted.

After take-off, the back should be arched and the head and neck extended then snapped forward to strike the ball with maximum force. Even a standing jump combined with the correct movement of the back and head can impart considerable speed and power to a header.

Diving to attack the ball
The greatest power of all is imparted to the ball by diving headers, especially if the dive takes place at the end of a short sprint. The

ADDING POWER TO THE BALL
Two body movements help impart force to a header.

⚽ *Arch the back. An arched back acts as a lever, bringing the head forward to strike the ball with force and power.*

⚽ *Nod the head. This is a complementary movement to arching the back; as the back straightens, additional force is transferred to the ball by a firm nodding movement of the head.*

Synchronizing these two movements will ensure that the ball is attacked with power.

full weight and momentum of the body is catapulted forward and transferred to the ball.

Some of the most spectacular goals are scored from diving headers and defenders are usually powerless to stop such a movement. Besides, it is often the only means of reaching a ball, and diving headers often produce a goal from what, at best, would only be considered 'half-chances'. It is important to remember however, that, as with all headers, the eyes should remain open and contact should be through the top half of the ball.

HEADERS FROM CROSSES

Crosses are a major source of goals and goal-scoring opportunities. The majority of these chances are for headers, and the majority of heading chances are for balls below head height. More goals would be scored from crosses if attacking players were better at getting into scoring positions and converting chances into headed goals.

GETTING INTO SCORING POSITIONS

Getting players into scoring positions is only half the battle in successful goal scoring. The other half, of course, is getting the ball into the right area at the right time.

As far as crosses are concerned, if the player crossing the ball plays it in early, and especially if he does so in the prime target area, behind the defence, the responsibility rests squarely on the shoulders of the attacking players to get on the end of the cross.

An attacking player's first objective is to be first to the ball, and his second is to put it in the net. The first will require him to outwit his marker; the second will need good qualities of character and sound technique.

The whole point of attackers moving in for a strike at goal is to make sure that it is they, not the defenders, who are first to the ball. Sometimes this is achieved by getting behind defenders; sometimes it is achieved by getting in front of them. Always, though, it is achieved by getting away from them.

There are three movements which central attackers should be aware of in order to outwit and wrong-foot their markers.

Pulling away from the marker

This is a simple technique of moving back away from the ball.

A1 is in possession of the ball. The task for D2 is to keep the ball and his immediate opponent, A2, in view. A2 will make that more difficult for D2 if he moves backwards, away from the ball. He must run backwards in order to continue watching the play and the movement of D2.

The distance A2 moves need only be three or four yards but he should get as far forward as possible without, of course, straying offside. D2 may now lose sight of A2 and watch the ball instead. If A1 were to cross the ball into the space behind D2, A2 is in an excellent position to move in to attack the ball on the blind side, behind D2.

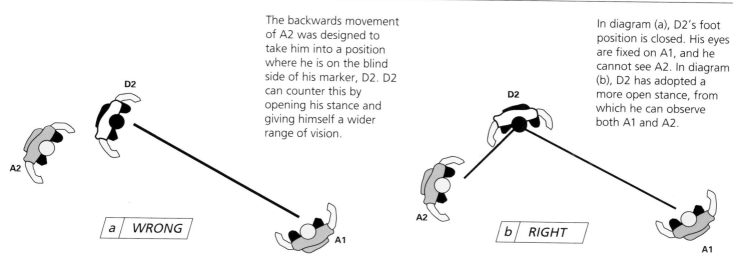

The backwards movement of A2 was designed to take him into a position where he is on the blind side of his marker, D2. D2 can counter this by opening his stance and giving himself a wider range of vision.

In diagram (a), D2's foot position is closed. His eyes are fixed on A1, and he cannot see A2. In diagram (b), D2 has adopted a more open stance, from which he can observe both A1 and A2.

Attackers should appreciate that good defenders will adopt an open stance in order to keep both the ball and their immediate opponent in view. They should also bear in mind that defenders will react both to the movement of the ball and to the movement of opponents. If, therefore, defenders position themselves to observe attackers, then attacking players should respond by moving so that the defenders have to adjust their positions.

Attacking a defender without the ball

The best way to make a defender react to the movement of an attacking player is to run at him. Note that this means running towards him, not into him. There should be no physical contact. The actual line of the run should be towards and behind the defender.

area, he should check his stride just for an instant. This simple act of stopping and starting, even without changing direction, will create two or three yards of space.

Movements aimed at pulling defenders out of position should be made **before** the ball is delivered. Afterwards, not only is it too late to make checking movements and still time a run correctly, but the defenders will probably be concentrating on getting to the ball first, and will not be distracted by opponents' runs.

Understanding the types of movements which will cause defenders difficulties is important. Understanding where and how to make these moves is important. Understanding when to make these moves is most important of all, for without correct timing, all else fails.

TAKING CHANCES FOR HEADING GOALS

Frequently all that is required at the end of a well-timed run is to use the head to steer or deflect the ball out of the reach of the goalkeeper. If the run is timed properly, the last thing the attacker need be concerned about is power. Bodily momentum, allied to the pace of the ball, will produce all that is needed.

The general principles involved in heading for goal are exactly the same as those for shooting with the feet. Placement is more important than power. Headers to the far post are usually more difficult to save because the ball is going away from the goalkeeper. Headers going down and away from the goalkeeper are the most difficult of all to save.

Near post headers

Headers at the near post must, inevitably, be steered or deflected towards the goal. Depending on whether the ball has been

A2 has slightly curved his run to aim at, and behind D2, who will react to cover the run to stop A2 getting behind him. In turning from an open stance to cover A2's run, D2 has a dilemma. If he turns to his right to track A2 he loses sight of the ball. If he turns to his left he loses sight of A2. This means he will be sprinting back towards his own goal, unsure either of the flight of the ball or of the position of his immediate opponent. Panic is likely to ensue, creating a classic recipe for an own goal!

Checking and changing direction

All of us have at some time played dodge and mark with an opponent. The essence of dodging is checking the stride and making quick changes of direction. If a player is closely marked as he runs in to meet a cross, particularly if he is running into the prime target crossed from the goal-line or further out on the flanks, the goalkeeper will either be positioned in the near half of the goal, towards the near post, or he will be arriving there having moved from a position in the far half of the goal.

Sometimes the goalkeeper can be caught moving towards his near post while the ball is steered or deflected across him, towards the far post. Of course, goals are also scored at the near post, but there is invariably an element of goalkeeping error when this happens. When the best goalkeepers are beaten, it is usually at the far post.

Mid-goal headers

It is easier to get a header on target from the middle of the goal because the attacker has the whole width of the goal in front of him. He should aim to direct the ball downwards into either corner of the goal. There is rarely anything to be gained by deflecting the ball, so the attacker can concentrate on generating power.

Far post headers

When heading at the far post, the most important consideration is the position of the goalkeeper.

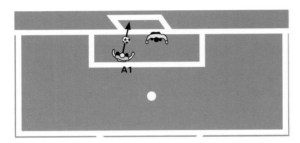

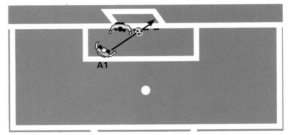

Sometimes the far post area is completely open, with the keeper stranded half-way across the goal. If this is the case, the ball should be accurately placed in the empty part of the net.

On other occasions, the goalkeeper will be moving into the area of the far post, having moved six or seven yards across his goal. When this happens, the header should be aimed across the

goalkeeper into the area he has just vacated.

Power headers, rather than glancing deflections, are almost always required at the far post and, as always, the most difficult balls to save are those that are headed downwards.

Diving headers

Overall, around two out of every three headed goals are scored from a contact on the ball below head height. The importance of diving headers should never be underestimated. Some players throw out a foot and miss the ball in situations where they could have reached it with a diving header. Defenders sometimes clear the ball in situations where, with a diving header, the attacker could have been first to the ball and would possibly have scored.

At every level, goals are there for the taking if players have the courage, the determination and the skill to launch themselves into diving headers.

A diving header transfers the whole weight and momentum of the body into the ball, producing great power.

64% of goals from crosses are scored with headers. All successful teams have aerial power. It is an essential quality in direct play and an essential element in The Winning Formula.

SHOOTING

No-one will be surprised to learn that shooting is the most important element in The Winning Formula. No amount of direct play will win matches if the players cannot shoot well.

Analysis reveals that a high percentage of opportunities to shoot are not taken. Any team can significantly increase its chances of winning matches if its players could guarantee that they would try a shot whenever they got a chance.

At the highest level of soccer the average number of shots per game is around 13 and one goal is scored for every seven attempts.

Another fact thrown up by our researches is that if a team can achieve ten shots on target during a game they will very rarely lose the match. Ten shots on target give an 86% chance of winning. In the hundreds of matches analyzed, we have never recorded a single match when a team achieved ten shots on target and lost the match.

These statistics clearly show that all teams would benefit from practice aimed at increasing the number of shots they take at goal in a game. Practice that improves accuracy is also important.

MISSED OPPORTUNITIES

The first step toward increasing the number of shots is to understand why players do not shoot when they have the chance. There are three main reasons.

Fear

Nothing destroys a player's performance quite as much, or quite as quickly, as fear. Basically, players are not afraid of shooting so much as of missing. This fear of failure can be brought on by crowds, coaches, parents or even team-mates. Eventually, players without the confidence to shoot will begin to avoid getting into positions which may produce shooting opportunities. The best that these players expect is praise for unselfish play, but in fact they are not really passing the ball so much as passing the responsibility.

Of course, fear may sometimes be physical;

players may fear the pain of 'going in where it hurts'. If a player is worried about physical contact he will not be able to concentrate on seizing every opportunity to score.

Lack of vision

Players who play with their head down often simply fail to see that a shot is possible. As a result, they pass or dribble – usually dribble – when there is a chance of a shot. All players should try to observe and understand the play around them, but in the attacking third, and especially the penalty area, the ability to quickly sum up situations becomes particularly important. Many chances occur which demand a first-time shot, but in order for a player to take a first-time shot he needs to orientate himself and know, not only where the goal is, but also where the goalkeeper is.

Lack of speed

There is no doubt that speed is a great asset in and around the penalty area, not just speed of movement but speed of thought and speed of reaction. All players will become quicker if put in realistic practice situations, not because they will cover the ground any faster, but because they will learn to pick up the cues more easily and react more quickly. This will give them more time, helping them to improve their composure and thus their accuracy and technical performance.

Lack of composure, which can be mistaken for lack of speed, leads to a poor first touch, to snatched shots and jerky movements that produce poor contact with the ball. A composed player will move more smoothly, ensuring a good contact on the ball.

DEVELOPING GOOD ATTITUDES TO SHOOTING

It is extraordinary that the most important, and most exciting part of attacking play should be the source of so much fear. All young players like shooting at goal, and shooting is the major fun element in the game. If we want more enjoyment in the game, and if we want to win more matches,

Previous page: Technique, skill and determination are needed to score goals. Diego Maradona hurdles a desperate tackle by Italy's Gaetano Scirea to score a World Cup goal for Argentina with a side-foot volley. Despite his being in mid-air, all Maradona's concentration is on the ball; he is well-balanced and has kept his head still.

then the one thing we need is more shots at goal. In the first instance, this requires improved attitudes to shooting.

Criticism

However bad a shot, credit should always be given for accepting an opportunity to shoot. Most criticism should be reserved for those who fail to take a chance to shoot. Any criticism of the shot itself should be constructive and followed up by purposeful practice. Criticism that is not constructive is worthless at best and may be damaging.

Teachers, coaches, parents and young players should ask themselves two questions.

⚽ *What is the purpose of criticism if it is not constructive?*

⚽ *Are those doing the criticizing responsible for improving the performance?*

If the answer to the second of these questions is no, then the real criticism should be aimed at the critics themselves. A better attitude to giving and taking criticism produces a better atmosphere in which to learn.

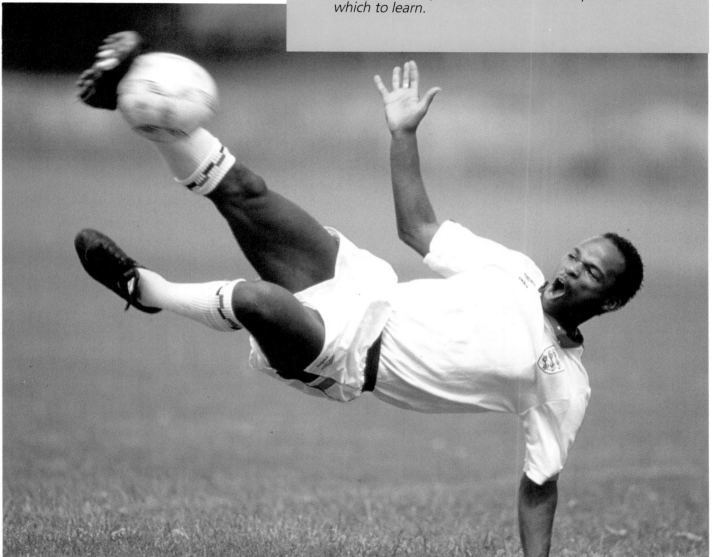

Assertion

Shooting is an act of self-assertion, of seizing the initiative. Players must learn, through correct practice, to recognize those situations where they must accept the responsibility for trying to score. Too often, players attempt to pass that responsibility (in the shape of the ball) to someone else.

Correct practice

A great deal of teaching and coaching in relation to shooting is not relevant; usually, it fails to simulate the situation which is causing difficulty in the game. Many players can shoot perfectly well in practice but have a problem when there is a defender challenging for the ball.

The bicycle kick is a spectacular volleying technique used when a ball is too high for a hook volley. It is demonstrated here by England Youth International Rod Thomas.

73

To be useful and relevant, shooting should be practised with opposition. Time spent on correct shooting practice is never wasted; shooting is the single most important skill to practice.

Courage

Shooting very often requires physical courage. Those afraid of physical contact should keep in mind that the real situation is not as bad as the one they imagine. The way to persuade someone that this is so is correct practice, complete with opponents. There can be no guarantee of success, but realistic practice is the best way to overcome this fear.

SHOTS OFF TARGET

Analysis shows that a high percentage of shots miss the target. In our sample there were 1,448 shots, and 760, just over half of them, missed the target. There are three ways of missing the target.

Shots over the crossbar

This is the worst type of inaccuracy, not only because it shows technical incompetence but because there is no possibility of secondary scoring chances through deflections.

Shots wide of the near post

Here there is some chance of a deflection, provided the shot is head height or below; the possibilities are not good, but at least they are better than with shots which fly high.

Shots wide of the far post

It is a fact that the great majority of secondary scoring opportunities occur at the far post. About one goal in four is scored at the far post. In many of these goals the ball has been deflected.

Very few shots are taken from directly in front of goal. Almost all shots are from an angle and allow for shooting toward the far post. Shots coming across defenders are likely to be deflected towards the far post as players lunge to make contact with the ball. This point will be returned to later. A shot actually going wide of the far post may be converted into a goal by a fellow attacker running in. One thing should be emphasized now: **if a player shoots wide of the goal, it is best if the shot is wide of the far post.**

SHOOTING LOW

Shots on the ground are more difficult to save than those in the air.

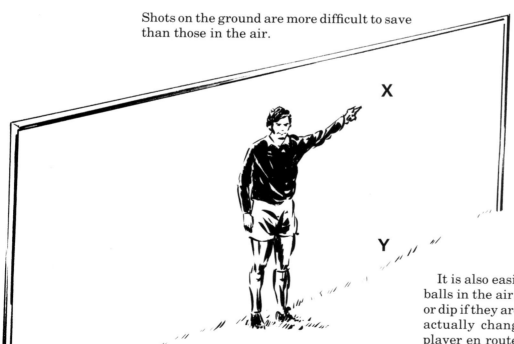

The goalkeeper will be able to move more quickly to save at point X than at point Y. He will have to move his whole body to reach a ball at Y, but may be able to reach a ball at X simply by stretching out an arm.

It is also easier for the goalkeeper to judge balls in the air. Shots can be made to swerve or dip if they are hit correctly, but no shot will actually change direction unless it hits a player en route. Shots along the ground, on the other hand, are likely to skid, stick or bump, making the shot more difficult to save. Young players like to hit the roof of the net and see it bulge, but in fact low shots are more likely to succeed.

DIRECTING SHOTS AWAY FROM THE GOALKEEPER

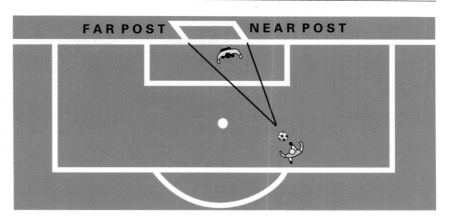

FAR POST   NEAR POST

The importance of shooting to the far post in gaining deflections has already been mentioned. There are other reasons for aiming at the far post.

If a goalkeeper can get his body into the line of flight he will do so. This represents his best chance of making a save and holding on to the ball. Near post shots always give him a better chance of getting into the line of flight than shots to the far post. Besides, if he has to reach for a shot at the near post and fails to hold on to the ball, it is likely to either go out for a corner or, at worst, drop outside the line of the goal.

If the shot is going away from the goalkeeper, towards his far post, it is more difficult for him to get into the line of flight, to hold on to the ball or to knock it away to safety.

Successful shots aimed inside the far post exceed scoring shots aimed inside the near post by four to one. Shooting low and aiming at the far post are of great importance and time should be spent on them in practice.

If the ball is going away from the goalkeeper it is clearly more difficult for him to get into the line of flight, and virtually impossible for him to get his body behind the ball. If he is reaching for a ball going away from him, he is, therefore, much less likely to hold on to it.

The consequences of failing to hold a ball travelling toward the far post are much more serious than failing to hold a near post shot. Virtually the whole of the goal is exposed. For the same reason it is more difficult to knock a far post shot away to safety.

A ball falling loose near the far post puts the goal in danger. The area around the far post is the prime scoring area. More goals are scored from there than from any other position. Just consider how many easy tap-in goals are scored in the area of the far post, compared with the area around the near post.

SWERVE AND POWER

A goalkeeper will always try to hold on to shots fired at goal. It is the attacker's job to make it as hard as possible for him to do this. Shots struck with power or swerve are difficult for a goalkeeper to hold on to, increasing the likelihood of secondary scoring chances. The number of secondary scoring chances is increased if the swerving or power shots are directed to the far post.

Shooting from outside the penalty area

The FIFA report on the 1982 World Cup pointed out that 38% of the goals in the competition were scored from outside the area. Our 20-year analysis of matches gives a lower figure, 16%, just under one goal in six. Neither figure however, takes into account the number of goals scored from loose balls and rebounds after a shot outside the area.

Of goals directly scored from outside the penalty area around 12% come from volleys, while 88% are the result of ground shots. This partly reflects the difficulty of controlling volleys – practice in this area is important – but it also emphasizes the effectiveness of ground shots, which are harder to save. Nearly three-quarters of long-distance goals are scored with the right foot. As most players are right-footed this is understandable, but it does indicate that players are rejecting chances that fall to their left foot. Players who can shoot with either foot will make the most of all their chances.

Long-distance power shots are of the utmost importance for a number of reasons:

⚽ *The shot may score direct. The chances of this are increased because the goalkeeper is often unsighted by defenders and attackers between him and the player shooting.*

⚽ *Deflections wrong-foot the goalkeeper. A power shot through a crowd of players may take a deflection into the net or set up a simple tap-in (past a stranded, off-balance goalkeeper) for a team-mate.*

⚽ *Even if the goalkeeper makes a save, he may not be able either to hold on to the ball or to push it out for a corner, leading to a secondary scoring opportunity.*

⚽ *The shot may be blocked by a defender, again leading to a secondary scoring opportunity.*

Undoubtedly the first and best way of increasing the number of shots in a game is for players to be more willing to shoot from outside the area. When players get within 30 yards or so of the goal, they usually have four options; pass, dribble, run with the ball or shoot. Of these options the one that will usually pay the biggest dividend is to shoot.

VOLLEYS AND HALF-VOLLEYS

Many chances to score come from balls dropping or bouncing in the penalty area. This sort of chance comes from set plays, crosses and forward passes over the heads of defenders, as well as from rebounds, deflections and poor headed clearances. Many fall into the 'half-chance' category. However, the result of a match very often depends upon accepting half-chances. They must be attempted if the number of shots at goal is to be increased.

The half-chance can be converted into a goal by a quickly taken volley or half-volley. Players therefore need to practise taking this type of shot, learning to adjust their body position quickly, so as to make contact through the top half of the ball. Far too many shots go over the crossbar, and many of these are volleys. Volleying techniques are dealt with in the chapter on *Passing and Support Play.*

One thing we can be sure of; if the shot goes over the bar, contact was made through the bottom half of the ball. If contact is made through the top half the ball it will never go over the crossbar.

Volleys are the most difficult shots of all to keep down. Much practice is required, more than is usually devoted to practising this skill, but the rewards for hard work are high. One goal in six is scored with a volley.

QUICKNESS

Speed of thought and movement are critical qualities in and around the penalty area, complemented by determination and courage. Players who possess these four qualities, plus good technique, are an absolute nightmare to play against in the penalty area; sooner or later they will find an opportunity to shoot for goal. Fortunately for defenders, very few players fit this description. Those that do usually have two particular physical qualities.

1. Low reaction time
This allows the player to react quickly to rebounds or deflections, for instance. This quality can be trained to a degree, but players with naturally quick reactions will always have more potential than ones with slower reaction times.

2. Low centre of gravity
Many situations requiring quick reactions also require turns through 90 degrees or more. Players with a low centre of gravity have a decided mechanical advantage in turning quickly.

While it is important that players with special natural attributes should play in those positions where their attributes will be most useful, their maximum potential will only be realized through correct practice. The ability to read the game, to pick up cues and anticipate situations are all enhanced by the simulation of match conditions in practice.

COMPOSURE

Composure comes from confidence, and confidence comes from knowing what one can do, of being sure of one's ability. The way to be sure of one's ability to perform is to repeat the performance over and over again. That is what practice does; it makes whatever is being practised permanent. Note the words: practice makes permanent, **not** practice makes perfect. Whether the technique or skill being practised is perfected depends on the quality and quantity of the practice.

Composure produces a smooth, unhurried performance. A composed, skilful player combines the maximum of speed and power with an effortless grace. That effortlessness is the result of great effort and long practice on the training ground. If genius is 10% inspiration and 90% perspiration, then great players put in the perspiration in training in order to display inspiration in a match.

Composure, then, is the result of correct practice. A composed player has a fraction longer to assess the time and space available and, where there is the chance of a shot, the position of the goalkeeper. This allows him to decide on whether a power shot or an accurate placement is the best option.

FIRST-TIME SHOTS

Analysis shows clearly that half of all goals are scored with first-time shots, that is without first controlling the ball. This does not include headed goals, almost all of which are first-time shots; when they are included, the proportion of goals scored with first-time shots rises to 71.5%. This figure does not include goals scored direct from free kicks or penalties.

There is a powerful message for everyone in these statistics, which should lead to a major rethink of many shooting practices.

SCORING WHEN CLEAR OF THE DEFENCE

A special type of composure is needed when a player breaks clear of the defence and has only the goalkeeper to beat. These situations appear to be easy, but they never are. It is essential that the player keeps a cool head. The four phases are: the approach, observation, making a decision and its execution.

1. The approach

The attacker will have broken clear of the defence either by dribbling past the last defender or by running into space behind the last defender to receive a pass. In these circumstances there is usually plenty of space between the attacker and the goalkeeper and so there is no need for close control. In fact, it is better for the attacker to play the ball well forward. This will allow him to cover the ground quickly and to check on the position and movement of the goalkeeper.

2. Observation

The goalkeeper's job when an attacker breaks clear of the defence is to narrow the shooting angle by moving towards the ball. He will want to stay on his feet and be steady and balanced when the shot is taken.

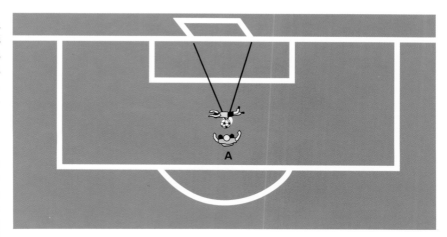

As the attacker runs forward he should observe the speed and angle of the goalkeeper's movements and assess the space.

Should the goalkeeper get near enough to the ball to eliminate the shot he will go down at the feet of the attacker, spreading his body in a barrier across the angle of the goal.

When an attacker gets clear of the defence, the goalkeeper's main aim will be to dive at the attacker's feet, smothering the ball before it is played past him. Here, Mark Hughes of Wales is frustrated by the Czechoslovakian goalkeeper.

3. Making a decision

Having weighed up the situation, the attacker must make a decision. There are three possible choices; shoot for goal, lob the ball over the goalkeeper or dribble it around him.

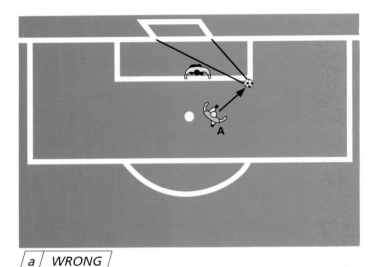

a | WRONG

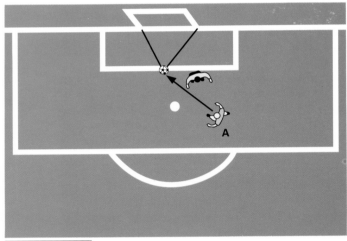

b | RIGHT

Shooting past the goalkeeper. Essentially, the ball should be passed into the goal. The attacker must be sure there is sufficient space to play the ball beyond the goalkeeper and into the net. It is possible to create more space for the shot by altering the angle just before shooting. Sometimes space can be increased by feinting to shoot, in order to draw the goalkeeper to one side, or at least unbalance him, before playing the ball firmly and accurately past him.

Lobbing over the goalkeeper. If space is available in front of the goalkeeper and especially if the ball is bouncing, it is often easiest to play the ball over his head as he comes forward. This technique is more difficult, however, when the ball is on the ground, rolling away from the attacker. This is not a reason for never lobbing the ball into the net so much as a reason for practising the technique in a realistic situation with a goalkeeper.

Dribbling past the goalkeeper. There are two important factors to be borne in mind.

The goalkeeper must be eliminated and the ball must be played out of his reach.

In eliminating the goalkeeper, the space and angle for shooting into the goal should be increased.

In order to eliminate him, the decision to dribble past the goalkeeper must be made

when the ball is far enough away for him not to be able to play it, but close enough to commit him and make it impossible for him to readjust his position. If a feint, or disguise play is to be made, this is the moment to do it – it can be devastating. The ball should then be played outside the goalkeeper's reach and preferably past him.

In (a), A has played the ball to his right, decreasing the angle for passing the ball into the goal. In (b) he has played the ball to his left, widening the angle for passing the ball into the net. Clearly, (b) is correct.

4. Execution

Once the decision to shoot, lob or dribble has been made, the execution should be characterized by two things.

⚽ A positive performance – with no changing of the decision.

⚽ A calm and clinical performance – with accuracy the first concern.

The more that players practise the four elements – the approach, observation, making a decision and its execution – the more assured they will become of their performance. With that assurance will come confidence.

Nearly one goal in every twenty is scored from a situation where a player is clear of the defence. It is therefore worth allocating time for solo attackers to practise beating the goalkeeper by shooting, lobbing or dribbling.

THE PRIME SCORING AREA

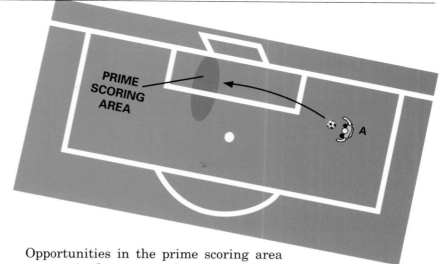

Analysis shows that 22.4% of all goals are scored from positions in the area of the far post. We have named that area the prime scoring area.

The prime scoring area is a position level with the far post. It is a narrow corridor, three yards or so in width and extending out eight or nine yards from the goal-line.

In every attack one attacking player should cover the prime scoring area. Rebounds and ricochets are highly likely to pass through it; the number of these rebounds and ricochets will increase as more shots are aimed at the far post area. A player should always be detailed to cover the prime scoring area at corners, free kicks from the flanks, crosses and long throw-ins.

Opportunities in the prime scoring area may come in the air or on the ground. Whatever height they come they are often clear chances with no opponent challenging for the ball and the goalkeeper stranded in the wrong half of the goal.

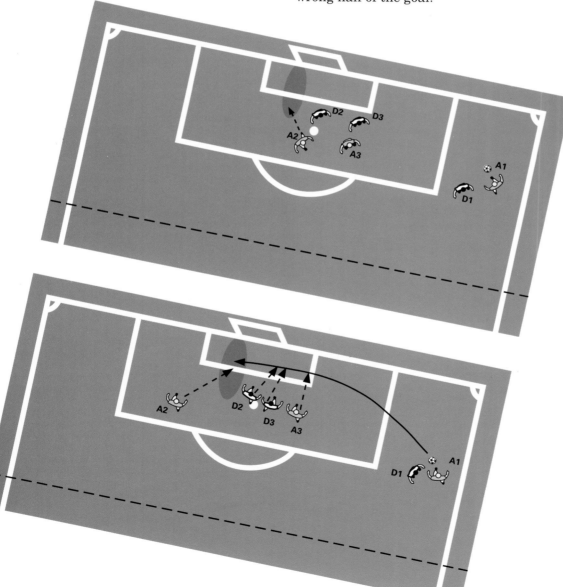

To get into position in the prime scoring area attackers will sometimes have to move away from a central position. In the diagram A2 is doing this, running backwards so he can watch A1, who has the ball, and his opponents. His position in the prime scoring area will be as far forward as possible while remaining onside.

On other occasions the attacker will move into the prime scoring area from a flank position, timing his run to arrive there at the same time as the ball. This is most likely when the ball is crossed in from the other flank. In the diagram, A1 has crossed the ball to the back of the defence. D2 has allowed himself to be drawn rather too far across goal. A2 must delay his run into the space until the last moment; if he moves too soon he may well attract the attention of D2.

When an attacker shoots from outside the penalty area a team-mate should move into the prime scoring area, anticipating a rebound or a deflection.

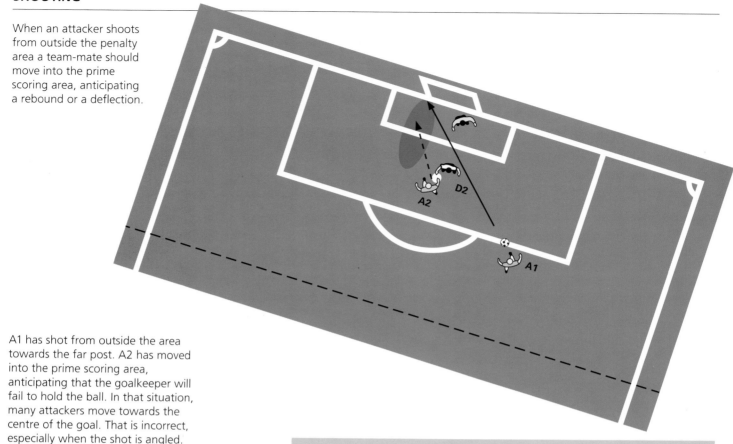

A1 has shot from outside the area towards the far post. A2 has moved into the prime scoring area, anticipating that the goalkeeper will fail to hold the ball. In that situation, many attackers move towards the centre of the goal. That is incorrect, especially when the shot is angled.

An attacking player should be detailed to take up position in the prime scoring area at all set plays in the attacking third. Set plays often lead to deflections and partial clearances, which present secondary scoring chances.

All these situations must be practised in order to make the most of the handsome opportunities that occur in the prime scoring area. Attacking players should learn to spot appropriate situations early so they can time their runs into the prime scoring area to best effect.

There is no doubt that attacking the prime scoring area at every opportunity will increase the rate of goal scoring. Direct play will markedly increase the number of opportunities to attack the prime scoring area.

Direct play will produce more chances to shoot and more set plays in the attacking third. Chances to shoot will come, directly or indirectly, from set plays. Many of these shooting opportunities will fall to players who only go into the attacking third on set plays, and it is important that those players get plenty of shooting practice in situations similar to those likely to occur at set plays.

SHOOTING – FACTS AND FALLACIES

Before concluding this chapter, it is worth restating some basic facts.

1. *Many shooting opportunities – we estimate as many as one in three – are missed because the shot is never taken.*

2. *Even at the highest level, more than half of all shots miss the target, so players should never shy away from shooting for fear of missing the target.*

3. *At the highest level the average number of shots each team will achieve on target per game is 6.2.*

4. *At the highest level the average number of shots on target needed to score one goal is 3.4.*

5. *At the highest level ten shots on target in a game gives an 86% chance of winning.*

6. *We have never recorded a single match when a team achieved ten shots on target and lost the match.*

Taken together these points should persuade players at all levels to spend more time on shooting practice. Realistic shooting practice (see the chapter on The Winning Formula for details) can pay high dividends.

CREATING SPACE

CREATING SPACE

Soccer matches are won by exploiting space. On many occasions this means first creating the space to exploit. Space can be created either by an individual player or by combined play between two or more players.

CREATING SPACE AS AN INDIVIDUAL

There are five essential techniques with which an individual can create space in which to play. Four of them involve techniques with the ball and the fifth an understanding of how to create space without it.

1. GOOD BALL CONTROL

The ability to bring the ball under control with one touch is an important technique for creating time and space in which to play. A player who can drop a ball at his feet with his first touch, so that it is ready to be played, gains room in which to manoeuvre and time to choose the most effective way of initiating direct play with his second touch.

There are three elements in good ball control.

(i) Moving into the line of flight
The controlling surface – the foot, thigh or chest – must be moved into the ball's line of flight. The head should be still. If the head moves out of line, it is very difficult to bring the controlling surface into line. It is rarely possible to watch the ball all the way to the actual moment of contact. Therefore, when practising, even without opposition, players should learn not to fix their eyes on the ball throughout its flight; they should look away to check on the position of their opponents and to look for any forward passing opportunities. It is not necessary, or advisable, to turn the head to do this. With practice, players will learn to read the play ahead at a glance. Once this is done, the most important thing is to keep the head steady and the controlling surface in line, and to concentrate on making a good contact with the ball.

(ii) Choosing the right technique
Controlling the ball is not simply a matter of presenting a controlling surface to the ball but also of choosing between wedge control and cushion control.

Wedge control presents a rigid controlling surface to the ball and is best used where power is needed to force the ball down or into space over a distance of possibly several yards.

Cushion control involves drawing back the controlling surface at the moment of contact to 'cushion' the ball, taking the force out of it and dropping it at the feet ready to play. This technique is best used where space is limited and marking tight.

(iii) Confident execution
Making an early decision about how to control and then play the ball gives a player time to concentrate on his technique. The best technical performances are always calm and unhurried. A player who is not calm and mentally relaxed is probably indecisive and will always appear to be in a hurry. His movements will be jerky, not smooth.

A mental state combining high concentration with relaxation is an ideal one for good ball control. Concentration and relaxation both come from confidence, and confidence comes from knowing what one can do. Knowing what one can do is the result of correct practice.

The importance of the first touch
Good ball control does not mean killing the ball dead beneath the foot. This is poor technique, as it requires another, 'setting up' touch before the ball can be played positively, wasting a precious second or two. The first touch should do three things; it should protect the ball from any challenging player, control it into available space and make direct play possible. Failure to bring the ball under control with the first touch will certainly mean the loss of a little time. If there is an opponent challenging, the ball may also be lost in a quick tackle.

Previous page: Ruud Gullit, captain of the Dutch team which won the European Championship in 1988, uses his great speed off the mark and turning ability to create space for himself, and intelligent runs forward to create space for his team-mates.

In (a), A1 has controlled the ball towards D1 and away from available space. He has also put it in a position where D1 will have little trouble preventing him playing it forward.

In contrast, in diagram (b) A1 has controlled the ball away from D1 into the available space, placing his body between D1 and the ball and screening it from him. D1 is in no position to prevent A1 from initiating direct play.

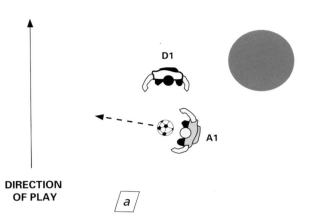

DIRECTION OF PLAY

a

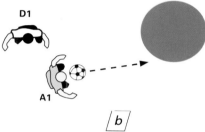

b

2. DISGUISE

One hallmark of an outstanding player is an ability to disguise his intentions. A feint, or a dummy, makes an opponent move in anticipation of a pass or dribble that does not occur and gives the attacking player space to exploit.

Defenders always try to make the play predictable; this makes their job much easier, as the players can anticipate the next move and position themselves ready to intercept or challenge for the ball. Predictable attackers make defenders look better players. Unpredictable attackers not only create space for themselves but also cause defenders to be less confident, more indecisive and more likely to make mistakes.

The most important element about disguise play is that it must seem to be real. If, for example, a player is moving off in one direction, checking, then moving in another direction, it is essential that his first movement is explosive. If he is feinting to kick the ball, there must be a substantial back-swing of the kicking foot or the defenders will not react.

Passes made with the inside of the foot are much easier to predict than those made with the instep. It is therefore worth practising passing with the instep in order to make one's play just a little less predictable. This technique is covered in the chapter on *Passing*.

3. TURNING WITH THE BALL

Every player should be able to turn with the ball. It is especially important, however, for those in midfield or forward positions. Defenders will always prevent opponents from turning if they can. This makes sure the ball is played away from the goal, slowing down the attack. Time, almost always, is on the side of the defence.

England midfielder Paul Gascoigne, here playing for the under-21 side, prepares to execute an outside hook turn with his right foot.

Awareness of space

Attackers should always be aware whether or not they have enough space to turn if the ball is played to them. If there is room, there is no need to move to meet the pass and the best position in which to receive the ball is 'half-turned', that is, sideways-on to the direction of play.

In (a), the player's feet are at 90°, sideways-on, to the direction of play. He has good forward vision, helping him make a quick decision about what to do next, and he can move forward quicker because he is already half-turned. On receiving a pass he can simply take the pace off the ball with a cushion technique and allow it to run into the space available, keeping up the attacking momentum.

In (b), where the player has his back to the direction of play, none of the advantages of being sideways-on apply; the attack will be slowed down as a result, and momentum lost through poor attacking rather than good defending.

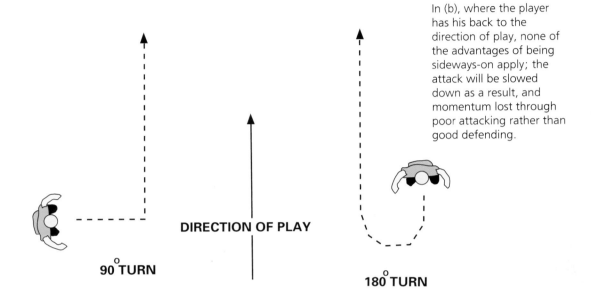

DIRECTION OF PLAY

90° TURN

180° TURN

In top-level soccer, however, players in midfield and forward positions are likely to be closely marked by defenders who will try to stop them turning. When this is the case attackers must move away from their markers to receive the ball; it is the player receiving the ball who should dictate the angle and speed of the pass.

Two things influence the decision to turn when marked; the player's position on the field and his technical ability to turn. It is inadvisable to turn in the defending third of the field, where losing the ball could prove disastrous. Players should always choose the safest option in the defending third. More than half of all goals scored originate in the attacking third of the field (which, of course, is the defending team's defending third); players who risk losing the ball in their own defending third are always likely to give away a goal.

As for technique, players who are not confident about their ability to turn with the ball are better advised to play it back to a supporting team-mate whenever they receive it with their back to the direction of play.

However, players who **can** turn with the ball are able to make a larger contribution to the team's direct play. Every player should attempt to master two or three basic techniques for turning with the ball.

By moving away at an angle, A can observe the movement of his marker, D. A could not do this if he were to move straight back down the field. He should now receive the ball on his outside foot so that his body is screening it from D.

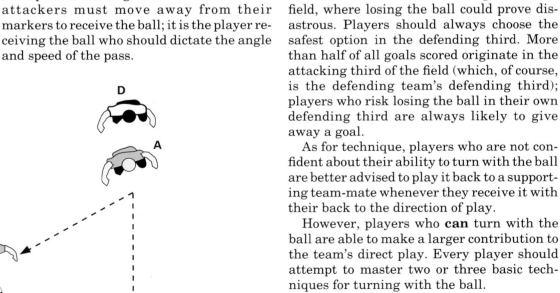

D

A

RIGHT

WRONG

The Cruyff turn

This turn is named after Johann Cruyff, the Dutch international of the 1970s, who used it to turn and lose many close markers.

1. Feint to kick the ball. This movement should be exaggerated so that the defender can see and react to it.

2. If the feint is with the right foot, pivot on the left foot and flick the ball with your right foot past the outside of your left foot at an angle away from the defender and behind him. The defender will almost certainly be caught off balance and facing in the wrong direction.

3. Accelerate away. This is most important. Once the turn is completed, and the defender beaten, he must not be given time to recover.

Though the Cruyff turn can be used to devastating effect in central attacking positions, it is an especially good technique to use on the flanks, where a feint at a pass inside leads to a turn and run outside the defender.

The step-over

1. Feint to pass the ball with the inside of the foot.

2. Instead, lift the foot and step over the ball, keeping the foot low and close to the ball.

3. Pivot on that foot and spin back to play the ball away with the other foot.

4. Accelerate away from the defender.

The inside hook

1. Take a long stride.

2. Reach and hook to turn the ball with the inside of the foot, while pivoting on the other foot.

3. Accelerate away from the turn.

The outside hook

This is a similar technique to the inside hook, but the ball is turned with the outside of the foot.

1. Take a long stride.

2. Reach and hook the ball with the outside of the foot while pivoting on the other foot.

3. Accelerate away from the turn.

There are two more simple techniques for turning and creating space, best used when an attacker is moving crossfield with the ball, closely marked, and unable to play the ball forward; the stop turn and the drag-back.

1.

2.

The stop turn

1. Trap the ball under the foot.

2. Turn through 180° and quickly play the ball with the outside of the other foot.

3. Accelerate away from the defender.

The drag-back

1. Pretend to kick the ball forward but lift the foot across the top of the ball and drag it back with the sole of the foot.

2. Turn quickly and accelerate away from the defender.

Players should practise all these methods of turning; in this way they will develop their own preferences and variations. Whatever the technique used, however, there are three common factors in all good turns.

⚽ *An element of disguise or surprise.*

⚽ *The attacker keeps his body between the ball and the opponent, screening the ball from him.*

⚽ *A change of direction, triggering an immediate change of pace.*

The ability to turn with the ball is vital. Our analysis clearly shows its importance in scoring. Turning was an element in one in five of all goals scored.

4. DRIBBLING

Players who can beat an opponent by dribbling not only make space for themselves but also, by taking defenders out of the game, often create a numerical advantage for their side. They are invaluable to a team, creating space and trouble where none existed. The technique of dribbling is dealt with in a chapter of its own. All that remains to be said here is that every player should master two or three dribbling techniques, as it is a vitally important way of creating space.

5. MOVING OFF THE BALL

Space is more often created by players without the ball than those with it. This is hardly surprising, since there will always be nine outfield players without the ball while only one can be in possession at any one time.

Players running off the ball to create space have two aims. First, to attract the attention of opponents in good defensive positions and draw them into less good positions, and second, to make the task of the player in possession easier. Various types of run, together with the way to recognize when a defender is in a good position, are covered in the chapter on *Forward Runs*.

As far as creating space is concerned, it should be understood that any movement is likely to cause trouble for defenders. Defenders react to the movement of attackers without the ball as well as to the movement of the ball. They much prefer, therefore, to play attackers who stay in fixed positions. The more often attacking players change positions, the more difficult it becomes for defenders to co-ordinate their teamwork.

CREATING SPACE AS A TEAM

The most critical points in a football match are when a side loses possession of the ball. This is when players are likely to lose their concentration. Sometimes when a team regains possession it will not be necessary to create space so much as make the most of the space presented by opponents.

At other times, though, the team as a whole will have to work hard to create the space in which to play. There are basically four techniques with which a team can create space.

1. SPREADING OUT FROM SIDE TO SIDE

Defences in retreat funnel back towards their own goal with the aim of sealing off space in front of goal from the attacking side.

Quite often, possession of the ball is regained when a team is in a 'retreated' position in front of its own goal.

When this happens the first thing the side regaining the ball should do is to spread out and stretch the opposition from side to side. If this is done quickly, the opposition will have problems marking and covering.

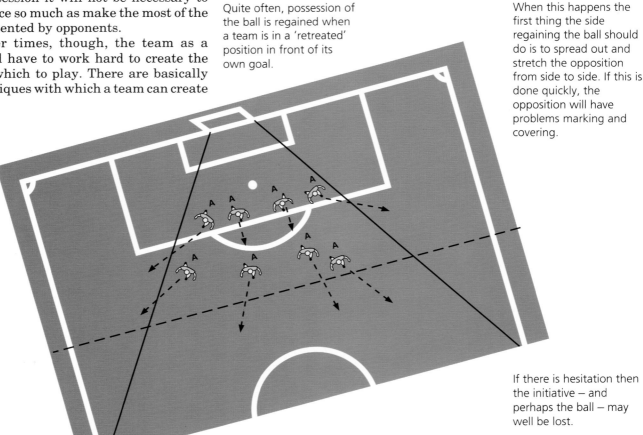

If there is hesitation then the initiative – and perhaps the ball – may well be lost.

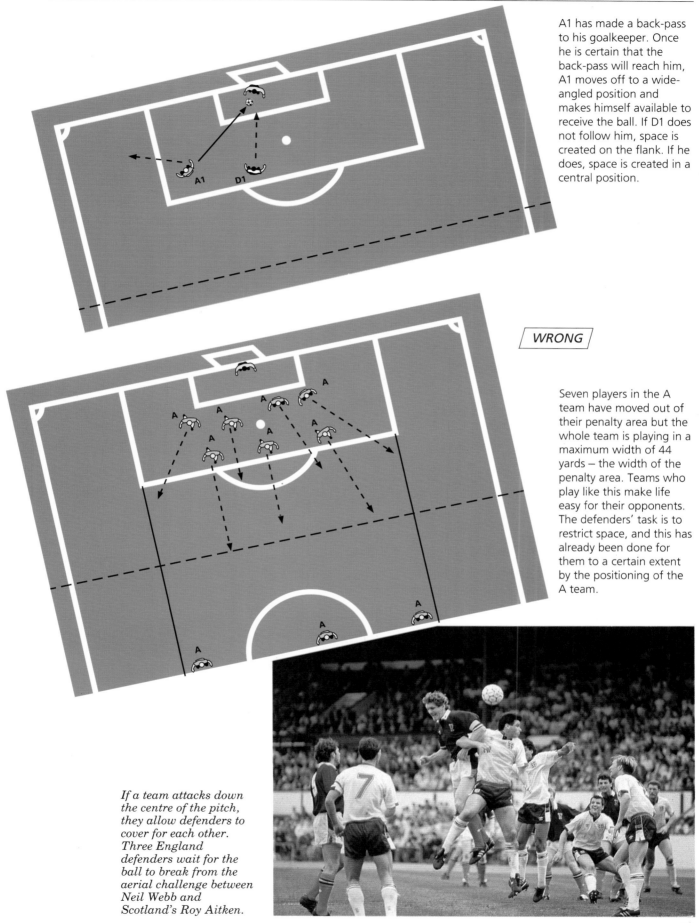

A1 has made a back-pass to his goalkeeper. Once he is certain that the back-pass will reach him, A1 moves off to a wide-angled position and makes himself available to receive the ball. If D1 does not follow him, space is created on the flank. If he does, space is created in a central position.

WRONG

Seven players in the A team have moved out of their penalty area but the whole team is playing in a maximum width of 44 yards — the width of the penalty area. Teams who play like this make life easy for their opponents. The defenders' task is to restrict space, and this has already been done for them to a certain extent by the positioning of the A team.

If a team attacks down the centre of the pitch, they allow defenders to cover for each other. Three England defenders wait for the ball to break from the aerial challenge between Neil Webb and Scotland's Roy Aitken.

The A team has spread out much more effectively. The runs of A2 and A3 have been almost parallel to the goal-line and A4 and A5 have also taken up wide positions, creating much more space in which to play and making the defenders' marking and covering jobs more difficult.

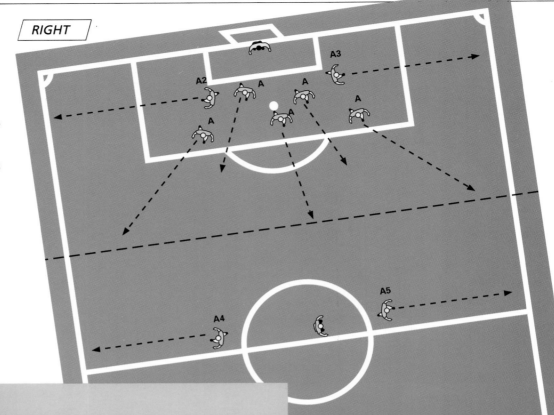

RIGHT

There are eight points to remember when a team spreads out side to side.

⚽ *The decision to spread out should be taken early and the ground covered as quickly as possible.*

⚽ *Wide means very wide – out on the touch-line.*

⚽ *Runs should be made at different angles into different spaces, but never at the expense of losing sight of the ball.*

⚽ *The positions taken up should make it difficult for the opposition both to mark an opponent and to cover each other.*

⚽ *Attacking players should take up positions giving them as wide a field of vision as possible in case they receive the ball.*

⚽ *The ball should be played out to the team-mate who is in the best position to exploit forward play, not simply in the biggest space.*

⚽ *The pass should be delayed until the player who is to receive it is in position to control it. A poor pass or poor control can destroy the space that has been created.*

⚽ *The next step must be to exploit the space that has been created with direct play. If players insist on playing the ball back, or square, possession might be retained but the initiative and the opportunity to exploit space will soon be lost.*

2. SPREADING OUT FROM END TO END

In order to defend well, a team needs to be compact, restricting the space available between defending players so that any opponent receiving the ball will be challenged, and the challenging player will always be supported.

For the attacking side, the opposite applies. Attackers have to spread out, side to side and end to end, to create space between defending players and make it more difficult for them to mark an opponent and cover a team-mate at the same time.

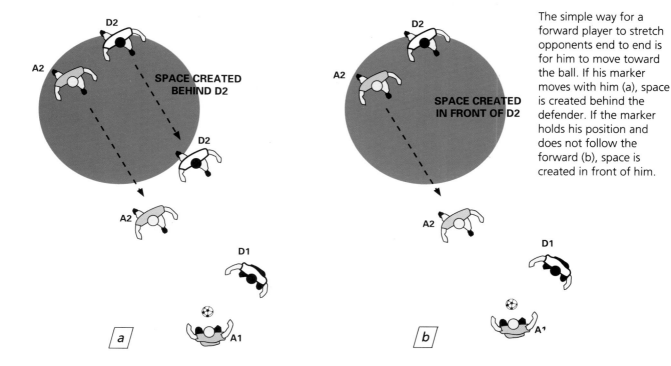

The simple way for a forward player to stretch opponents end to end is for him to move toward the ball. If his marker moves with him (a), space is created behind the defender. If the marker holds his position and does not follow the forward (b), space is created in front of him.

Defenders are always concerned about the space behind them and so, on occasions, space can be created in front of them. Attackers can encourage this to happen by a simple move away from the ball, to the back of the defender, before checking back towards the ball.

A2 has made a quick movement to the back of D2. The move had to be quick so that D2 was sure to react to it and A2 could create more space when he changed direction towards A1, who has the ball. Space is created in front of D2 for A2 to collect the ball, turn, and beat the recovering D2 by dribbling or passing the ball past him.

An attacker can also create space by moving toward the ball, drawing the defender forward, before checking and moving into the space behind him.

A2 has run back towards A1, who has the ball, drawing D2 with him. A2 checks back behind D2's run, moving into the space behind him to receive the ball.

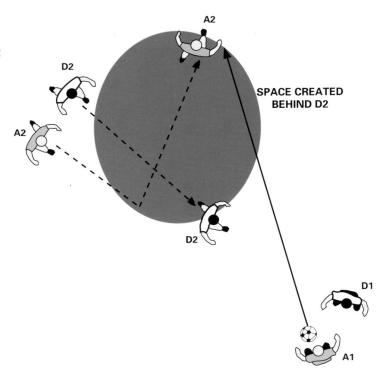

SPACE CREATED BEHIND D2

Overlap runs

Overlap runs have two functions; to create space end to end and to allow the overlapping player or the player in possession to exploit that space.

Overlap runs are always made from behind the ball to a position in advance of it. The run is always to the outside of the player with the ball. Overlaps are usually made on the flanks, but they can also be effective in more central positions.

A2 has run outside A1 into a position ahead of him and behind both D1 and D2 to receive a forward pass from A1. The timing of this pass may be crucial if D2 is the last defender, as A2 will be offside if the ball is delivered too late.

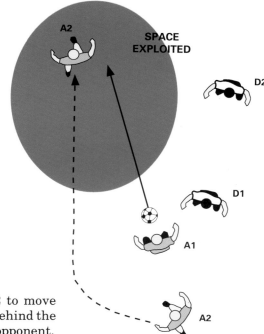

SPACE EXPLOITED

Normally, D2 will not allow A2 to move into a position in unmarked space behind the defence. D2 will usually cover his opponent.

At every level of soccer, a player who can steal a march on his opponent is always likely to be first to the ball when it is played forward.

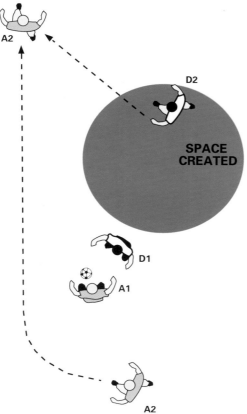

SPACE CREATED

D2 has moved to track A2's run, but in doing so has moved away from a position where he can support D1. A2 has therefore succeeded in his primary objective of creating space end to end between D1 and D2.

The modern game increasingly requires players who know where and how to move into position in front of the ball. If these moves are made at the right time, they open up splendid opportunities for direct play. If they are made at the wrong time, they will be defensively irresponsible at best, disastrous at worst.

As far as overlap runs are concerned the issue is clear cut. The time to make a run, to move from a supporting position to one in front of the ball, is when the player with the ball no longer needs support, when he has turned and has the space to play the ball forward. This is the time when extra forward players are needed and the time when supporting players should break forward.

3. CHANGING THE DIRECTION OF PLAY

The better defenders are, the more important it is for the attacking side to know how to create space by changing the direction of play.

Cross-over runs

A cross-over run is a simple, but usually very effective, move between two attackers. While space is usually created by increasing the distance between defenders, in this case the opposite applies. The purpose is to draw defenders together and thus to create space on either side of them.

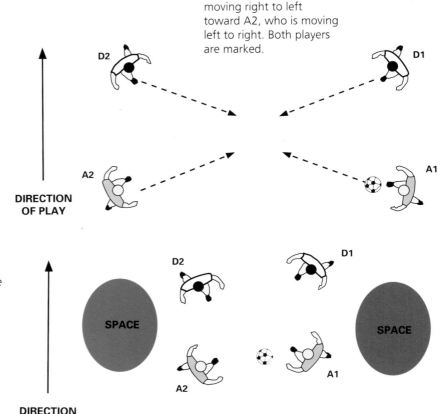

A1 has the ball and is moving right to left toward A2, who is moving left to right. Both players are marked.

DIRECTION OF PLAY

This shows the position just before A2 takes the ball from A1. Space has been created on either side of the knot of four players.

DIRECTION OF PLAY

Cross-over plays can be made side to side across the field or end to end down the field. As they cross, sometimes the player with the ball gives it to his team-mate, and sometimes he takes it on himself, using his team-mate's run as a decoy. A successful cross-over play relies on three factors.

⚽ Change of pace. As the players cross, they should accelerate away in opposite directions. If both players change pace quickly and simultaneously, the defenders will not have time to recover and mark them adequately. The space and time for direct play will have been achieved.

⚽ Screening the ball. The player with the ball should play it with the foot furthest from his opponent, screening it from him. If the ball is screened correctly, defenders will find it very difficult to get a clear sight of it.

⚽ Good communications. Both players must know who is going to take on the ball and who is the decoy. Confusion can lead to embarrassment and the loss of the ball. The best way to avoid this is to establish within the team that the player without the ball will always call either 'take' or 'leave'.

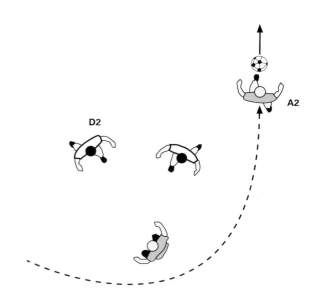

A2 takes the ball from A1, moves into the space created, and passes the ball forward.

Long cross-field passes

Defenders want to keep the play in front of them, denying space behind them, and to make play predictable by forcing it in one direction. Attackers have to achieve the opposite, and make the play unpredictable. If space is not available and forward play impossible the best plan is to change the point of an attack.

Defenders very often find it more difficult to position correctly on the side of the field away from the ball than they do in the general area of the ball. There are a number of reasons for this which attacking players would do well to understand.

Lack of concentration. Some players only really concentrate when they are actively involved in the play. This problem applies in both attack and defence. As a result, it is entirely a matter of chance if they find themselves in the correct position when the ball is switched in their direction.

Concentrating only on the ball. Some defenders concentrate on the ball to the exclusion of all else. They are known as ball watchers. Such players are often drawn towards the ball, leaving too much space behind and/or to the side of them. Ball-watching defenders on the opposite side of the pitch from the play – for example a full-back when the play is all down the other flank – may find themselves as much as 20 yards out of position if the play is suddenly switched.

Over-compensation. Defenders react to the movement of the ball and the movement of opponents. Because of this they may also be forced to react to the movement of their fellow defenders. Defenders in flank positions, especially those on the opposite side of the pitch to the ball, must be aware of potential danger in the centre and position themselves accordingly. There is always the danger, though, that defenders will over-do this and move into too central a position, unbalancing the defence and leaving it shorn of challenge and cover on the flank.

Long cross-field passes seek to exploit unbalanced defences. Sometimes they will be square passes, sometimes diagonal. Either kind will usually create space for forward play, and the long forward diagonal pass to the back of the defence is potentially one of the most lethal of all passes.

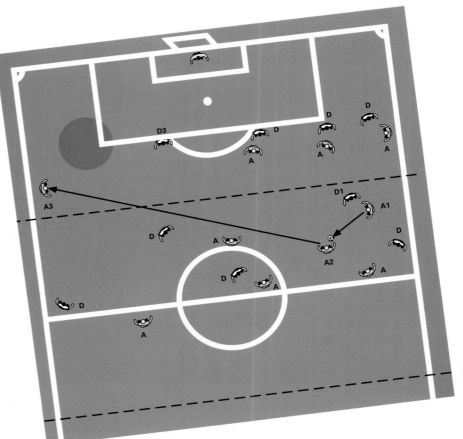

A1 could not pass the ball forward and has therefore passed back to the supporting A2, who can then hit a long cross-field ball to A3. D3 has come too far in and will not be able to cover the ground to challenge A3 while the ball is in flight, leaving A3 with the ball and time and space for direct play.

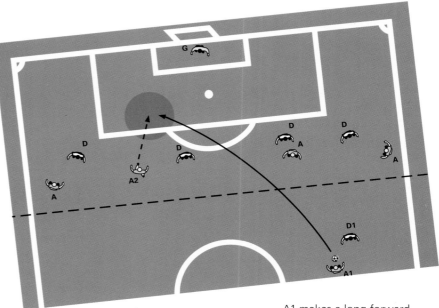

A1 makes a long forward diagonal pass to the back of the defence for A2 to run on to.

Despite the misgivings of some modern coaches and commentators the technique of passing the ball over long distances, in the 30-60 yard range, is all-important. The ability to deliver the ball accurately over such distances, either forward or across the field, is a very useful weapon in the armoury of any team.

Reverse passes

The technique for making reverse passes is simple enough. It involves running with the ball in one direction and passing, on the run, in the opposite direction.

A1 runs with the ball from left to right, marked by D1. As D1 follows A1, D2 adjusts his position to support. A2, however, can hold his wide position. There is now space into which A1 can play a reverse pass for A2 to run on to. If D1 is marking tightly, preventing A1 from passing on the run, then A1 should use one of the techniques for turning in order to create time and space for the pass.

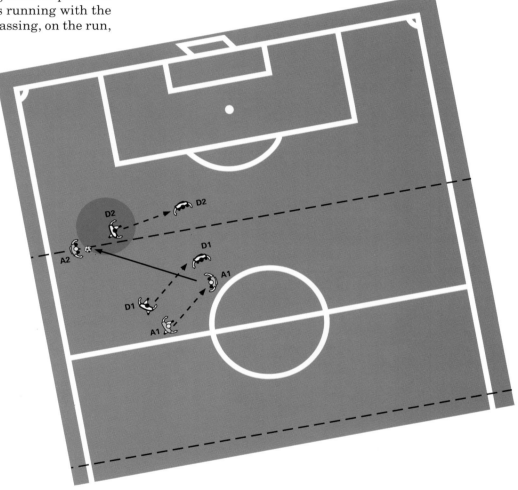

4. One-Touch Play

Teams playing at the highest level must be able to play accurate one-touch football. The nearer a team gets to its opponents' goal, the more restricted space is likely to be and the more important one-touch play becomes.

Defenders will react to the movement of the ball, but since the ball can travel quicker than any defender, two or three consecutive, accurate, one-touch passes will beat any defender and create space.

Defenders will react to the movement of players. If attackers receive the ball and play it off with one touch, then move to a new position, the defenders' jobs are made much more difficult.

The more a team practises their one-touch play, the more they will improve their **vision** – the ability to recognize situations quickly, their **decision-making** – the ability to choose the best pass quickly before the ball arrives, and finally their **confidence** – confidence comes with accuracy and accuracy comes with correct practice.

When a team has mastered all the various individual and team techniques to create space they become potentially extremely formidable opponents. Whether the team realizes that potential depends on the players being equally good at exploiting the space their efforts have created.

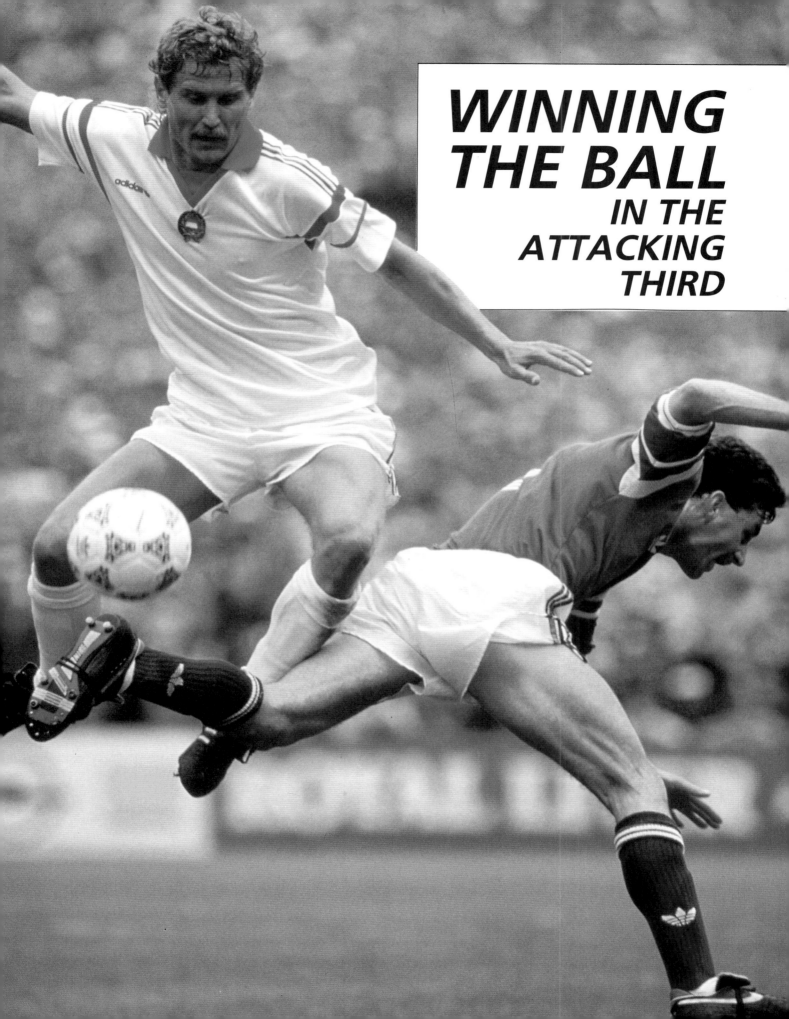

WINNING THE BALL
IN THE ATTACKING THIRD

WINNING THE BALL
IN THE ATTACKING THIRD

Soccer matches are won in the attacking third of the field. In one sense this is an obvious thing to say, because hardly any goals are scored from outside the attacking third, but this is not the whole story. There are some people who would argue, for instance, that though the goals are **scored** in the attacking third, most of them are **created** in the middle of the field. This view is most definitely not supported by our detailed analysis of hundreds of matches.

No less than 52.5% – more than half – of all goals scored come as a result of moves that start in the attacking third of the field.

The importance of this single fact – that over 50% of all goals come from moves starting in the attacking third – cannot be overstated. It means, for example, that teams which retreat back towards their own goal whenever they lose the ball in the attacking third are not only distancing themselves from their opponents' goal, they are distancing themselves from victory.

The idea that it is strategically better to fall back and reorganize defensively as soon as the ball is lost is one of two mistaken notions that have contributed, more than any others, to the general reduction in goal-scoring over the last thirty years or so. The other mistaken notion, of course, is that possession play – trying to prevent the opposition from scoring by preventing them from getting the ball – is the key to successful soccer.

Already, more than half of all goals scored originate in the attacking third. This figure is likely to increase as more teams adopt the strategy of direct play. Part of this strategy involves attempting to regain possession as soon as possible. This chapter is concerned with a team's making the most of its opportunities to win back the ball in the attacking third, thus maintaining pressure.

Previous page: It is a vital part of The Winning Formula that players in forward positions must work just as hard as those in defensive positions to gain possession of the ball. Here, the Republic of Ireland's John Aldridge has just failed to dispossess the Hungarian Imre Garaba.

THE IMPORTANCE OF CONCENTRATION

Lapses of concentration on the part of defenders help create scoring opportunities for opponents who keep their own concentration. There are three occasions when defenders' concentration is most likely to fail.

The first of these is when the game stops and has to be restarted, that is at set plays. Some players only concentrate when the ball is in play. When play stops they think about something else, and when play restarts there is a time-lag before their attention is refocused on the game. The lag may be just a split-second, but often that is enough for the damage to be done.

Concentration also tends to fail when the ball is won and lost. The player who wins the ball may be guilty of this, slowing the making of the decisive pass which will clear the danger. It also affects the players on the team who have just lost the ball. Their thoughts will not always immediately turn to defending; they show their disappointment by holding their head in their hands or by remonstrating with their team-mates, the officials and sometimes, it seems, the Almighty! Once again, there is a time lag before concentration is restored. This is why attacking players are so often caught offside when their team wins back the ball soon after losing it.

The more often the ball is won and lost, the more chances there are for players to lose concentration. By definition, possession changes less often when a team is playing possession football than when their strategy involves direct play. The ball is also more likely to be lost in the attacking third when a team is using direct play, simply because the ball is more often played into the attacking third.

The third occasion on which concentration is easily lost is when tiredness sets in. Tired players are likely to find their minds wandering. Even their will to win will be affected under the physical and mental stress of fatigue which saps their energy.

PRESSURING DEFENDERS

One simple message emerges from the statistics on goal scoring from set plays and especially from regained possession immediately following set plays.

Once a team gets the ball in the attacking third of the field they should try and keep it there by making it as difficult as possible for the defenders to clear the ball.

This is not an invitation to possession play, which is ineffective in scoring goals, but rather a reason for the team without the ball to adopt a compact shape. The details of this strategy are covered in the chapter *Key Factors in Defending*. Basically, it involves keeping the team compact as a unit, and avoiding getting stretched.

If the team maintains compactness the distance between players is small and, wherever the ball is, there will be someone there to challenge for it and someone else to support him. The strategy keeps the opposition under constant pressure and frequently forces errors. If the opposition can be forced into errors in their own defending third, so much the better.

When attackers enter the attacking third of the field it is important that they retain, or increase, the momentum of the attack. When the momentum is slowed, defenders have time to recover from bad positions to good ones and the object of the attack is switched

Players get more tired as the game goes on. The quicker the tempo of the game, the quicker players will tire. Direct play always increases the tempo of the game, and teams which are not physically prepared for such a match will struggle, as tiredness saps not only their concentration but also their judgement, technical proficiency and speed of reaction.

The more tired a player is, the more he can be pressured and the more unforced errors he is likely to make. If these errors occur in a position in his own defending third – and the chances are that at least some of them will – that is good news for his opponents.

from penetrating the defence to retaining possession, usually by playing the ball back to the middle third of the field. The ball is retained but the initiative is lost.

Increasing momentum in the attacking third forces defenders to play under pressure. They may be caught in bad positions and have less time to recover. This kind of pressure may result in a direct goal-scoring opportunity or in a set play from which a goal may well be scored.

For attackers to function best, they have to understand what makes defenders uneasy. When a defender is attempting to clear the ball from inside his own penalty area, he will want to gain height, distance and width, in that order of importance. Putting him under pressure makes this much more difficult to achieve. Less height means less time for the defence, less distance and less width mean more danger if the attacking team regains possession.

ATTACKING IN NUMBERS

The greatest single source of goals is a combination of set plays and regained possession immediately following set plays. This is dealt with in detail in the chapter *Attacking from Set Plays*.

Set plays are an opportunity for teams to increase the number of players in the attacking third, with eight, or even more of the team in advance positions. Even when free kicks are awarded in the middle third many players are pushed forward ready for the kick to be delivered into the attacking third.

Having this many players forward not only brings goals directly from set plays but also makes it more difficult for defenders to clear, which accounts for the number of times possession is regained in the attacking third. Sheer weight of number is one reason why so many goals are scored following set plays.

REGAINING POSSESSION AFTER SET PLAYS

The organization of the team for attacking at set plays should take into account two things. First, some players should be positioned to give the team the best possible chance of scoring directly from the set play; that is, without the opponents touching the ball. This is covered in the chapter *Attacking from Set Plays*. Second, other players should be positioned to give the team the best possible chance of regaining possession should the defenders clear the ball from the set play.

When planning which players should cover the areas at a set play, it is best to assume that the delivery of the ball from the set play will be reasonably accurate and certainly according to plan. If the plan, for instance, is to take inswinging corners, any change to outswinging or short corners will make all the planning irrelevant.

Worse still, if eight or nine players have come forward to attack from a set play and the agreed delivery is changed, they are all likely to be caught out of position. They will not be able to challenge for the ball, and will be helpless to intervene if their opponents win it and sweep out of defence to create a scoring opportunity of their own.

Long throw-ins
The arrangement of attacking players will to some extent be determined by the positions taken up by defenders.

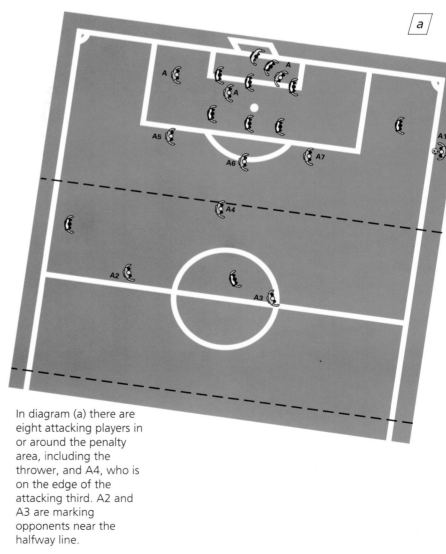

In diagram (a) there are eight attacking players in or around the penalty area, including the thrower, and A4, who is on the edge of the attacking third. A2 and A3 are marking opponents near the halfway line.

In diagram (b) there are only seven attacking players forward, as A4 has been withdrawn to a position in midfield where he can support A2 and A3. The positioning in (b) is often adopted to secure against breakaways if possession is lost, while that in (a) offers a better chance of regaining the ball in the attacking third of the field if possession is lost.

Positive thinking and the principles of direct play point to position (a) as the best option. This is based on the principle of keeping only equal numbers in rear positions, as well as an appreciation of the importance of space in front of a defence and the effect both those considerations have upon the compactness of a team.

With A4 marking the space in front of the defence and providing support for three players – A5, A6 and A7 – he not only increases the attacking options but also guards against breakaways, making it much more difficult for the opposition to break out of their defensive positions should they regain the ball.

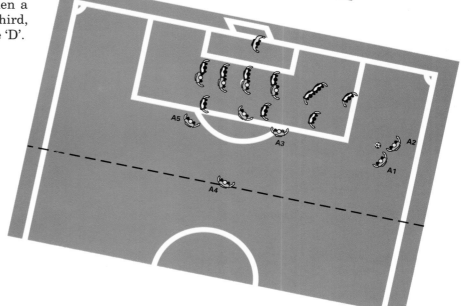

Free kicks

It is not unusual to see all eleven players withdrawn into defensive positions when a free kick is conceded in the defending third, especially if the kick is in or around the 'D'.

The defending team has pulled all its players back into the penalty area for a free kick from the flanks. A4 is the rearmost player of the attacking team. He should be positioned on the edge of the attacking third, rather than on the halfway line. Should the D team manage to play the ball away outside the penalty area, the A team is well positioned to be first to the ball anywhere in the attacking third.

Strong challenges by attacking players often force defenders into giving away free kicks in dangerous positions. At right, the Dutch forward Marco van Basten tangles with England central defender Tony Adams.

The defending team may choose to leave one or two players in forward positions.

Here, D2 and D6 have taken up wide forward positions. They are marked by A2 and A6, and as a result there have been minor adjustments in the penalty area and there is now only one man on the ball, A1. There are still two players on the edge of the area to challenge for partial clearances. A4 should retain a central position which will enable him to challenge for any ball played out of the penalty area in a central position and also to move in support of A2 or A6 should the ball be cleared out to the wings.

If the free kick is in or around the 'D', in a central position, it is more likely than ever that all eleven players will be brought back to defend, since four or five of them will be required to form a defensive wall.

Here, the teams are positioned for a free kick from the centre of the 'D'. A4 again takes up a position on the edge of the attacking third, while two attacking players will hold their position on the edge of the penalty area to pick up partial clearances. One of these will be A3 and the other will be the player who elects to take the kick, A1 or A2.

Corners

Every team should decide a policy for corner kicks and stick to it. Two of every three successful corners are played to the near post, almost all of them inswingers (see the section on Corners in the chapter *Attacking from Set Plays*). Any inswinging ball, whether from a corner, a flank free kick or a cross in open play, is difficult for a defender to clear properly. A defender trying to play a ball swinging in to him, inside his six-yard box, is unlikely to be able to clear it much further than the edge of the penalty area.

The defending team has nine men in the penalty area for this corner and one man marking the kicker, leaving D2 in an advanced position. The attacking team has just one man, A2, marking him. A3 is positioned on the edge of the attacking third, and A4 and A5 are positioned on the edge of the penalty area to pick up partial clearances. This arrangement gives the attacking team an excellent chance of regaining possession should the ball be cleared to any part of the attacking third.

If the defending team had brought back all eleven players to the penalty area then A2 would have gone forward into the area himself, leaving A3, positioned on the edge of the attacking third, as the rearmost outfield player in the attacking team.

A corner flicked on from the near post allows a team-mate running in at the far post to use all the momentum of his run to leap above the defence and put power into his header at goal. England's Tony Adams does just that, outjumping Majed Abdullah of Saudi Arabia to head home an equalizer.

Choosing the support players

At every set play described in this section, two players have been positioned on the edge of the penalty area, primarily to challenge for partial clearances. These players should be carefully chosen. If possible, one should be primarily left-footed and the other right-footed. Both should be good volleyers of the ball – almost all of the shooting chances that will come their way will be volleys. It is also important that both players have quick reactions and a cool head so they can take their chances and not be intimidated by opponents charging at them.

REGAINING POSSESSION IN OPEN PLAY

There are three particular situations where there is an excellent chance of regaining possession following the breakdown of a move in the attacking third; after crosses, from headed clearances of long balls forward, and after a defender has been first to a ball to the back of the defence.

1. Crosses

If a defender is first to a good cross – one played early, to the back of the defence and into the prime target area (see the chapter on *Crosses*) – the attacking side should have few problems regaining possession. At the very least, attacking players should be able to put the defender under such physical pressure that he is pleased to put the ball out for a corner.

If the cross is not so good – it does not penetrate to the back of the defence, for example, or is hit too deep and too high, two other factors come into play.

First, attackers should ensure that defenders are not allowed to clear unchallenged. The defender will probably be heading the ball and will be attempting a long, high clearance. If he is put under pressure his header is much more likely to be short and low and can be picked up by an attacker.

Secondly, it is possible to predict the area where the clearance will land; we have called this the anticipation area. An attacking player, and preferably two, should be moving into that area as the cross is made to anticipate the defensive header.

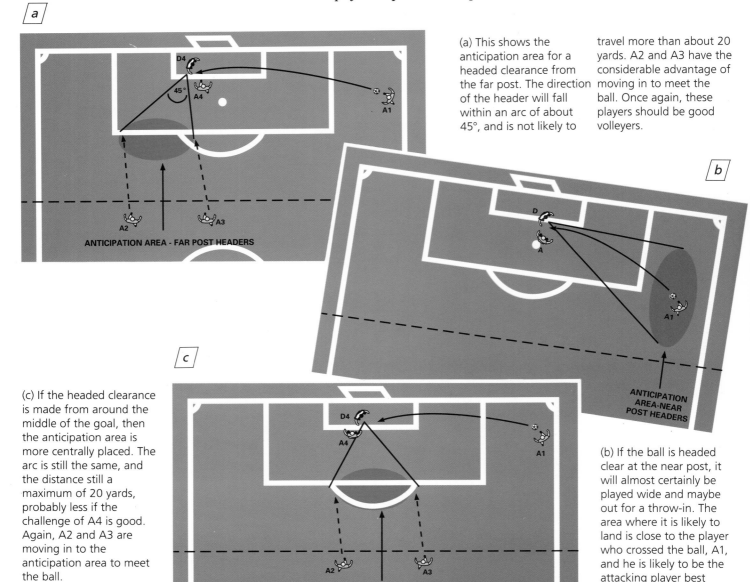

(a) This shows the anticipation area for a headed clearance from the far post. The direction of the header will fall within an arc of about 45°, and is not likely to travel more than about 20 yards. A2 and A3 have the considerable advantage of moving in to meet the ball. Once again, these players should be good volleyers.

ANTICIPATION AREA - FAR POST HEADERS

ANTICIPATION AREA - NEAR POST HEADERS

(b) If the ball is headed clear at the near post, it will almost certainly be played wide and maybe out for a throw-in. The area where it is likely to land is close to the player who crossed the ball, A1, and he is likely to be the attacking player best placed to try and regain possession of the ball.

(c) If the headed clearance is made from around the middle of the goal, then the anticipation area is more centrally placed. The arc is still the same, and the distance still a maximum of 20 yards, probably less if the challenge of A4 is good. Again, A2 and A3 are moving in to the anticipation area to meet the ball.

ANTICIPATION AREA - MID GOAL HEADERS

2. Long forward passes

Long forward passes are usually intended for the space behind the defence. Inevitably these passes sometimes fall short and are headed clear. Much of what has been said about headed clearances of crosses applies to headed clearances of long forward passes.

The worst that can happen is that the defender is allowed to move forward to meet the ball. A good header of the ball can achieve good distance and pick out his target if he can take a run at the ball. If, however, the defender has to run back toward his own goal, before jumping to try and head the ball in the opposite direction, things are very different. The defender will find it difficult to put power in the header, as his body is moving in the opposite direction. Also, because he is trying to turn at the same time, he will find it very difficult to control the direction of his header. The ball may even skid off his head and go out for a corner or a throw-in.

Here, A1 has aimed a long ball forward, looking for the space behind D2. A2 has run into the space to receive the ball, but D2 has moved back to intercept the pass with a header. The header lacks power and direction and will fall in front of D2 in an arc of something less than 45°, a maximum of 10-12 yards away. A3 has moved into the anticipation area to pick up the ball, while A2 must move back onside. A3 should be capable of passing the ball on his first touch or controlling it at speed for a run, a dribble or a shot.

Glenn Hoddle, generally recognized as one of the most skilful midfield players ever to play for England, was a specialist in long forward passes, which he hit with backspin so that they would drop invitingly for forward players to run on to.

Some self-appointed purists feel that playing long balls over the heads of defenders is not good soccer. Potentially, though, it is excellent soccer and should be encouraged as a vital element in the strategy of direct play. It is just as important to position players to anticipate interceptions of long forward passes as it is to position them to anticipate clearances at set plays.

3. Balls to the back of the defence

A defender always has problems when he has to turn back to gather the ball. The first task of the attacking team is that he should not be given space in which to turn back upfield to play the ball forward. The second task, if possible, is to seal off the safety route back to the goalkeeper.

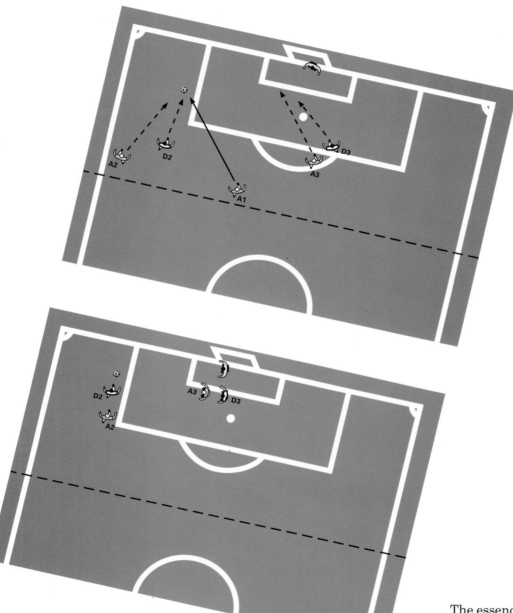

A1 has made a pass inside D2 to the back of the defence. However, D2 has recovered quickly enough to get to the ball before A2. A2 must pressure D2 immediately, and prevent him from turning upfield. A3 must react quickly and seal off the route back to the goalkeeper.

A2 and A3 have both moved to put pressure on the defenders. D2 now has a problem and will probably play the ball off for a corner or throw-in. Even if D2 had the space to turn, A2 would still have to challenge him and make it as difficult as possible for him to pass the ball forward, while A3 would still be required to cut off the safety pass back to the goalkeeper.

The essence of all these tactics for winning the ball in the attacking third is teamwork and compactness to pressurize defenders. If a team is not compact, good teamwork is not possible, as situations are bound to arise where players may need help but do not have a team-mate close enough to provide support. The subjects of teamwork and compactness are dealt with in detail in the chapter *Key Factors in Defending*.

ATTACKING
FROM SET PLAYS

Just under half of all goals scored in the matches we have analyzed came from a set play or when possession was regained immediately following a set play. This makes set plays by far the most important single factor in scoring goals and winning matches.

Further analysis revealed the importance of direct play in gaining set plays. Almost 90% of set plays in the attacking third of the field were won from moves of five passes or less. Direct play helps to increase the number of set plays, and set plays help to win soccer matches.

Teams do not generally set out with the aim of gaining set plays. Set plays come as a by-product of positive play which puts pressure on opponents. For example, a corner may result from a deflected shot at goal, or a free kick from a beaten defender's despairing challenge. Set plays are second prizes when direct play has just failed to succeed.

Basically, there are five things an attacking team can do which make it likely that defenders will concede a set play – either a throw-in or a free kick of some kind.

WAYS TO GAIN MORE SET PLAYS

1. Passing to the back of the defence.
2. Crossing to the back of the defence.
3. Dribbling.
4. Pressuring defenders.
5. Shooting.

---

1. Passing to the back of the defence
Passes to the back of the defence always cause defenders problems. If the ball is played past him, a defender will be in the uncomfortable position of having to turn and run towards his own goal. Safety should be at the top of his mind – assuming he can be first to the ball.

His best option would be a pass back to the goalkeeper, but if this route is blocked he will either have to attempt to turn – which is very risky unless there is plenty of space – or play the ball out for a throw-in or a corner. If in doubt, good defenders will always play the ball dead. Safety first is the golden rule in the defending third.

Lofted passes to the back of the defence often cause defenders more problems than ground balls. Passes that call for the defender to turn and head the ball are especially difficult and often the ball skids off the defender's head and out of play. A pass over a defender's head calls for him to turn and play an awkward bouncing ball. Most defenders are uncomfortable in this situation and are happy to play the ball into touch.

2. Crossing
Crosses to the back of the defence, especially into the prime target area (see the chapter on *Crosses*), cause defenders maximum discomfort. Most of them, running back towards their own goal, will settle for putting the ball behind for a corner kick.

Players attacking down the wings sometimes dwell on the ball, trying to find more space for a cross, then end up passing the ball back to a supporting player. Most of the time they would do better to take a chance and try to get the cross in early. If they succeed, the ball will get into the prime target area at the back of the defence. If they fail, quite often it is because the cross is knocked away by a defender for a throw-in or a corner.

3. Dribbling
Most defenders would consider they had won a duel with a dribbler if they had put the ball out for a corner or a throw. In fact, if a set play results from a dribble, the attacker, not the defender, has come out on top. A set play, particularly in the attacking third of the field, is a perfectly acceptable result from a dribble, and another good reason for more players to dribble more often in attack.

Dribbling does not only produce throw-ins and corners. The FIFA report on the 1982 World Cup reported that three of every five penalties and free kicks around the penalty

area were given for fouls on people dribbling. More goals are scored, directly and indirectly, from free kicks than from corners and throw-ins combined.

Dribbling is an important part of the game in the attacking third, and most teams could boost their goals tally simply by dribbling more in advanced positions.

4. Pressuring defenders

Pressure is exerted on a player in possession of the ball by challenging him or moving toward him, cutting down on the time and space he has available in which to play. If a defender is first to the ball when it is played to the back of the defence, an attacker should challenge him as soon as possible. When time and space are limited, high demands are put on technique, and defenders who are not confident about their technique will frequently panic. When this happens the ball can go anywhere. When a defender has once been forced into a position like this in a match, he will start to worry about it happening again – which leads to more uncertainty and more panic.

Any tactic which discomfits defenders and encourages them to panic is useful to an attacking side in increasing the number of set plays they are awarded. Making sure that defenders on the ball are continually put under pressure certainly comes into this category.

5. Shooting

The evidence that direct play increases the number of shooting opportunities, and that the more shots a team has, the more likely it is to score, is overwhelming. It is dealt with in detail in the chapter on *Shooting*. It is equally true that the more often a team shoots, the more secondary shooting opportunities it creates. Some of these come from rebounds and others from corners, either because the shot hits a defender or because the goalkeeper pushes it wide or over the bar.

Teams that are prepared to shoot at every opportunity are difficult to defend against. Defenders are under extra pressure not to allow the attackers a sight of goal and are therefore more likely to make a mistake or give away a set play.

Applying these five positive principles will increase the number of set plays a team is awarded in a game. This is not to say that a team should go out looking for set plays, simply that direct play and a positive approach will produce more set plays as a matter of course. And with set plays involved in nearly a half of all goals scored, more set plays can only mean more goals.

Even the best organized walls are vulnerable to free kicks curved over or round them. This shot by England's Glenn Hoddle, a master at playing the dead ball, beat the Dutch defensive wall but hit the near post and was cleared.

WHY SET PLAYS PRODUCE GOALS

Set plays have always been a major factor in winning soccer matches. The more important the match and the closer the contest, the more likely it is that the match will be decided by a set play. Twenty-seven goals were scored in the six World Cup finals between 1966 and 1986. Of these, thirteen came from moves started by set plays and five more when the ball was regained immediately following a set play.

There are four major reasons why set plays are such an important source of goals.

1. A dead ball
The ball is still and on the ground or, in the case of a throw-in, safe in the thrower's hand. A still ball is much easier to play than one which is moving.

2. Lack of pressure
Defending players must be at least ten yards from the ball at corners and free kicks, making it difficult to disturb the kicker or put on the kind of pressure that causes inaccuracy. This does not apply to throw-ins, but there the thrower has the considerable advantage of using his hands.

3. Extra attacking players
At set plays teams can put seven or eight players in attacking positions, something that never happens in the normal course of play. Having so many players forward makes it more difficult for the defenders to clear the ball, which is why so many goals come from regained possessions following set plays.

The advantage does not come simply from weight of numbers. A set play allows players to take up positions that suit their individual strengths; tall central defenders can get into position to head for goal, for example, while one or two good volleyers of the ball take up positions to fire back half-clearances (see the chapter *Winning the Ball in the Attacking Third*).

Players can be positioned for all eventualities. For instance, a back-header from a near post corner might go into the goal, but it might also be flicked into the mid-goal area or to the far post, and players should be positioned to take these chances.

4. Rehearsal
The more teams practise and rehearse their set moves, the more accurate and well-coordinated their performance will become. The more accurate and well-coordinated their performance, the more successful a team will be, and with success comes more confidence. First, however, comes practice.

There is a further benefit from rehearsing moves. It helps players develop their concentration. It is not enough for a player to know what he should be doing. He must concentrate in order to do it effectively and to do it whenever it is required. Players who lose concentration tend to drift out of the game.

Rehearsing pre-planned moves helps players to be alert and watchful. The whole process of rehearsal improves their concentration and leads toward a disciplined team performance, with every individual correctly performing the task he has been given.

There is one final point to make about set plays in general before moving on to particular kinds of set plays. **Variety is not a virtue where set plays are concerned.** At least, if there is variety, it should be variety around a single theme.

THROW-INS

Players seem to relax their concentration more at throw-ins than at any other time. Throw-ins are underestimated as attacking weapons, and may be looked on as simply a method of restarting the game. They should, in fact, be looked on as a possible route toward winning it.

There are six key things to remember to make a throw-in an attacking move.

1. Take the throw quickly
If defending players' concentration lapses – as it often does when the ball goes out of play – this should be exposed immediately. The throw must be taken as quickly as possible, which means that the man nearest the ball should take the throw.

The only exception to this rule is for a long throw in the attacking third of the field (see below), when time needs to be taken for extra players to move forward into attacking positions and the ball given to the long throw specialist.

2. Throw to an unmarked player
An unmarked attacking player should be able to initiate forward play faster than any other, so he will be the best player to receive the ball. If for some reason he is not in a position to initiate forward play, then he should not be given the ball.

3. Throw forward
In accordance with the principles of direct play the ball should be thrown forward where possible. There are, of course, exceptions to this rule, such as a throw back to the goalkeeper in the defending third of the field. In the attacking third of the field, though, the ball should always go forward if possible, and preferably to a player who can turn with the ball. If the player who is to receive the ball is marked, he should always be supported.

4. Throw for ease of control
A throw-in is a pass. The ball should be delivered with the same consideration as a pass, and thrown at a pace, and an angle, which makes it as easy as possible for the receiver to bring it under control and as difficult as possible for any defender to challenge him for it.

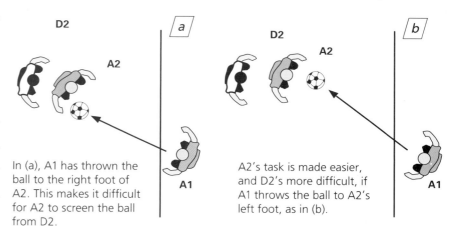

In (a), A1 has thrown the ball to the right foot of A2. This makes it difficult for A2 to screen the ball from D2.

A2's task is made easier, and D2's more difficult, if A1 throws the ball to A2's left foot, as in (b).

If the thrower wants the ball headed back to him, he should aim to deliver it chest high. This will make it easy for the receiver to move towards the ball and head it through its top half, directing it down to the feet of the thrower.

111

5. Create enough space for the throw to be effective

Players often make a mistake in standing too close to the thrower. In fact, they should spread out at a throw-in. This makes it more difficult for defenders to mark them and to cover each other and it creates space to exploit.

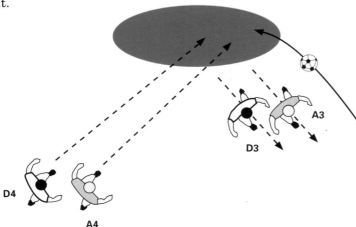

A2 and A3 have both made runs toward A1. Their markers have followed them. Space has as a result been created behind D3, into which A1 can throw the ball for A4 to run on to. A4 will be marked by D4, but D4 will be in a one against one situation with no cover.

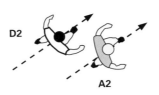

The pause in play at a throw-in makes it easy for attackers to move about and interchange positions. Since defenders have to react instantly to pre-planned and rehearsed moves, it becomes extremely difficult for them to mark and cover effectively.

6. Get the thrower back into the game

The player taking the throw-in should not think his task is finished once he has delivered the ball. If the player he has thrown to is marked, the thrower should move towards him to give support. At the very least the thrower should provide an extra man in the area of the ball.

Defending teams sometimes position a man near the thrower to stop the ball being played back to him. This marker may well feel his job is done if the ball is not played straight back to the thrower, who should put him to the test by joining in the attack once the throw has been taken.

LONG THROW-INS IN THE ATTACKING THIRD

Long throws into the penalty box are an excellent attacking technique and all teams should include at least one specialist thrower.

The most effective long throw is fast and low to the area of the near post. An attacker who is tall and a good header of the ball should take up position here to flick the ball into the mid-goal area or to the far post. The rest of the team should be positioned in support across the whole penalty area, ready to attack the ball when it is flicked on or to challenge for any partial clearances.

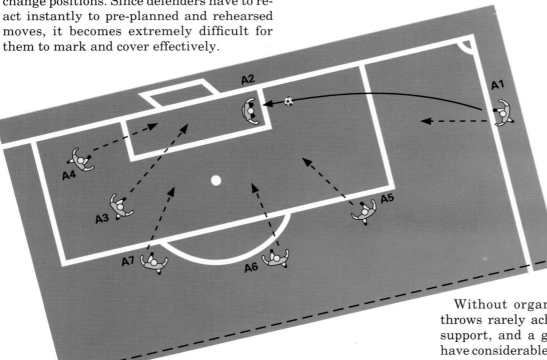

A1 has thrown the ball to A2. A3 is positioned to attack the mid-goal area and A4 the far post. A5, A6 and A7 are in support positions ready to challenge for half-clearances. Note that A1 follows his throw into the area to support A2 and pick up on half-clearances in that area. All the attacking players should delay their runs forward to the last possible moment in order to make it as difficult as possible for the defenders to mark them.

Without organized team support, long throws rarely achieve anything. With that support, and a good throw, the defenders have considerable problems and goals will inevitably come.

DIRECT FREE KICKS

More goals are scored as a result of free kicks than from corners and throw-ins combined. They are potentially a very important factor in scoring goals and winning matches. Sometimes kicks present a good chance of scoring with a direct shot; sometimes there is very little chance of scoring direct, and the aim of the kicker should be to set up a chance of a goal for a team-mate. Whatever the situation, though, one rule should always be kept in mind when taking free kicks.

If the goalkeeper takes responsibility for setting the defensive wall at a free kick, the defenders' attention is often distracted. Quick-thinking attackers can exploit this to score.

Free kicks outside the attacking third

There is little or no chance of scoring directly from a free kick outside the attacking third, and the emphasis should be on taking the kick quickly, to take advantage of any lapse in concentration on the part of the defenders.

As soon as the kick is awarded, two players should move to the ball to take the kick promptly and possibly change the direction of play, while players in advance of the ball should try to get in a position on the goal side of their immediate opponent, while remaining onside (players can be ruled offside at a free kick, though not at the moment a throw-in or a corner is taken). There is no need for set moves; simplicity plus the general principles of direct play are all that are required for success.

Free kicks in the attacking third – the flanks

The wider the angle from which a free kick is taken, the more important it is to do two things; play the ball to the back of the defence and challenge the free defending players.

Defenders dread balls played in behind them, but if a free kick is accurately taken they are powerless to stop it. Ideally the ball should be played with inswing and spin toward the near half of the goal (this means a left-footed kick from the right flank or a right-footed kick from the left flank). This forces the defenders to turn and try to deal with a ball which is spinning and swerving away from them.

> **The simpler the play, the greater the chance of success.**

A1 has played the ball with inswing past the two-man wall and over the head of D2. D3, D4 and D5 have to turn and attempt to clear a ball which is swinging away from them. To make their job even more difficult, each of the defenders should be challenged by an attacker.

D2 is positioned to block the direct shot to the far post, as the goalkeeper has taken up position in the front half of the goal. A2 stands a couple of yards in front of him. A1 will try to play the ball over both their heads. Should the ball be played too low, A2 should be able to prevent D2 clearing. A3, A4 and A5 challenge the other defenders, putting them under heavy pressure. The attacking players will move around before the kick is taken, trying to pull the defenders out of position so they can be first to the ball.

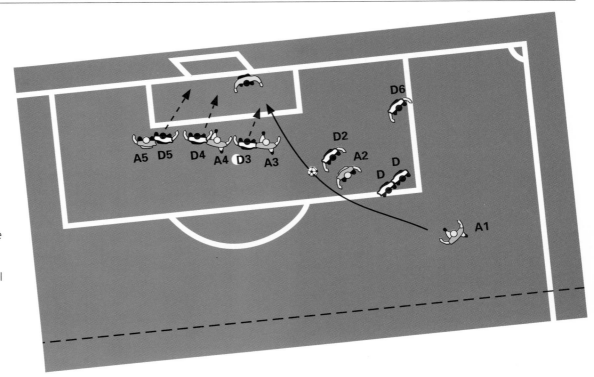

Our analysis shows this to be the most effective method of taking free kicks between the edge of the penalty area and the touch-line. When the ball is delivered correctly, a goal results once in every five attempts.

In the diagram above, D6 is occupying a space on the outside of the two-man wall. Sometimes this space is not defended, and for this reason the attacking team should always position two players on the ball.

The space on the outside of the wall is not defended. A2 and A1 are on the ball. A2 runs into the space at the back of the defence. A1 plays the ball to him so that he can drive the ball across the back of the defence.

Attacking teams must not make the mistake of sending too many players forward to attack the back of the defence. Two attacking players — A7 and A8 in the diagram — should be positioned at the edge of the penalty area to pick up balls that are only partially cleared.

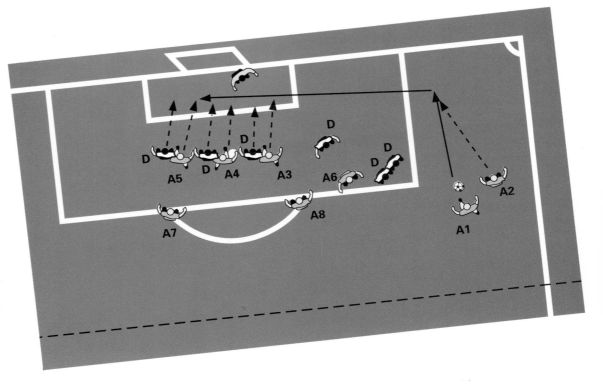

Free kicks in the attacking third – central positions

If a team is awarded a free kick in or around the 'D', the defending team will erect a wall to block part of the goal against a driven shot. The goalkeeper will position himself just off-centre in his goal, to the side of the defensive wall. This allows him to cover both a drive into the part of the goal not protected by the wall and a chip over the wall into the other half of the goal.

The goalkeeper will only feel comfortable behind his wall if he can retain a clear sight of the ball; it is up to the attacking team to deny him this. This is done by positioning two attacking players slightly in front of and to the side of the wall, completing it and blocking off the whole of the goal. The attackers must not stand level with the wall, or they would be offside.

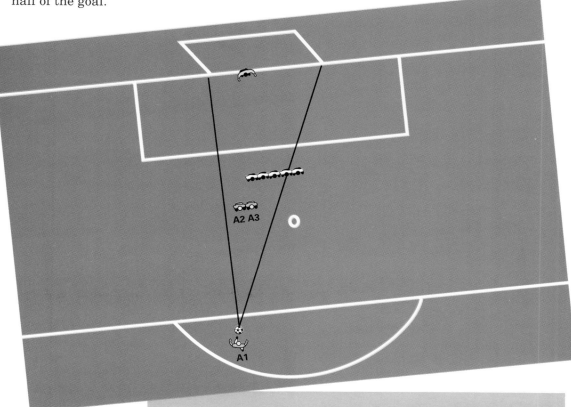

There are five players in the defensive wall. A2 and A3 are positioned to complete it, though leaving a small gap just inside the post for a driven shot. A2 and A3 are just seven yards from the ball. The defenders, of course, must be ten yards from the ball. A2 and A3 could, of course, position themselves just a yard from the ball, but this position has its disadvantages. The main one is that they will then be too far out to attack the six-yard box for possible rebounds.

Six or seven yards from the ball is the best position, as this blocks the goalkeeper's view of the kick and allows the attackers to move in on any rebounds. The attackers in the wall should stand close together and keep their feet together, or the goalkeeper will be able to catch a glimpse of the ball.

It is important that the attackers hold their position until the moment the kick is taken, at which point they should break, spinning round to move in on the goal and look for any rebounds.

Two players should come up to take a free kick in or around the 'D'. There are four reasons for this.

⚽ *The defenders will not know who is going to strike the ball.*

⚽ *The attackers approach the ball at speed from different angles, making different types of kick possible. Ideally one player should be left-footed and the other right-footed.*

⚽ *Decoy play is made much easier.*

⚽ *The player who does not strike the ball can act as a screen, blocking the defenders' view of the kicker.*

The two attackers on the ball will have decided between them what type of kick will give the best chance of getting a goal, and which one of them is best equipped to take it.

One possibility is that one player will make his run slightly earlier than the other, acting as a decoy while the second player strikes the ball. In this case, the decoy run should be made just in front of the ball rather than over it, to effectively screen the player taking the kick.

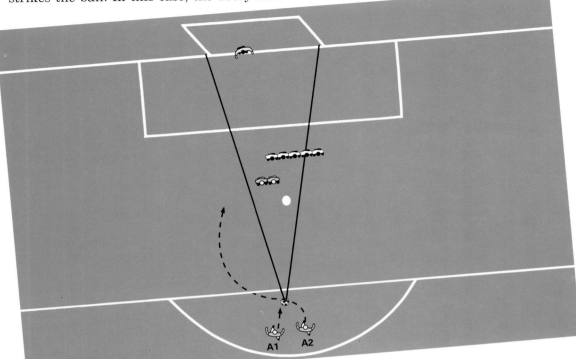

A2 has made his run so that he is positioned directly in front of the ball as A1 enters his kicking stride. As A1 hits the ball, A2 should have moved out of the line of the goal, bending his run towards the goal to look for rebounds.

The two players positioned on the ball should practice synchronizing their runs, and also establish a good understanding with the two attackers on the end of the wall.

The attackers on the end of the wall should stand firm for the player making the first run, concealing the ball from the goalkeeper. (This does not mean that the player making the first run will never play the ball, simply that he will not try to drive it through his own wall.) They should always break for the second player, continuing to watch the ball as they turn to look for rebounds.

An attacker should always challenge any defender who gets the ball from a free kick. It makes him uncomfortable and makes a clearance more difficult. Most teams withdraw all eleven players into the penalty area to defend against a free kick in the 'D'. The attacking team can therefore afford to send nine forward, including the two players on the ball, leaving just one outfield player to cover against a break. Every defender marking space to the side of the wall should be closely marked. Defenders do not like being treated this way and defend less well as a result.

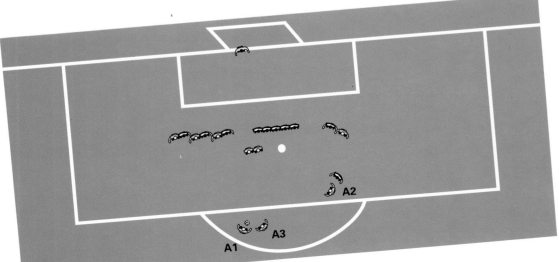

All the defenders except those in the wall are marked. A1, the kicker, and A2 stay at the edge of the area when the kick is taken, to take advantage of any rebounds. A3, the decoy runner, and the rest of the attackers converge on the six-yard box as soon as the kick is taken.

INDIRECT FREE KICKS

There are two areas where special consideration has to be given to indirect free kicks; in the 'D' and inside the penalty area, positions from which a shot at goal would be taken in normal play.

Indirect free kicks in the 'D'
All the principles outlined for direct free kicks in the 'D' apply to indirect free kicks, the difference being that the shot must be made on the second touch rather than the first. A slight adjustment in the position of the attacking wall is the main tactical requirement.

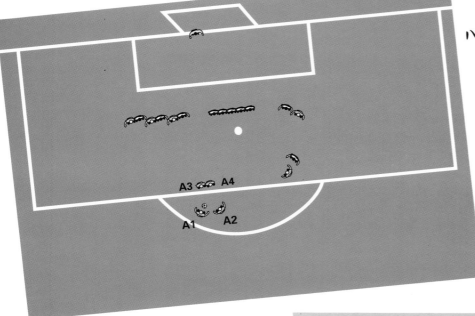

A1 is going to make a short pass for A2 to shoot. A3 and A4 are positioned just a couple of yards from the ball, blocking the goalkeeper's view of it. They should hold this position as long as possible, giving the goalkeeper very little chance to see the ball.

Indirect free kicks in the penalty area
Indirect free kicks in the penalty area are not awarded very often, but teams should prepare for the rare occasions that they are. All eleven defenders will almost certainly be pulled back into the penalty area. If the kick is less than ten yards from the goal, the probability is that all eleven will be ranged along the goal-line between the posts. When this happens, the whole defending team usually moves toward the ball in a block when the kick is taken and before anyone can shoot.

There are four things for the attacking team to consider. First, if the kick is taken from a wide position, the ball should be played to give the player taking the shot a wider angle. Second, if the ball is less than ten yards from goal it should be played back, allowing more time and space for the shot.

There are four key factors in a successful free kick, direct or indirect.

⚽ *Understanding which technique will pay the highest dividend.*

⚽ *Keeping the play simple and direct.*

⚽ *Playing the ball accurately.*

⚽ *Challenging opponents not in the wall and getting to the ball first.*

Third, the shot should ideally be placed over the heads of the defenders and as far from the goalkeeper as possible. Finally, the chances of success are greatly increased if the players involved remain calm in a situation where confusion and panic usually rule.

PENALTY KICKS

The importance of penalty taking has increased in recent years, with penalty 'shoot outs' now widely used to decide matches in cup competitions. As a result of this, all players, not just one or two specialists, should practise taking penalty kicks.

Successful penalties come as the result of the combination of the right temperament and the right technique. The ideal penalty taker should have a calm, even temperament. He should be able to shut out everything around him and concentrate on a confident, positive technical performance.

There are basically two techniques for taking penalties; placement and power. Placement kickers use a side-footed technique to stroke a shot along the ground just inside a post; power kickers attempt to beat a goalkeeper with the simple force and speed of their shot. Whatever the choice, penalty takers should make up their mind what they are going to do and stick to it. Nothing is worse in a penalty-taker than indecision.

My own preference is for power, especially as so may goalkeepers move before the ball is kicked. This is, of course, against the laws of the game, but goalkeepers frequently go unpunished for it. If the goalkeeper anticipates correctly and the ball lacks pace, then the shot is likely to be saved. The best technique is to aim for either of the stanchions and hit the ball low with pace.

The kick should be supported in case there is a rebound.

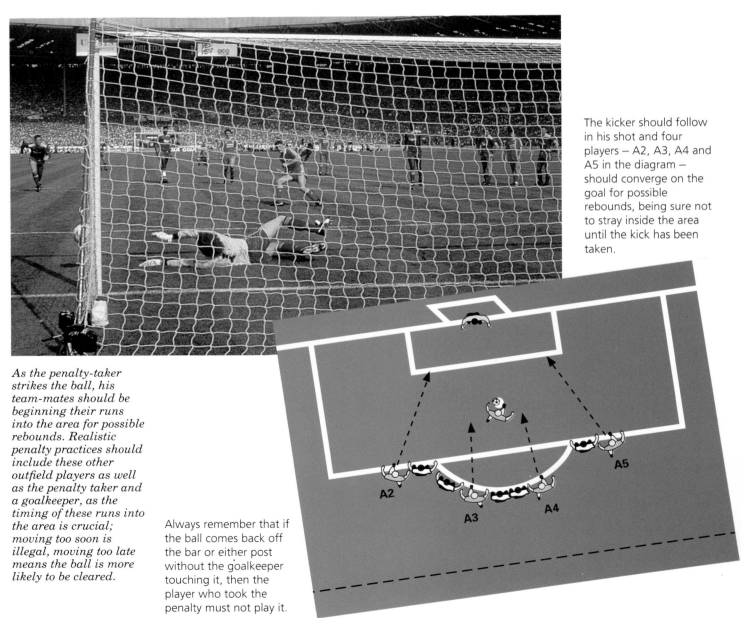

The kicker should follow in his shot and four players — A2, A3, A4 and A5 in the diagram — should converge on the goal for possible rebounds, being sure not to stray inside the area until the kick has been taken.

As the penalty-taker strikes the ball, his team-mates should be beginning their runs into the area for possible rebounds. Realistic penalty practices should include these other outfield players as well as the penalty taker and a goalkeeper, as the timing of these runs into the area is crucial; moving too soon is illegal, moving too late means the ball is more likely to be cleared.

Always remember that if the ball comes back off the bar or either post without the goalkeeper touching it, then the player who took the penalty must not play it.

CORNER KICKS

Though not as important as free kicks, corners are a prolific source of goals. There are two basic types of corner, short and long.

Short corners

The purpose of playing the ball short at a corner is to produce a numerical advantage of two against one or three against two in the area of the corner flag, taking advantage of the law which keeps defenders at least ten yards from the ball. This advantage is then used to engineer a more dangerous position closer to goal and at a better angle. Players who move out to support the short kick should move back into the danger area once it is taken.

However, short corners are not a major source of goals and there is nothing to be gained unless the attacking team has a numerical advantage – and thus an unchallenged player – in the area of the ball.

Long corners

There are two types of long corner, depending on which way the ball is swung into the penalty area.

Outswinging corners do produce goals but are less effective than inswinging deliveries. They should only really be used as a last resort, as for instance when a corner is won on the right and there is no-one on the team who can play the ball in accurately with their left foot.

Inswinging corners are by far the most effective. Inswinging corners directed to the area of the near post are the most effective of all. The FIFA report on the 1982 World Cup recorded that two of every three corners from which goals were scored were played toward the near post.

Some players and coaches have a mania about variety. They think that an outswinging corner after a series of inswinging ones will have the advantage of containing an element of surprise. In fact it will be more likely to provide an element of relief for the defenders.

If the team organization is good, there will be an element of variety, but it will be a variation on a theme, and the theme that pays the highest dividends is an inswinging corner to the near post. Perfecting this type of corner and persisting with it will markedly increase the number of goals a team scores from corners and from regained possession immediately following a corner.

Attacking players should be carefully selected for the various roles required. The most important is the kicker, who must be able to guarantee an accurate service; 80%, or four accurate kicks in every five, is an acceptable rate. The kicker should regularly practise his delivery as well as participating in the equally important team practice.

The kicker should try to deliver the ball into the six-yard box between head and bar height, ideally swinging into the front half of the goal. He will be aiming for area A from the left-hand side of the field and area B from the right-hand side.

It is up to the rest of the team to support the kick and get the maximum out of it. Four players are needed in the six-yard box. Their precise positions and functions are important.

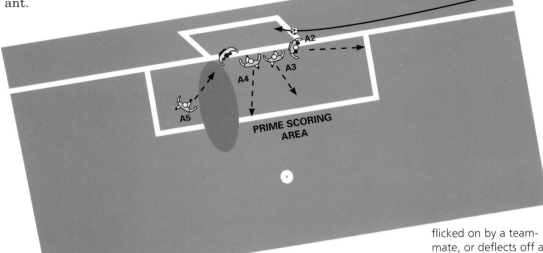

A2 is positioned at the near post for a corner from the right. His job is to move towards the ball and flick it on across the goal if it is low in flight. He must be tall and capable of performing well under physical pressure.

A3 stands close to the goal-line inside the near post. As the kick is taken he moves out towards the edge of the six-yard box, where he can attack any ball entering the area below bar height. This may entail his moving out then in again. There are two reasons for this. By standing on the goal-line both A3 and the player deputed to mark him will be obscuring the

goalkeeper's view, and by moving in and out A3 is more likely to create space for himself than he would by standing still. A3 should also be tall and a good header of the ball. Sometimes he will head

for goal; often it will be better if he heads across goal to the area of the far post.

The task of A4 is similar, but he starts from the back half of the goal. His move to the edge of the six-yard box when the

corner is taken should allow him to watch the ball all the time; if it is flicked on he should be looking to attack it.

The job of A5 is critical. He attacks the prime scoring area, by the far post (see the chapter on *Shooting*). If the ball is

flicked on by a team-mate, or deflects off a defender, it is very likely to drop invitingly into the far-post area for a relatively simple scoring chance.

All four players should be careful not to be caught offside in the six-yard box if the corner kick is partially cleared.

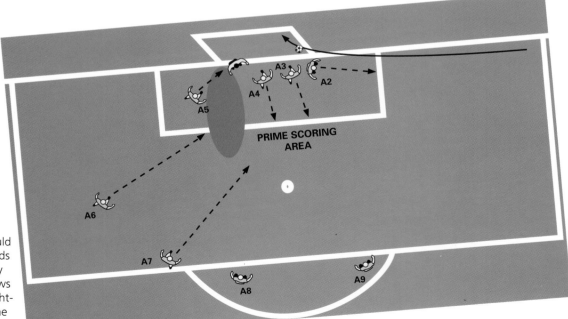

Four more players should support the kick towards the edge of the penalty area. The diagram shows their positions for a right-side corner. A6 is on the far side of the penalty area, ready to attack the far post. A7 is near the edge of the penalty area, looking to attack the mid-goal area just outside the six-yard box. A8 and A9 hold their positions at the

edge of the penalty area to pick up any rebounds or partial clearances. It is best if these two players are good volleyers of the ball.

Eight players are shown here in advanced attacking positions, on the assumption that the opposition have pulled back all eleven players into defensive positions. If they choose to leave one player upfield then either A8 or A9 should go deeper, to the edge of the attacking third of the field.

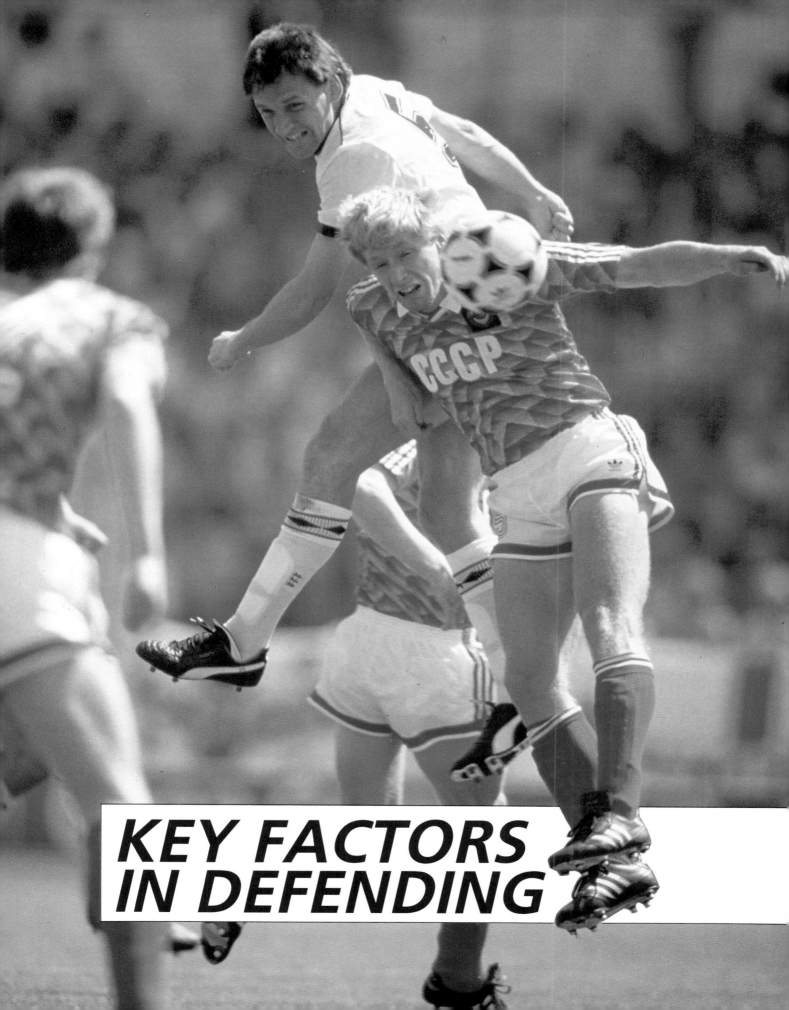

KEY FACTORS IN DEFENDING

KEY FACTORS IN DEFENDING

Previous page: England defender Dave Watson climbs high to beat Alexei Michailichenko of the USSR.

Challenges and physical contact are part of the excitement of soccer. Below, West Germany's Matthias Herget attempts to get in a tackle on Italy's Gianluca Vialli.

Direct play is based on playing the ball forward whenever possible. This involves such techniques as turning with the ball, running with it, dribbling, crossing, making runs behind opponents and passing to the back of the defence. Good defending consists of stopping opponents doing these things, or at least making it extremely difficult for them. More important, perhaps, players should remember that good defending is the first stage in launching an attack.

Some players will read this chapter only out of curiosity. Seeing themselves as attackers, pure and simple, they think they need know nothing about defensive techniques. This belief is based on the idea that the roles of attack and defence are determined by the player's customary position on the field of play. This is a mistake. The crucial factor is, in fact, possession of the ball. The team with the ball is attacking. The team without the ball is defending. When his team does not have the ball, a player in the attacking third is defending. Similarly, a player positioned in his own penalty area becomes an attacker the moment his team wins the ball. To emphasize this point, in all the diagrams in this chapter, and indeed in the book, the A side is the team with the ball and the D side is the team without it, no matter where they are on the pitch.

It is an essential part of The Winning Formula that as soon as their side loses possession, every forward player should start to think defensively – that is, they should be working to get the ball back. In fact, good defensive play is especially important in the attacking third of the field. As is explained in the chapter *Winning the Ball in the Attacking Third*, the chance of a move resulting in a goal is greatly increased if possession is won in the attacking third. Goals are less likely to come from moves that start in the middle third, and least likely of all from those beginning in the defending third.

LOSS OF POSSESSION

Players are more likely to lose concentration when their team loses the ball than at any other time. Whether it is out of despair, frustration, disappointment of simply the mistaken notion that defending is not their department, players lose vital seconds and with them the opportunity to win the ball back immediately.

Some attacking players believe that they should save their energies purely for attacking, and they should not be expected to challenge for the ball. What those players fail to realize is that if they did challenge for the ball – especially in the attacking third – more and better attacking opportunities would be created. A player who loses the ball in the defending third will invariably try to win it back immediately, because he is aware of the danger. Those who do not try to do so in the attacking third can only be unaware of the opportunities.

PRESSURE

A player's first objective in defending is to restrict the time and space available to the attackers, putting them under pressure. Players put under pressure in this way in their own defending third often panic and give the ball away.

All players, whatever their position, should start pressuring as soon as possession is lost. It is just at this moment that some players lose their concentration. Football, like most games, is often decided by mistakes, and failure to concentrate is one of the main reasons why mistakes happen.

In maintaining concentration and putting on pressure, a defender has made the first step toward winning back the ball. An effective challenge is the second step.

CHALLENGING FOR THE BALL – THE RECOVERY RUN

Before a player can challenge for the ball, he must recover to a position at least level with the player on the ball and preferably goal-side of him. It is a mistake to recover much beyond the player with the ball, as the whole objective of the exercise is to make direct play difficult and to prevent the ball being played forward.

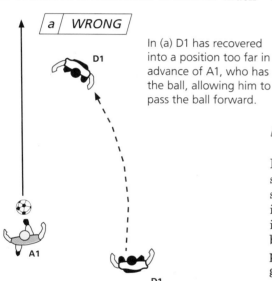

In (a) D1 has recovered into a position too far in advance of A1, who has the ball, allowing him to pass the ball forward.

In (b) D1 has recovered into a position just goal-side of A1, blocking the forward passing routes.

DIRECTION OF PLAY

It is not possible to put a player under pressure from five or ten yards away. The ball can still be played forward past a defender standing at that distance. Two yards away is the ideal distance to aim for, ensuring that the ball has to be played square or back to a supporting player. That is good pressuring and good defending.

CHALLENGING FOR THE BALL – RECOVERY LINES

A defending player's best line of recovery will always be the shortest route back. Players on the flanks should follow a line back to their near post and players in central positions should run towards their own penalty spot.

There are three main mistakes players must guard against in making recovery runs. The first is failing to recover – either the run is not made at all, or it is made too slowly or too late; the second is recovering too far beyond the ball and the third is relaxing and allowing their concentration to lapse once goal-side of the ball.

Once a player gets into a position goal-side of the ball he must think again about his line of recovery and about his responsibilities for marking or challenging an opponent. He will have to do one of five things.

- ⚽ *Challenge the player with the ball.*
- ⚽ *Cover a team-mate challenging the player with the ball.*
- ⚽ *Mark an opponent in the area of the ball.*
- ⚽ *Occupy important space goal-side of the ball.*
- ⚽ *Track an opponent making a run to the back of the defence.*

CHALLENGING FOR THE BALL – THE GOAL-SIDE CHALLENGE

Having recovered goal-side of the ball, the defender will be in a position to challenge for the ball or in a position to challenge should the ball be played to his immediate opponent.

There are four possibilities in challenging for the ball. The angle of approach to the challenge will depend on which option is chosen.

1. Interception

If the defender feels that he can intercept the pass, this is by far the most effective way to win the ball. It puts one opponent, at least, out of the game and gains time and space for direct play.

DIRECTION OF PLAY

A1 attempted to play the ball to A2 but D2 has intercepted the pass, leaving A2 on the wrong side of the ball and D2 with time and space to play the ball forward. The line of approach is into the line of the pass.

Players should avoid going to ground when making a tackle unless they are sure of winning the ball or playing it dead.

2. Tackling

If the defender feels that he can reach his opponent at the moment the ball arrives then his best chance of winning the ball will be with a tackle.

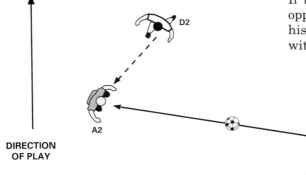

DIRECTION OF PLAY

D2 has judged that he can reach A2 at the same time as A1's pass. His angle of approach is thus in a direct line towards A2.

3. Forcing the player outside

Forcing a player outside means making him move at an angle away from the goal. A typical example would be a full back forcing a winger down the line.

A1 has received the ball near the touch-line. D1's angle of approach is on a line to occupy the infield space, making A1 play in the space down the touch-line. If an opponent is to be forced down the line, the defender's angle of approach must always seal off the inside route.

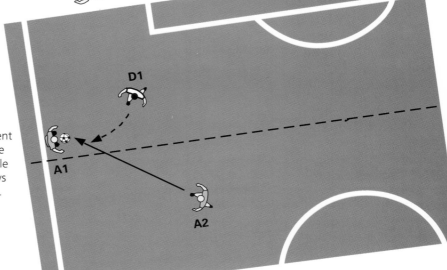

4. Forcing the player inside

If a defender wants to force an opponent inside, his approach should cut off the route outside for the player with the ball. This is done, for example, to deny the flanks to a team that is particularly good at playing crosses into the prime target area (see the chapter on *Crosses*).

As A1's pass was in flight, D2 moved to challenge A2, curving his run to close off space down the line and force A2 inside.

Whatever the line of approach, the key to an effective challenge is speed. In football, speed is not only about how quickly a player can run, but about how quickly he can start running – his reaction time. The time to start running is when the pass is made to one's opponent and the time to run quickly is while the ball is in flight.

It is important, however, for the defender to have slowed his approach by the time the ball arrives at his opponent. If he continues to move at speed, he will find it difficult to change direction and the attacker will be able to beat him with a quick movement. The defender should, therefore, slow down and adopt a balanced position just before the opponent brings the ball under control.

It sometimes happens that a defender will have to slow down in this way when he is still several yards short of an ideal challenging position. Three techniques can help a defender when this happens.

1. Sideways-on position

Taking up a slightly crouching position, edging in slowly towards the attacker, is the best way to close down the last few yards. This position, sideways-on to the direction of play, means that the defender is already half-turned should the ball be played past him. The crouch keeps him balanced and ready to move off either foot. Neither of these advantages apply if the defender's stance is square on, facing up the field.

2. Feinting to tackle

Any player who can seize the initiative in a one against one confrontation is likely to win it. A defender can often gain the initiative by pretending to tackle. One of two things might happen. Perhaps the attacker will look down at the ball, to protect it from the tackle; if this happens the attacker has surrendered the initiative, as he is now thinking of defending the ball rather than attacking his opponent. Alternatively, the player with the ball may attempt to move it away from the tackle, and lose control.

3. Focusing on the ball

The attacker will also be thinking in terms of trying to unbalance the defender with feints or trick plays. The defender's best plan in these situations is to concentrate solely on watching the ball, so that he is not distracted by the movements of the player. He must react only to the movement of the ball.

CHALLENGING FOR THE BALL – STAYING ON ONE'S FEET

Players should always keep their feet when challenging for the ball. Players who go to ground unnecessarily, even for just a second or two, reduce their team for that space of time to just ten effective players. This is known as 'selling oneself'. Besides, going to ground frequently is a waste of energy. Getting up is hard work in itself, and then there is often a long chase after an opponent who should not have needed chasing.

There are really only two occasions when a player can be justified in going to ground to dispossess an opponent with a sliding tackle. First, if the opponent gets clear of the defence then this is an emergency, calling for emergency measures. Second, if the opponent is at the edge of the pitch the defender can play the ball dead for a corner or a throw-in, giving himself time to recover his feet.

Albanian defender Gega fails to win the ball with a sliding tackle, allowing England's John Barnes to run on.

CHALLENGING FOR THE BALL – PREVENTING PLAYERS FROM TURNING

The ability to turn with the ball is an important part of attacking and an important element in direct play. It is a factor in one of every five goals scored. Preventing players from turning with the ball is an equally important part of defending. Defenders, especially rear defenders, must master the technique of not giving attackers room to turn.

There are five elements to this technique.

1. Watching the player with the ball
Defenders should not be so obsessed with marking their immediate opponent that they forget about the player with the ball.

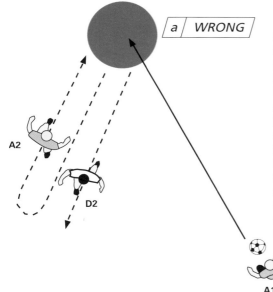

In (a), A1 has the ball. A2 has moved outside, into space, and his marker, D2, has gone with him, leaving space in the centre. A1 plays the ball forward into the space and A2 doubles back to receive the ball behind D2, who has reacted to the player he is marking and forgotten about cutting off the passing avenues of the player with the ball.

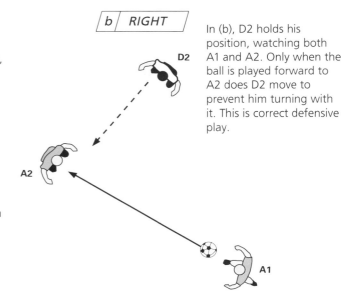

In (b), D2 holds his position, watching both A1 and A2. Only when the ball is played forward to A2 does D2 move to prevent him turning with it. This is correct defensive play.

2. Making up ground when the ball is travelling

It is once the pass has been hit towards his immediate opponent that a defender must move in close to prevent him from turning.

In (a), D2 is too close to A2, leaving space behind D2 into which the ball can be played. In (b), D2's position closes off that space but he is still close enough to A2 to make up the ground between them when A1's pass forward is in flight.

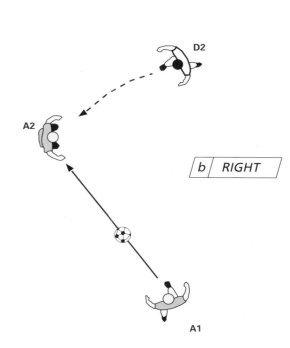

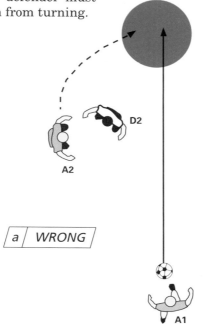

a | WRONG

b | RIGHT

3. Keeping a distance

Once the defender is in a position to challenge, he must watch the ball. To do this he has to keep three or four feet from the attacker. Any closer and he will find it difficult to see the ball. Besides, if a defender gets too close to an attacker, the attacker will be able to turn past him, rolling around the defender's body and not allowing him to get a tackle in.

4. Timing a challenge

A distance of three or four feet should be close enough for the defender to challenge for the ball should the attacker attempt to turn with it. The time to challenge is when the opponent is half-turned. At this point the ball is no longer being screened by the attacker and the defender has a good view of it. The attacker will also be slightly off-balance, with his weight on one foot.

Defenders who challenge for the ball while the attacker has his back to them run a very great risk of giving away free kicks. Since free kicks are a major source of goals, it makes no sense at all to give them away with reckless challenges.

5. Being patient

Once the defender has taken up the ideal position behind an attacker who is facing his own goal, it is the attacker who has got all the problems. Time is on the defender's side; all he has to do is hold his position and wait for the attacker to make his move. If the defender is impatient, and tries to win the ball from an unwinnable position, the attacker's problems are solved at a stroke. He either has a free kick for a foul or the defender has 'sold himself' in the tackle and is beaten.

Patience will always be rewarded in this situation, as in many others. It ranks alongside concentration as an essential quality for all defending players.

Liverpool's John Aldridge is closely watched by two Wimbledon defenders as he attempts to race clear.

CHALLENGING FOR THE BALL – DETERMINATION

When a player moves in to win a ball he must do so with speed, accuracy and timing. The chance of winning the ball should preferably be better than 50-50, and the determination must be 100%.

The full body weight should be transferred into the tackle. It should be remembered that Association Football is a body contact sport. Providing the tackle is within the laws of the game, players should not shrink from bodily contact.

A game of soccer is a whole series of one against one contests, all over the field; some involve speed, some technique, some physical contact. The more of these contests the players of a team can win, the more they can gain a psychological dominance over their opponents. This too is part of The Winning Formula.

SUPPORT PLAY

A player pressuring and challenging the player with the ball needs support. No matter how good a defender he is, he should always have the security of being correctly covered.

The correct covering position is a combination of the right angle of support and the right covering distance.

The angle of support
There are three possible angles of support, depending on what is happening in the game.

When the opponent is being forced down the line, the correct covering position is down the line and just infield of the player being supported.

When the opponent is being forced across the field the correct covering position is infield of, and just a little behind, the player being supported.

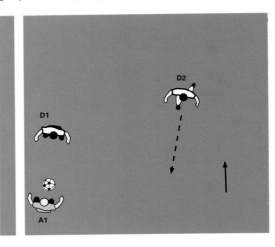

Again, A1 is forced to travel in one direction, across the field. D2 hangs back a little to prevent A1 turning inside and dribbling toward the goal.

When the challenging player is not close enough to the ball, the covering player should support at an angle of 45° from the challenging player.

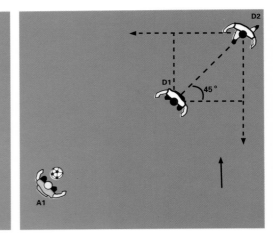

D1 is too far from A1, who therefore has the choice of attacking the space either inside or outside him. D2 must cover in a position where he has a chance of dealing with either possibility, poised between the two at 45° from D1.

D2's covering position ensures that A1 must continue where D1's challenge has sent him – down the line. He hangs back just a little to prevent A1 making a move inside, which must always be D2's prime concern.

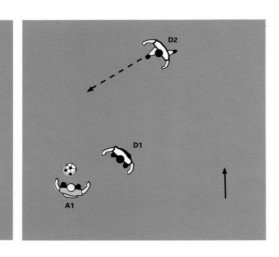

Supporting distance

The ideal covering distance is some four to six yards from the challenging player. This both limits the space available to the opponent and is close enough to challenge immediately if the player being covered is beaten.

Four other factors ought to be taken into consideration.

1. The speed of the opponent. If he is very fast it is better to stand a little further back.

2. The ability of the opponent. If he likes to kick the ball ahead and sprint past opponents, then stand a little further away. If he likes to bring the ball up to opponents and dribble round them then stand a little closer – four yards away rather than six.

3. The position of other defenders. If the supporting defender is the last man then he may well have more players to mark and more space to protect. Sweepers often face the dilemma of whether or not to move out of a central position to give support against an attack down the flanks. The golden rule here is, if in doubt, hold the central position.

4. The area of the pitch. If a defending team is stretched and has lost its compactness (see below), both the challenging and the supporting players are presented with problems; this is particularly true in the middle third of the pitch and in flank positions, where a player may be forced to cover a little further away than the ideal distance. In order to cover effectively a team must retain its compact shape.

These are all important points, and must be considered, but the single most common fault in supporting players is that they take up a position too far from the challenging player.

Verbal support

The supporting player has another responsibility in addition to covering at the correct angle and distance. It is up to him to provide the challenging player with information, advice and encouragement – verbal support as well as physical. For example, the supporting player should tell the challenging player whether the player with the ball should be forced inside or outside.

It is important that players should practice supporting one another as a team. They must agree on what calls to use. When a supporting player shouts 'Force him outside,' the challenging player must know which side 'outside' is. This is an obvious point to make, but a necessary one. There is no guarantee of understanding if the calls have not been worked out beforehand. Good teamwork means not leaving this sort of thing to chance.

As well as this essential information, the supporting player, who has a good view of the whole situation, should also lend encouragement to the challenging player, calling on him to move closer to the opponent perhaps, or to remain patient and keep watching the ball. This form of support is also part of good teamwork.

Supporting players can judge how well they are doing this part of their job by the number of times they have to try and win the ball. The better the verbal support they give, the less often the player they are supporting will be beaten and the less often they will have to attempt to win the ball themselves.

Unless defenders continually call to one another and offer verbal support, they will not function as a unit to the best of their ability. Here, Scotland's Alex McLeish directs a team-mate into position.

COMPACTNESS

If a team allows itself to get spread and stretched all over the field, large spaces will appear between and behind players, making it impossible to pressurize and support effectively.

In order to defend successfully a team must keep a compact formation and avoid being stretched. This enables it to attain the first objective of defending – to keep the ball in front of the defence and deny opponents the chance of passing the ball behind the defence.

Three things must be done if a team is to work as a compact unit.

1. Forward players

Forward players must work hard to recover and to exert pressure the moment their side loses possession.

A2 has intercepted an inaccurate pass from D1. The seven D players in advanced positions now become defenders and immediately make recovery runs to achieve compactness. They have three aims in view: to get goal-side of their opponents; to challenge the player with the ball; and to decrease the space between the rearmost player (apart from the goalkeeper) of their team and the one furthest forward.

Should A2 delay making his pass, allowing D2 to challenge, the initiative might well pass back to the D team.

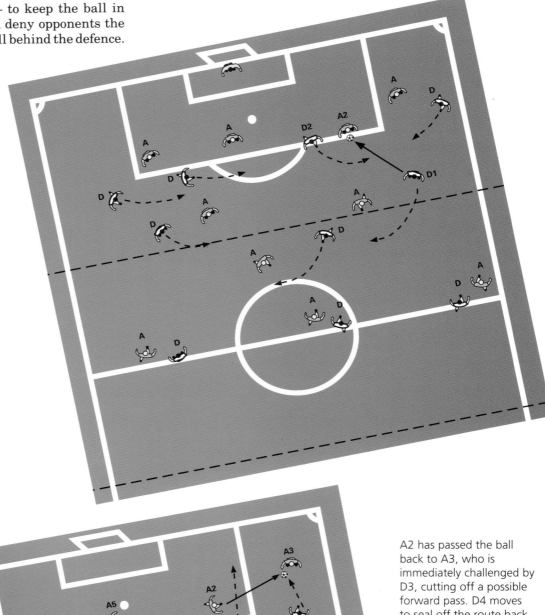

A2 has passed the ball back to A3, who is immediately challenged by D3, cutting off a possible forward pass. D4 moves to seal off the route back to the goalkeeper, and both D5 and D2 have moved cross-field to support D3 and D4 by marking A5 and A2. From this position, the D team has an excellent chance of winning the ball back in the attacking third.

2. Rear players

Just as it is important for forward players to recover and exert pressure when the ball is lost, it is equally important for rear players to move up when it is played forward. Failure to do this stretches a team and makes it difficult for them to sustain direct play. If the ball is played forward quickly, as it should be, then rear players must move up quickly, to maintain support. This is physically demanding and most teams will need to improve their fitness levels, especially their powers of endurance, to keep up the strategy of direct play.

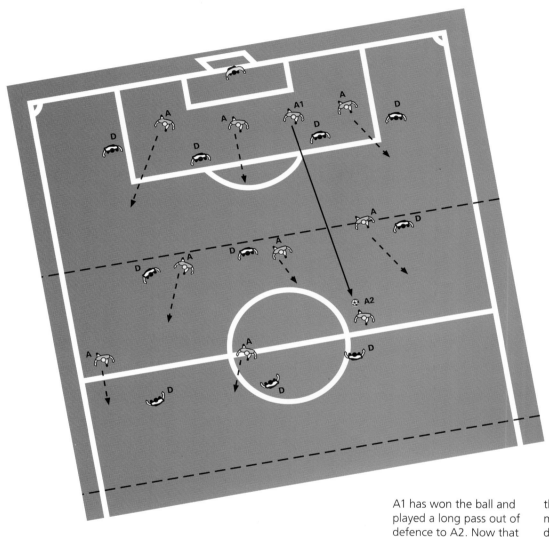

A1 has won the ball and played a long pass out of defence to A2. Now that their team has possession, the rest of the A players move out of their defensive positions to support the attack.

As a team, the attackers have three objectives: to support the man on the ball, decreasing the pressure on him; to move into space behind opponents; and to stretch the opposition end-to-end and side-to-side. This is exactly the opposite of what a team will try to do when it loses the ball.

It quite often happens that the forward players of the team which has lost the ball recover slowly when the opposition's rear players move up to support their own forwards. Two or more players will be stranded in offside positions. In this way a team moving forward quickly can reduce their effective opposition to nine or even fewer players.

Moving up in this way should not be confused with playing the offside trap. Catching the opposition offside may be one of the by-products of moving up, but it is not the reason for it. The offside trap is a risky tactic; this is not, as the team moving up is in possession of the ball. It is actually an example of positive, attacking thinking, rather than the negativity of offside tactics.

3. Quartering the field

Sometimes it is not possible to keep the opposition playing in front of the defence. The best alternative is to restrict passing angles and make the play predictable. The ball can be locked in a quarter of the field when the opposition has the ball on a flank.

A1 is in possession and is challenged by D1, who is not able to get into a position goal-side of the ball. He has therefore positioned himself to force A1 to play through a narrow gap with only A2 and A3 as possible targets, making A1's play predictable. The defending team has moved across to its right flank and, excluding the goalkeeper, outnumbers the attacking players seven to five in that quarter of the field. If the defending team stops the ball being played out of that quarter of the field it will always have the upper hand.

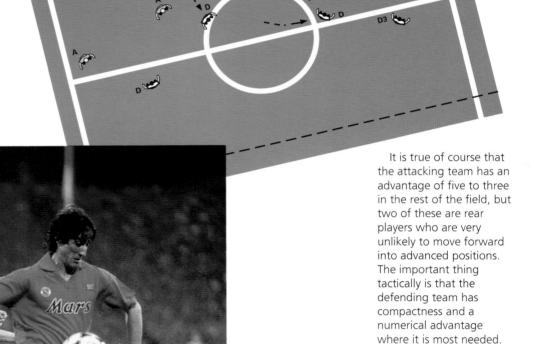

It is true of course that the attacking team has an advantage of five to three in the rest of the field, but two of these are rear players who are very unlikely to move forward into advanced positions. The important thing tactically is that the defending team has compactness and a numerical advantage where it is most needed.

Attackers will always strive to make their play unpredictable, which makes defenders indecisive and slow in taking up the right position. Defenders must try to do the opposite, making the attackers' play predictable and helping their team-mates move into the right positions early.

Defenders should be close enough to attackers to follow every move, but far enough away not to be easily turned. Here, Napoli's Fernando de Napoli is shadowed by Bayern Munich's Jurgen Wegmann.

TRACKING RUNS TO THE BACK OF THE DEFENCE

According to our analysis, runs made to the back of the defence without the ball are a factor in one goal of every four scored. It comes as no surprise, then, that tracking such runs is a key factor in defensive play.

This is easier said than done. The problem is not so much defenders allowing their opponents to move into the space behind them, so much as not seeing what they are up to before it is too late. There are three things that defenders must get right.

1. Starting position – the guiding triangle

The first rule in tracking players is to keep goal-side of them. It is important to understand what this means – there is more to it than just being nearer to your own goal.

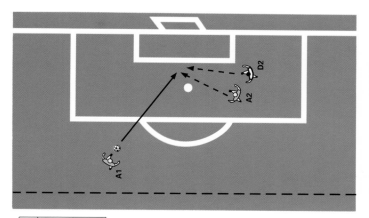

a	WRONG

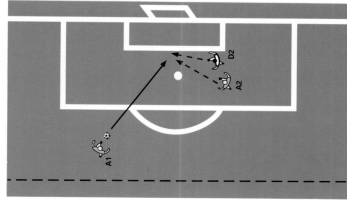

b	RIGHT

In (a), D2 is not goal-side of A2; he is in fact on the corner-flag side and will lose a race against A2 for the ball played forward by A1 in front of goal. Diagram (b) shows D2 in the correct, goal-side position.

As a general guide, defenders should try to stay within a triangle formed by the position of the ball, the position of their immediate opponent and the centre of the goal. Their exact position should enable them to do three things.

- ⚽ If the ball is played behind them, they should be able to beat their immediate opponent to the ball.

- ⚽ If the ball is played to their immediate opponent, they should be able to make up the ground while the ball is in motion.

- ⚽ They should be able to keep the ball and their immediate opponent in view at all times.

D2 and D3 are both correctly positioned within their own guiding triangles. One or other of them is sure to be first to any ball A1 plays into the space behind them; equally they will both be able to make up the ground between themselves and A2 or A3 when the ball is in motion, should A1 play it to either of these attackers. D2 and D3 are also in a position to see both their immediate opponent and the player with the ball.

2. Avoiding ball watching

Ball watching – watching the play to the extent of losing sight of one's immediate opponent – is a common defensive fault, especially on the opposite side of the pitch to the ball. Avoiding it is a matter of adopting the correct stance.

A closed stance provides an excellent view across the field but no view at all of the situation unfolding behind the defender.

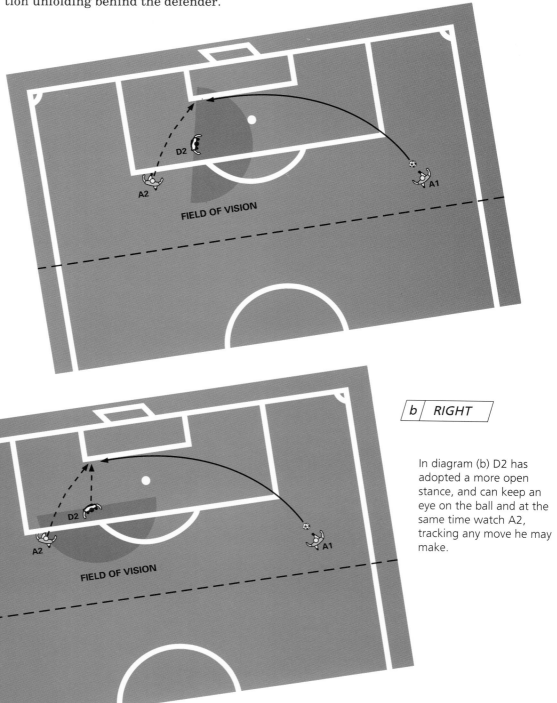

a | WRONG

In diagram (a) D2 has an excellent view of what is happening across the pitch but cannot see A2 moving into a dangerous position behind him, ready to meet a possible cross. Because D2 does not know where A2 is, he cannot keep goal-side of him.

b | RIGHT

In diagram (b) D2 has adopted a more open stance, and can keep an eye on the ball and at the same time watch A2, tracking any move he may make.

Ball-watchers are often attracted towards the ball and move too far across the field.

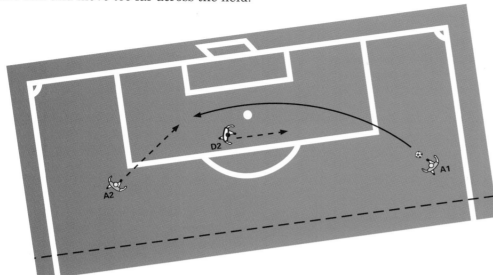

Here, D2 has been ball-watching and as a result has left space behind himself for A1 to play the ball into and for A2, who has hung back, to exploit.

Good defenders are constantly glancing over their shoulders to see what is happening behind them, and adjusting their positions accordingly. It is not only the rearmost defenders who have problems with attackers moving into space behind them. Midfield players should also recognize their defensive responsibilities and track players making forward runs from midfield positions.

If a forward runner's move is tracked immediately, the runner often gives up. Indeed, players making forward runs from the defending third or the middle third of the field quickly become nervous of the space left behind them if their runs are tracked. Midfield and forward players should take espe-

cial note of this. If they work hard at their tracking, deterring opponents from launching forward runs, they will actually save themselves a lot of running in the course of a match.

3. Keeping position

Defenders must be careful that their enthusiasm for tracking runs does not allow them to be drawn out of position. Not all forward runs are made with the idea of exploiting space; some are aimed at creating it by pulling defenders out of position. Dealing with such runs is not simply a matter of not following, but of knowing how far to go and the right line to take.

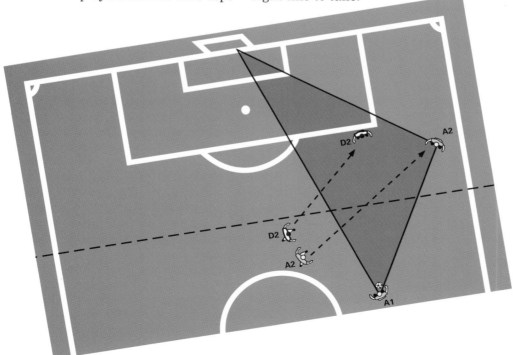

A2 has made a diagonal run toward the right flank. D2 has tracked the run but dropped off A2, taking a line into a position within the guiding triangle where he can see both the ball and A2. He is close enough to challenge A2 should the ball be played to him, and will be first to any ball knocked in behind him by A1. D2 has covered less distance than A2 and is still in an excellent position.

CLEARING UNDER PRESSURE

However well a team defends, sooner or later it will be placed under pressure near its own goal. At every level goals are scored because defenders do not clear adequately from this position. More than half of all goals scored come from moves originating in the attacking third. In other words, the majority of goals come from moves begun when defenders surrender the ball in their own defending third.

A defender has four objectives in clearing from near his goal; to be first to the ball, to play it high, to play it long and to play it wide.

Defending at the top level requires both a cool head under pressure and the courage to risk injury by challenging for the ball in dangerous situations. Scotland's Alex McLeish stoops to head away against concerted English pressure in a 1988 international at Wembley.

Being first

There are no second prizes for defenders challenging for the ball in front of their own goal. No matter how well a player can head a ball or how safely he can kick it, his technique counts for nothing if he is not first to the ball.

Being first to the ball means moving to meet it as early in its flight as possible. Defenders, especially in their own penalty area, normally have the great advantage of facing the ball coming towards them. This makes it much easier to move into the line of flight and attack the ball. Attacking the ball is not simply a matter of technique; it is very largely a matter of determination and, in the case of headers, courage. If a player is good at attacking the ball, he should be good at clearing it, because the considerable force of his body momentum will always be applied to his clearances.

Going for height

Height means time, and time in the penalty area favours the defence. It is better to play the ball straight up in the air, even in the six-yard box, than to play it down to an opponent on the edge of the penalty area.

Playing for height means striking through the bottom half of the ball. If a ball is hit through its bottom half, whether with the head or a foot, it will always rise.

Going for distance

Height without distance brings only temporary relief of the pressure. Clearances should ideally clear the crowded penalty area; the further they go the more likely it is that the danger is over.

Going for width

Balls cleared to central areas – especially those dropping around the edge of the penalty area – are often played straight back in by supporting attackers. Those cleared high and wide usually drop safe. Even if there is an opponent to pick up the ball he will very likely not have an angle for a first-time shot at goal.

If possible, balls crossed from the left should be headed out to the right, and vice versa. As a rule, there are fewer opponents on the opposite flank to a cross.

Going for touch

There will be times when it is correct to play the ball out for a corner or over the touch-line for a throw. Although set plays can be dangerous, at times they will be a safer alternative than the situation the defender is having to deal with. Some purists may decry this as bad play, but if the alternative is to risk losing the ball in the defending third then it can only be seen as good play, the option most likely to bring success.

DEFENDING THE FAR POST

Elsewhere in this book the area of the far post is called the prime scoring area. More than one goal in five is scored from there. Many of these goals come from rebounds or deflections; some, however, come from crosses or set plays. In this case, understanding that the problem exists is more than halfway to solving it. Many defenders do not appreciate the dangers, but it is a fact that teams are four times more vulnerable at the far post than at the near post.

The remedy is simple. When the opponents attack down a flank, the defender on the other flank should make it his first priority to defend the area of the far post, making sure he is first to any ball played into that area.

DEFENDING
AT SET PLAYS

Previous page: Just one outfield player should be chosen before the game to organize any defensive walls. Mexico's Hugo Sanchez, here playing for Real Madrid, checks the position of the wall with the goalkeeper while his fellow-defenders concentrate on the player taking the kick.

Set plays combined with possession regained immediately after set plays account for just over half of all goals scored. A team which can avoid giving away set plays in their own defending third will make it more difficult for their opponents to score.

More goals are scored from free kicks than from corners and throw-ins combined, and most free kicks are awarded for fouls. Players should avoid making reckless challenges and learn to be patient and to avoid going to ground save in an emergency (see the chapter *Key Factors in Defending*).

When players gain possession in the defending third of the field, they must expect their opponents to put them under pressure. Many set plays are given away in this situation because the player on the ball panics under pressure. The best defensive players keep calm and usually find they have more time and space than they thought.

Even the most confident and competent of teams will concede some set plays, of course. Set plays are difficult to defend against as the attacking team has three great advantages.

⚽ They can move a large number of players into pre-planned attacking positions.

⚽ A player taking a kick cannot be pressured, as defending players have to be ten yards from the ball.

⚽ A player taking a kick or a throw has the advantage of a dead ball.

The defence's problems may be deepened by two common mistakes.

⚽ The defence may not be properly organized to cope with the types of situation that arise during and after a set play.

⚽ Players' concentration may lapse because the game has stopped; sometimes, having moved into their assigned position, they feel the job is done and fail to concentrate on what they should be doing there.

Faulty technique accounts for a large number of set plays. Players in defensive positions are often required to make first-time clearances, sometimes of ground balls, sometimes volleys, and sometimes headers. Without a sure-footed, confident technique many of these attempted clearances will go out of play for a throw or a corner or, worse, fall to a dangerously positioned opponent.

SUCCESSFUL DEFENDING

Set plays often decide the result of a match. The defending team should appreciate this, and also that they are not only defending against the set play but against a possible secondary scoring chance immediately following it. Three qualities are needed for successful defending.

1. Planning and organization. Planning is necessary in order to make the opponents' job as difficult as possible, not only at the set play itself, but also if they regain possession following the set play. The aim is to get the best out of players as individuals and to combine their talents to produce the best possible team. Players must be carefully selected to fill specific positions.

2. Individual and team discipline. The efficiency of a team as a whole depends on each individual player thoroughly doing the job he has been given. This is true at all times, but particularly at set plays.

3. Concentration. Lapses in concentration are a major problem at set plays, but concentration is vital if players are to successfully do the jobs they have been given.

Defensive organization needs to be thought out in detail. Players must be detailed to specific tasks and each situation should be rehearsed. When players are drilled in what to do, they are more likely to keep their concentration, and the danger from set plays is thereby reduced. Once the ball has been cleared the whole defence

should move up and out of the penalty area as quickly as possible in order to support the player with the ball and to play as many opponents as possible offside.

In tactical terms, the basic problem for the defending team at all set plays is to achieve the best possible balance between marking players and marking space. It is not so much that one method is better than the other, simply that no team should rely on either method in isolation. The rest of this chapter is about the way this problem can best be solved at different types of set play.

THROW-INS

Throw-ins occur more frequently than any other type of set play. Some players regard them merely as a way of restarting the game, unaware of how often goals are scored from moves begun with a throw. Because of this, many players lose concentration at throws and leave opponents unmarked.

Defending against throw-ins is usually just a matter of applying the basic principles of defending. Special tactical arrangements such as those at free kicks and corners are usually neither practical nor necessary. The only exception to this rule is when the opposition set up for a long throw in their attacking third. At ordinary throw-ins, however, defenders need to do just three things.

1. They should move into marking positions quickly, while the ball is being retrieved. As usual, defenders should take up positions in a triangle drawn between the goal, their immediate opponent and the ball. They should stand where they can watch both their immediate opponent and the ball.

2. They should mark all the players in the area of the ball, including the thrower. Defenders tend to mark too closely at throw-ins. This mistake can be costly, for the attacker can create space for himself with a quick change of direction. At a throw-in, attackers usually stand around 15 to 20 yards from the thrower. If this is the case, the defender should stand two or three yards goal-side of the man he is marking. At that distance he can cover any quick move by his opponent and also make up ground to challenge should the ball be thrown to his attacker.

3. They should put the player receiving the ball under heavy pressure, making control and one-touch play more difficult for him. The receiver has to pass or control a dropping ball, a particularly difficult task under pressure.

Long throws

The long throw, rarely seen 30 years ago, has become a major set piece in modern football and a useful source of goals. Players' throwing techniques have improved. Not only can many players throw the ball long distances, but they can do so with a relatively low, flat trajectory, flinging the ball at speed into the mid-goal area. Defending against such a throw is no easy task.

The one thing attackers do not have on their side is surprise. Everyone can see when a long throw is coming. Defenders should go into pre-set positions, chosen with regard to the following factors.

1. The player taking the throw should be marked by a defender standing two or three yards away in a line between the thrower and the goal. The defender's job is to try to force the thrower to steepen the trajectory of the throw. The higher the trajectory, the longer the ball is in the air. Time, as ever, works in favour of the defence.

2. The player positioned to receive the throw should be marked from behind, but not too closely. The defender must have the space in which to move forward and attack the ball.

3. Someone should mark the space in front of the player receiving the throw. The ideal position is two or three yards in front of him. Placing a defender here not only puts pressure on the receiver, but also on the thrower.

4. The goalkeeper should stand in the near half of the goal. It is rarely possible for him to make a realistic challenge for the ball from the far half of the goal.

5. As much space as possible should be sealed off in the penalty area. The attacking team will push several players forward to support the long throw, ranging them across the width of the penalty area to challenge for partial clearances or flick-ons. One player will be detailed to attack the far post area. All these players must be denied space.

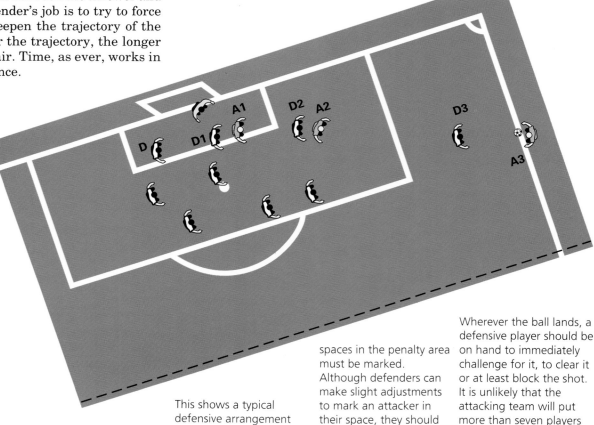

This shows a typical defensive arrangement against a long throw. Nine outfield players have been brought back to meet the threat. Apart from D1, D2 and D3, all the others are marking space. All the spaces in the penalty area must be marked. Although defenders can make slight adjustments to mark an attacker in their space, they should not leave the area which they are responsible for marking in order to mark a player. Their job is to deal with secondary shooting opportunities. Wherever the ball lands, a defensive player should be on hand to immediately challenge for it, to clear it or at least block the shot. It is unlikely that the attacking team will put more than seven players in the penalty area and the number and position of the defending players shown here should be enough to deal with seven attackers.

FREE KICKS OUTSIDE THE DEFENDING THIRD

Players are mistaken if they think that goals are only scored from free kicks conceded in their defending third. Goals do, in fact, result from moves begun by free kicks conceded in both the middle and attacking thirds of the field, though of course only very rarely from a direct shot.

Teams awarded a free kick outside the defending third will usually try to take it quickly, to take advantage of any lapse of concentration on the part of the defending players and also to make good use of the space that is awarded to them with the kick, as their opponents must retreat ten yards.

It is a basic defensive principle at any dead-ball situation that one player should threaten the kick. Essentially this means standing ten yards from the ball in line with the goal, blocking the direct route forward. This delays the attack. Either the opponents will have to use a less direct route or a more difficult technique, such as lofting the ball over the challenging defender's head. Even if the kick clears the defender, the lofted ball will make control more difficult for the eventual receiver.

The time gained by challenging the kick should be used to mark all the attacking players who are in front of the ball and to seal off all important spaces against the pass. Defenders goal-side of the ball must be particularly watchful for attackers making runs to the back of the defence. All such runs should be tracked by defenders.

Players who dispute the award of free kicks and argue with the referee not only offend the spirit and laws of the game, they also do their team a disservice in not immediately taking up an effective defensive position. Players who argue with referees succeed only in demonstrating their own indiscipline and lack of concentration. They are a liability to their team and are not part of any winning formula. The same thing applies to players who refuse to position themselves ten yards from the ball. A match played within both the letter and the spirit of the laws of the game is more enjoyable to watch and more enjoyable to play in.

Defenders are often prepared to concede free kicks in the middle third of the field rather than let an opponent run free. However, a quick free kick can often restore the attacking team's advantage. This foul by West Germany's Buchwald gave the Italians just such an opportunity.

DIRECT FREE KICKS IN THE DEFENDING THIRD

The danger from free kicks obviously increases the nearer the kick is to the penalty area. The danger is greatest from free kicks in and around the 'D', although the majority of goals from free kicks in fact come from the flanks; this is because more free kicks are conceded there than in central positions. Defensive positions and techniques for a free kick from the flanks are much the same as those for a corner kick or a cross. Free kicks from more central positions require special techniques, however.

Defensive walls

The greater the threat of a direct shot into the goal, the more important it is to protect part of the goal by building a defensive wall.

Many goalkeepers like to take charge of setting the wall, but to direct operations properly they have to stand at a post, leaving the whole goal vulnerable to a quickly taken kick. It is better, then, that an outfield player sets the wall. He does this simply by making sure that one player – which player this is should be pre-planned – is in a direct line between the ball and the post furthest from the keeper. The other players in the wall position themselves with regard to this key player while the player setting the wall moves quickly to his agreed defensive position.

The number and identity of the players in the wall at any given situation should be pre-planned. It is important to get into position quickly, so it is essential that every player should know exactly where to go and what to do in every situation. If five players are needed then the whole team should know which five players.

This means that players should not only know that they are in the wall, but where in the wall they should be. Generally speaking, the tallest player should be on the outside of the wall and the shortest on the inside. The tallest player should stand **outside** the key player who is in line between the ball and the post; his job is to stop the ball being bent around the wall. The other players should line up inside the key player in descending order of height. The reason for having the tallest players on the outside is that they will present the largest possible barrier to the most vulnerable part of the goal – that furthest away from the goalkeeper.

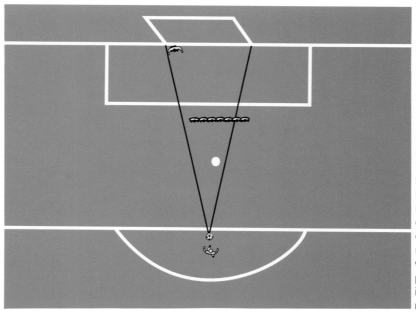

This diagram is a guide to the number of players who should form the wall in various parts of the defending third. It is just as much a mistake to put too many people in the wall as too few, for two reasons. First, the goalkeeper must be able to see the ball while retaining a position near the centre of the goal. Second, defenders will be better used marking attacking players and vulnerable space.

There are seven players in the defensive wall. In order to see round the wall, the goalkeeper has to stand just a yard or so inside his right hand post, leaving him vulnerable to a chip over the wall to the left of his goal. Besides, seven players in the wall leaves just three players to mark space on either side of the wall and cover the opponents – probably as many as seven of them – who take up attacking positions. Even six players in the wall would be too many.

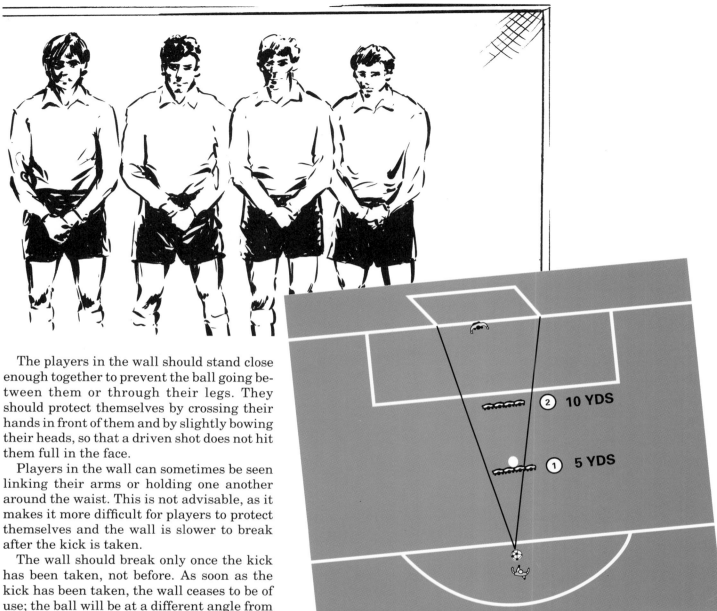

The players in the wall should stand close enough together to prevent the ball going between them or through their legs. They should protect themselves by crossing their hands in front of them and by slightly bowing their heads, so that a driven shot does not hit them full in the face.

Players in the wall can sometimes be seen linking their arms or holding one another around the waist. This is not advisable, as it makes it more difficult for players to protect themselves and the wall is slower to break after the kick is taken.

The wall should break only once the kick has been taken, not before. As soon as the kick has been taken, the wall ceases to be of use; the ball will be at a different angle from the goal. The best idea, therefore, is for the whole wall to attack the ball together. This is especially so if, instead of a shot, a short pass is made to change the shooting angle.

There is probably more cheating around the placing of a defensive wall than any other aspect of the game. Ignorance of the law is no excuse for this; if a player knows why a wall is being built he also knows that he should be ten yards from the ball. Ignorance of distance is no excuse either; walls are only erected in the vicinity of the penalty area where there are plenty of pitch markings to help assess distance; if there is a free-kick on the edge of the 'D', for instance, the wall should not advance beyond the penalty spot.

If a wall is carefully set, the last thing the defending team wants is for it to be moved by the referee because it has been set too close.

One final point needs to be made about forming defensive walls. Though the principle is simple enough, it is not so simple as to make practice unnecessary. Time spent on the practice field drilling players into their roles at free kicks will pay dividends in matches.

Sealing off space

It is a good idea to withdraw all eleven players to defend against free kicks around the penalty area – these are a major source of goals. How many of these players are in the wall and how many are deputed to mark

Obviously four players will seal off more of the goal at point (1) than at point (2). Equally obviously the referee will move a wall formed at point (1) back to point (2), leaving the team vulnerable to a direct shot past them inside the goalkeeper's unguarded right-hand post. It is pointless to cheat in this way, in the hope that the referee will not enforce the law, because it is likely to result in a gap in the defence that the attackers will be quick to exploit.

143

players or space depends mainly on where the free kick is being taken. There are basically three positions for the ball.

Free kicks in the 'D' are the most dangerous of all. The area to seal off stretches from the edge of the six-yard box to the edge of the penalty area.

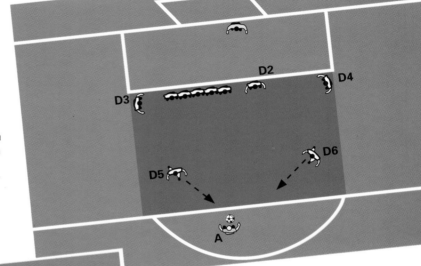

All ten defending outfield players are positioned to seal off space between the six-yard box and the edge of the penalty area. D2 is in line between the ball and the far post to block any shot aimed inside it. D3 and D4 may have to make slight adjustment in their positions to mark opponents but they should not be positioned outside the width of the six-yard box. They should be half-turned, so they can move quickly into the six-yard box to clear possible rebounds or blocked shots. D5 and D6 are positioned to threaten the kick, ready to move in to block the shot if the ball is played sideways for another player to shoot.

Free kicks between the 'D' and the corner of the penalty area represent less of a direct threat to goal, but the vital space to seal off increases.

There are only three players in the wall. The kick is threatened by one player, D2. D3 is positioned to protect the space on the outside of the wall. D4 is in a line between the ball and a point just inside the far post, ready to block a shot towards that post. D5, who must be a good header of the ball, is in the area of the far post to deal with high crosses.

Free kicks down the side of the penalty area represent even less of a direct threat but require even more vital space to be covered.

There are two players in the defensive wall. D3 defends the space outside the wall. D2 threatens the kick from a square position inside the kick. D4 is positioned not only to block a shot to the far post but also to deal with a greater danger, an inswinging cross to the front half of the goal. While other players may adjust their positions to take into account the position of opponents, the player filling D4's role should always hold his position.

INDIRECT FREE KICKS IN THE PENALTY AREA

Indirect free kicks in the penalty area are not awarded very often, but a well-prepared team should always have a plan for dealing with them.

A direct shot is unlikely unless the kicker blasts the ball, hoping for a deflection into the goal. Usually he will play it to one side, changing the angle and setting up a shot for another player on the second touch.

If the ball is from the side of the penalty area then the defence should organize as if for a direct free kick from the flanks. If the ball is in a good, central shooting position – which it will be most of the time in the penalty area – the defence should do two things.

1. It should cover as much of the goal as possible with a defensive wall. If the ball is less than ten yards from the goal this will effectively mean placing all eleven players between the posts, with the goalkeeper in the centre. For a central kick from further out the ten outfield players should form two walls, building in from each post, with the goalkeeper positioned in the centre and slightly in front of them. If there is a gap between the walls it must be in the central position covered by the goalkeeper.

2. As soon as the kick is taken, and before a second touch is made, everyone in the wall or walls should converge on the ball. Not only does this give the best chance of smothering a shot, it can also catch some of the opposing players offside.

PENALTY KICKS

There is nothing outfield players can do to defend directly against a penalty kick. Their job is to be first to any rebounds there might be off the goalkeeper, the posts or the bar. Four or five defenders should position themselves around the penalty area – taking care not to stray into it until the kick is taken – ready to run in and clear any rebound, or put the ball out for a corner or a throw.

CORNERS

Generally speaking, teams are not as well organized for attacking at corner kicks as they should be. Nevertheless it seems to be generally appreciated by attackers at the highest level that the most dangerous kick is an inswinging one aimed to the near post. Defenders too should be aware of this.

Defending against corner kicks involves exactly the same principles as defending against free kicks.

If no-one has been given the responsibility of organizing the defence against free kicks, the result is a milling crowd rather than an efficient defensive wall. The Spanish wall is seen here in argumentative disarray in a match they lost to West Germany.

Threatening the kick

A player should be detailed to threaten the kick from a distance of ten yards. There are two reasons for this. First, it may disturb the kicker.

The second reason for positioning a player wide to threaten the kick is the possibility that the opponents might decide to take a short corner. If they do, the player positioned to threaten the kick can challenge the player with the ball and try to prevent him from crossing it, or at least delay him. It should be understood, though, that the two against one advantage in the attackers' favour is unsatisfactory from the defensive point of view, and another player must come across to equalize the numbers (see the end of the chapter).

Position (1) threatens an outswinging kick. Position (2), further out from the goal-line, threatens an inswinging kick. The technique of threatening a kick involves positioning a yard inside the anticipated line of flight and moving into line as the kicker approaches the ball. This late movement can often cause the kicker to take his eye off the ball or change his mind about the line of the kick; in either case, the quality of the kick will be affected.

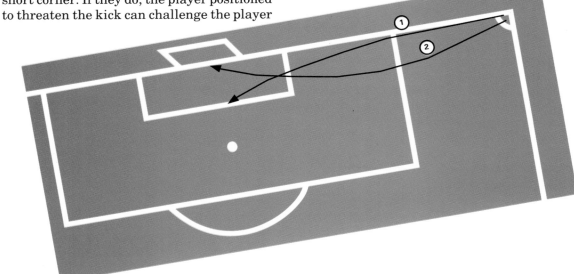

The position of the goalkeeper

The greatest threat from corners is at the near post. Attacking teams will place two players at the near post and, almost certainly, a third player on the goal-line.

If the goalkeeper stands at the far post he will find his way obstructed and it will be difficult, even impossible, for him to move across goal to the near post. If he stands at the near post he will be helpless if the ball is played or flicked on towards the far post. The best position for the goalkeeper to adopt for corner kicks, then, is in the centre of the goal.

The goalkeeper's body position is also crucial. He should be half-turned toward the kicker. This open stance will allow him to keep an eye on what is happening in the penalty area as well as watching the kicker.

Liverpool (in red) pack their penalty area to defend against an Everton corner in the 1989 F.A. Cup final at Wembley. Liverpool's keeper Grobbelaar has moved from the centre of his goal to cover a near post cross. His stance is good.

Positioning defenders on the posts

A defender should guard each post at corners.

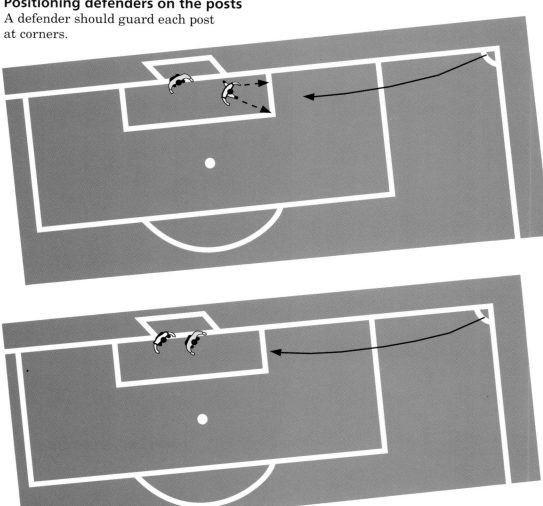

The player on the near post should be a yard off the goal-line and a yard outside the line of the post. His main concern is for the space in front of him. He may have to deal with an inswinging ball hit with pace. There may be no alternative but to play such a ball out for another corner; should this happen he should move well forward of the post to attack the ball.

If the ball is crossed in high the goalkeeper may come out to take it. If he does, the defender at the near post should retreat to a position on the goal-line, just inside the post, to defend the goal.

If the goalkeeper is correctly positioned in the centre of the goal the defender assigned to the far post should stand on the goal-line just inside the post. He should adopt an open stance to give him the best possible field of vision.

Defending the area around the near post

The defender positioned on the near post must be supported by other players ready to defend the front half of the six-yard box. Two players are needed for this. Ideally both of them should be good headers of the ball, and have the determination to attack the ball and be first to it.

D1 is positioned on the near post. D2 and D3 occupy the supporting defensive positions. D2 is a couple of yards inside the six-yard box. He is concerned with the space in front of him and between him and D1. His foot position is important. He should be balanced and on his toes as for a standing sprint start; this will allow him to move forward quickly to attack the ball.

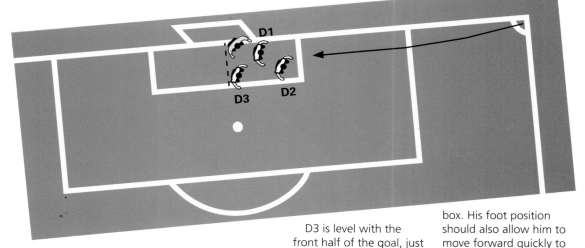

D3 is level with the front half of the goal, just a yard inside the six-yard box. His foot position should also allow him to move forward quickly to attack the ball.

Defending the area around the far post

While the near post is unquestionably the most vulnerable area at corner kicks it should not be assumed that goals will never be scored at the far post. Teams often play to flick the ball on from a near post position to pitch in the general area of the far post. Defenders must always be on the alert for this sort of play, especially those in the far half of the six-yard box.

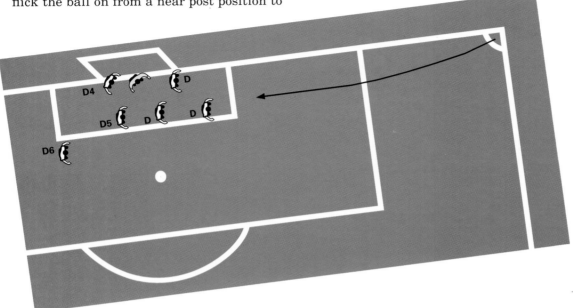

D5 is positioned level with the back half of the goal and on the edge of the six-yard box. D6 is at the back of the six-yard box and a yard outside it. Both players are positioned to challenge for balls in the air in the area of the far post. Each should take up a position that will give him the field of vision to watch for movement by attackers in the back half of the penalty area.

Defending the rest of the penalty area

The further out the ball is from the six-yard box, the less the danger. However it is perfectly possible that the corner will be played directly into the area between the six-yard line and the edge of the penalty area, or that the ball will be partially cleared there. A good attacking team will position players to take advantage of this, so the final three defending players should be positioned there to stop them from doing so.

D7, D8 and D9 are positioned in line with the penalty spot. This is only a rough guide to their positions, which can be adjusted to take into account the positions of the opposing players. Their main task is to prevent a strike at goal from the edge of the penalty area. D7, though, has an additional job; he must watch the area close to the kicker. If the attacking team bring up a second attacker to create a two against one situation for a short corner, D7 must move out to challenge. If he does so then D8 and D9 will have to adjust their positions to cover the space he leaves.

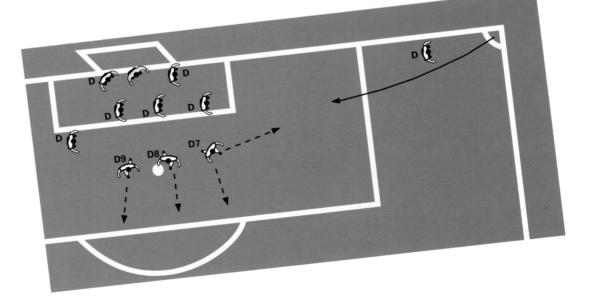

GOALKEEPING

GOALKEEPING

Previous page: The result of a game more often turns on the skill and reflexes of a goalkeeper than the contribution of any one outfield player. This penalty save by Wimbledon's Dave Beasant helped win the 1988 FA Cup final for his club.

The goalkeeper is the single most important player in a soccer team. If he plays badly he can lose matches on his own account. If he plays well he gives his team-mates confidence and makes their performance more assured. Despite this, he is probably also the most neglected player from a training and coaching point of view.

As we have seen in earlier chapters, most goal-scoring opportunities result from crosses or set plays. The goalkeeper's role as the final defender is critical in these situations. He should, therefore, be closely involved in any discussion of team tactics and should practise what is to be done at these and other situations along with the defence, rather than simply practising shot-stopping.

Although such situations can be rehearsed, the goalkeeper often has to make instant decisions and must rely on his reflexes, positioning and skills. The first requirement, then, is a correct technique.

HANDLING

Starting position

The starting position is important. The weight should be on the balls of the feet, which should be roughly shoulder-width apart. This ensures a balanced position from which it is possible to move quickly in any direction.

As shown in the picture on the left, the hands should be at waist height, with the palms open and outside the line of the body. The head should be slightly tilted forward in order to bring the weight of the body onto the balls of the feet. This is an alert position, helping make quick movement possible. The head should be steady at all times to help keep a balanced position.

Taking the ball above head height

The photograph on the left shows a side view of the position of the hands. The ball is taken early, with the hands in front of the line of the body. This allows the goalkeeper to watch the ball into his hands, something that is not possible if the catch is attempted directly above the head.

The hands should be behind and slightly to the side of the ball, as in the picture above, with the fingers spread and the thumbs roughly two inches apart. The position of the hands in front of the body allows the goalkeeper both to watch the ball into his hands, and to cushion it, taking the pace off the ball. The hands should be roughly 12 inches in front of the body. The distance between the hands and the line of the body is known as the cushioning space.

Taking the ball at chest height

There are two basic techniques for taking a ball at chest height. It can be caught or trapped against the chest.

Above, the hands are positioned palm outwards to catch the ball early in front of the body. This gives a cushioning space of about 12 inches and allows the goalkeeper to keep his eyes on the ball. The head must be steady.

The goalkeeper positions his body in the line of flight of the ball. On the right, the hands have been positioned palm upwards to 'cup' the ball. The forearms are wrapped around the front of the ball, cushioning it and securing it to the chest. The head and shoulders lean forward to assist the trapping of the ball against the chest.

Taking the ball at waist height

Here (top left) the goalkeeper has got his body into the line of the ball with the palms of the hands facing upwards in readiness for cupping the ball, with the hands coming underneath and then over the ball to secure it against his stomach.

The cupping technique is completed (below left) with the forearms around the front of the ball, cushioning it to the body. The head and chest are over the ball to ensure it is fully secure.

Taking the ball at thigh height

The cupping technique can also be used for taking the ball early, as on the right. It is particularly useful for balls that pitch approximately two yards in front of the goalkeeper, who leans forward to scoop the ball into his stomach. The technique is very similar to that for balls at waist height, except that the ball is usually cushioned at thigh height.

This (above left) is the position for taking the ball in front of the body at thigh height. Once again, the hands make contact with the ball approximately 12 inches in front of the body to allow a cushioning space.

The feet (above centre) are at an angle to the line of the ball. The right knee bends inwards toward the left knee in order to ensure that the ball cannot pass between the goalkeeper's legs. This is the 'K' leg position.

Taking the ball at ground level

Balls at ground level can be taken either from a stooping position or from a kneeling position.

The picture on the right shows a perfect example of a stooping position, taking the ball as early as possible and allowing once again for a cushioning space. The whole body is behind the line of the ball and the feet are close together so the ball will not go through the goalkeeper's legs if it goes through his hands.

Ground balls can be taken equally well from a kneeling position. Having scooped the ball into the body (below right) the hands secure it there. The knee of the right leg is in front of the left heel, making it impossible for the ball to go through the goalkeeper's legs.

Above, the kneeling position seen from the side. The hands are behind the ball, taking it early and allowing for a cushioning space.

SHOT STOPPING – TYPES OF SAVE

Diving saves – collapsing

Ground shots just to the side of the body are extremely difficult to save and require the goalkeeper to make a quick collapsing movement to get his body behind the ball.

On the left, the goalkeeper has moved both feet to the side, away from the ball, to enable him to fall or dive into a position behind it.

And then (left) the hands are positioned to secure the ball to the body.

Diving saves – buckling

Another way of getting down quickly behind a low shot is to allow the body to buckle. A knee is bent beneath the body (below) to lower it quickly to one side, behind the ball.

The photograph below shows the position of the hands behind the ball in the buckling technique.

Waist height and below – catching the ball

The thrust comes from the foot nearest the ball, putting the body in a sideways-on position when the ball is caught. As the picture on the right shows, the hands are positioned to the side of and slightly behind the ball and the eyes are watching it into the hands.

Waist height and below – deflecting the ball

The body weight is thrust off one foot to get the body airborne.

Contact is made with the ball (left) with the aim of deflecting it round the post. The hands are flat and open to ensure a firm contact.

The save ends with a landing on the side of the body, not the stomach. This sort of landing always results when the thrust is made off the foot nearest the ball, in this case the left foot. If the thrust is made off the foot furthest from the ball, the body twists in flight and the goalkeeper will not only land on his stomach but will almost certainly lose sight of the ball in its flight.

Saves away from the body above waist height

The technique of thrusting off one foot to get the body airborne is identical whatever the height of the ball.

Left, a strong thrusting movement has allowed the goalkeeper – Bruce Grobbelaar of Liverpool – to catch the ball well above waist height.

Above, Bruce Grobbelaar falls toward the ground, holding the ball in his hands and turning in mid-air.

The mid-air twist has allowed Grobbelaar to trap the ball between his hands and the ground as he lands (right), so that it will not be jarred loose by the impact.

Everything is right technically about this save away from the body. The goalkeeper's hand position allows him to watch the ball all the way and provides a cushioning space.

Deflecting the ball

Deflections over the bar are sometimes made by the first hand – the one nearest the source of the shot, as in these photographs – and sometimes by the second hand. Whichever hand is used, the important thing is that contact on the ball is made with an open palm.

The goalkeeper is airborne from a very powerful thrust off the right foot and he deflects the ball up and over the goal. The hand is spread wide, providing the maximum surface for deflection.

Recovery saves

The technique of making a recovery save, of stopping a ball which has been played over the head of the goalkeeper, is to run backwards, watching the ball all the time, and turning only at the point when the body is underneath the ball and close enough to make contact.

At this point the body turns sideways and the hand furthest from the goal comes up within the line of the body to make contact with the ball. The goalkeeper here, in the yellow No. 1 shirt, is Northern Ireland's Pat Jennings.

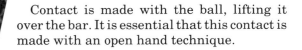

Contact is made with the ball, lifting it over the bar. It is essential that this contact is made with an open hand technique.

The goalkeeper falls to the ground with the ball safely lodged on the roof of the net.

Double saves
Goalkeepers have to make double saves when they fail to secure the ball first time.

Here the goalkeeper has blocked a shot but the ball has actually dropped behind him.

The goalkeeper then dives on the ball and secures it to his chest. Many goals are scored from rebounds off goalkeepers, and they must always be ready to pounce on the ball and make the second save. This often means diving at attackers' feet and requires courage.

SHOT STOPPING – GENERAL PRINCIPLES

Narrowing the angle – getting into line

The most important basic technique of shot-stopping is to give the attacker the smallest possible target to aim at on either side of the goalkeeper. This is known as narrowing the angle.

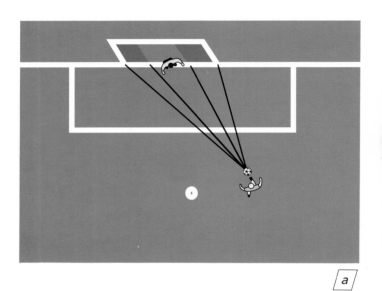

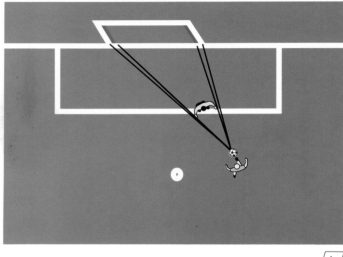

a

b

(a) If the goalkeeper stays on his line he will have to move very quickly to save a shot aimed at the shaded area of the goal.

(b) By moving a few yards off his line towards the attacker, the goalkeeper decreases the target area – he narrows the angle at which the attacker can shoot.

Goalkeepers should always try to get into a position in a line drawn between the ball and the mid-point of the goal. This minimizes the distance the goalkeeper will have to move either side to make a save. To cut down the shooting space even further, his position should be in advance of the goal-line – how far in advance depends on the position of the ball. This will be dealt with in detail in the next section.

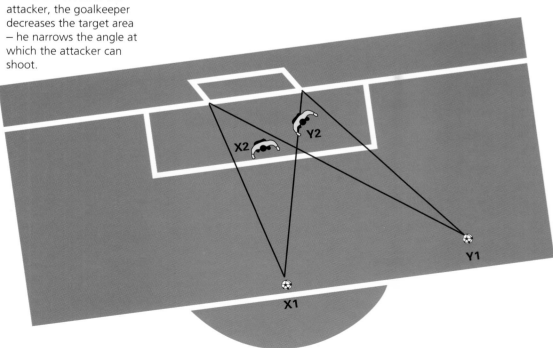

This diagram shows the ideal position for a goalkeeper faced with an attack at the edge of the penalty area. With the ball at Y_1, the goalkeeper should be at Y_2, in line between the ball and the centre of the goal and approximately three yards off the goal-line. When the ball is at X_1, the best position is at X_2, four yards off the goal-line and in line between the ball and the centre of the goal.

To get into the right position the goal-keeper must be quick on his feet. Good, quick footwork is a technique that all goalkeepers should work on. The feet should move as close to the ground as possible, with the studs literally brushing the turf. Essentially it is a quick shuffling movement; the feet should be kept roughly shoulder width apart so that the goalkeeper is always balanced in readiness for a shot. It is a mistake to bring the feet close together and an even worse mistake to allow them to cross, as both positions will guarantee a lack of balance.

Narrowing the angle – finding the right distance

When the ball is close to goal, inside the penalty area, it is critical for the goalkeeper to be precisely in line between the ball and the centre of the goal. The further the ball is from goal, the more important it becomes for the goalkeeper correctly to judge his distance from the line. Staying precisely in line becomes less important, as the ball has to travel further before reaching the goalkeeper, giving him time to make any necessary adjustment.

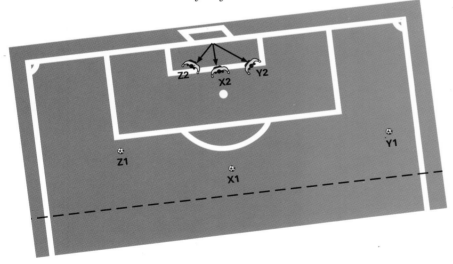

When the ball is in the middle third of the field the goalkeeper should take up a roughly central position, though still in line between the ball and the centre of the goal, and between six and twelve yards from the goal-line, that is between the six-yard box and the penalty spot. The pitch markings will help him fix his position.

When the ball is in the attacking third of the field the goalkeeper again takes up a roughly central position in line between the ball and the centre of the goal. He should be between 12 and 22 yards off his line, between the penalty spot and the edge of the 'D'.

Narrowing the angle when an attacker breaks free

When an attacker breaks clear of the defence, putting the goalkeeper in a one against one situation, the goalkeeper should position himself in a line between the ball and the centre of the goal, and then advance down that line towards the ball. The correct time to advance is when the ball is outside the playing distance of the attacking player. When the ball is close enough to the attacker for him to shoot, the goalkeeper should not move forward, but be balanced and in the starting position ready to make the save.

Blocking

Sometimes the goalkeeper has time to get near enough to the ball to block the shot. When this happens it is essential that the goalkeeper attacks the ball, and the ideal time to do this is when the attacker drops his head to look at the ball and has drawn his kicking foot back to strike the ball.

The goalkeeper has attacked the ball, successfully blocking the shot.

Having blocked the shot the goalkeeper gathers up the ball.

This diagram shows the goalkeeper's position when the ball is in the defending third. In all three positions of the ball the goalkeeper is in line between the ball and the centre of the goal and is just inside his six-yard box.

Spreading

When an attacker tries to dribble past the goalkeeper, he will do so by changing the angle of the ball, dragging it to one side. The goalkeeper can counter this by using the technique of spreading.

The attacker has moved the ball to his left to find a new angle, but the goalkeeper spreads his body across the line of the new angle.

The goalkeeper takes possession of the ball while the attacker is forced to hurdle over him.

If there is any doubt in the goalkeeper's mind over whether or not to spread himself he should stay on his feet and force the attacker to make a further movement with the ball.

Fly kicking

One of the reasons for the goalkeeper taking a position off his goal-line when the ball is in the middle or the attacking third of the field is to enable him to advance still further to defend the space at the back of his defence which is vulnerable to through passes.

If the goalkeeper is sure he can reach the through ball first he should move towards the ball at speed and concentrate on kicking it as high, as wide and as far as possible. This technique is called fly kicking. Almost invariably this technique is only used outside the penalty area where the goalkeeper cannot use his hands.

DEALING WITH CROSSES

The majority of attacks do not come through the centre of the defence but are deflected towards the flanks. Crosses into central positions are therefore of vital importance to the success of attacks, and dealing with crosses is vital to the security of a defence. The goalkeeper's great advantage in being able to use his hands makes him the key figure in dealing with crosses.

For all crosses, goalkeepers must position themselves to obtain the widest possible angle of vision.

An open stance, such as that shown here by Peter Shilton, enables a goalkeeper to watch a cross coming from his left while giving him a sufficiently wide range of vision to see any movements made by attacking players to his right.

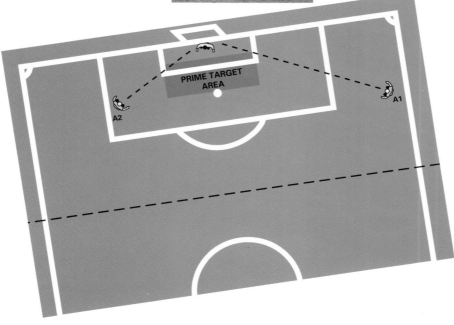

PRIME TARGET AREA

An open stance gives the goalkeeper a field of vision of almost 180°. This gives him a view of the whole of the prime target area (shaded in the diagram). More than four of every five goals scored from crosses are scored from this area (see the chapter on *Crosses*).

Positioning

Basically there are six points on the field from which the ball is likely to be crossed, each requiring a different position of the goalkeeper.

Position (1) is where the ball is on the flanks at the edge of the goalkeeper's defending third of the field. The goalkeeper should be in the centre of his goal but six yards out, on the edge of the six-yard box. This is a case where the distance from the goal-line is more important than the angle between the ball and the goal. It places the goalkeeper in command of the prime target area, enormously increasing his chances of dealing with any ball played into that area from position (1).

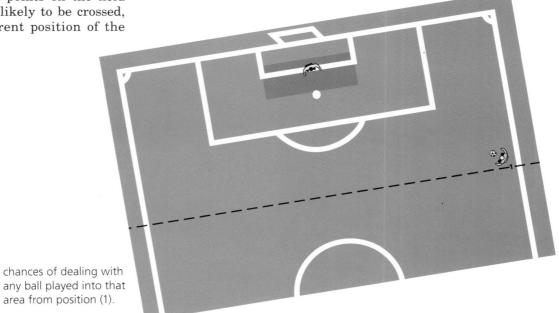

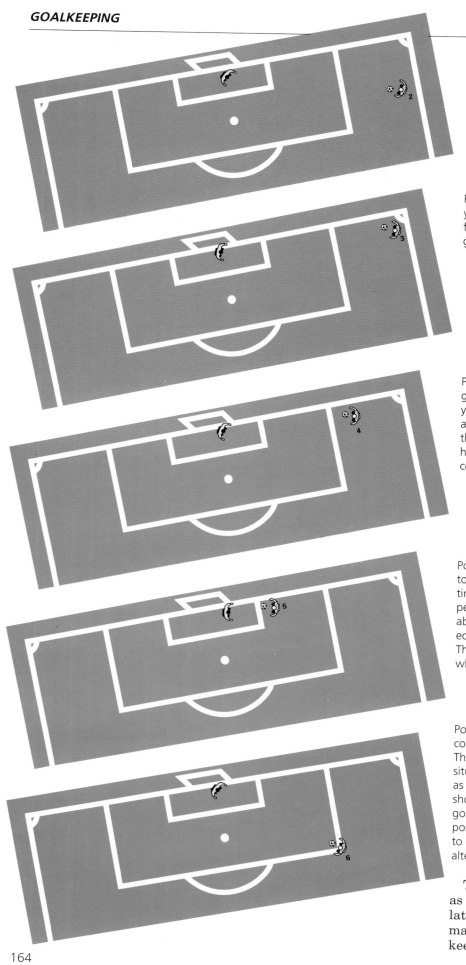

Position (2) is also wide on the flank, but some 10 or 15 yards out from the goal line. The goalkeeper again stands in the centre of his goal, but this time just two or three yards out from the goal-line.

Position (3) is within a yard or two of the corner flag. Again, the goalkeeper is in the centre of his goal, but this time just a yard or so off his line.

Position (4) is close to the goal-line just four or five yards outside the penalty area. The goalkeeper is in the front half of his goal, halfway between the centre and the near post. His front foot is on the goal-line and his rear foot is positioned to give him an open stance so that he can see the movement of players in the back half of the penalty area.

Position (5) is again close to the goal-line but this time the attacker has penetrated to within about two yards of the edge of the six-yard box. This is the only situation where the goalkeeper should come level with his near post. He should stand about one yard out from the goal-line, allowing him to touch the post with an outstretched hand.

Position (6) is near the corner of the penalty area. This is a particularly tricky situation for goalkeepers as it threatens either a shot or a cross. The goalkeeper must adopt a position that allows him to cope with either alternative. He should stand just in the front half of his goal and just off his line. If the ball were four or five yards inside the area, a cross would be less likely and the goalkeeper would be further off his line to guard against the shot.

The ability to make fine judgements such as this, continually adjusting position in relation to the whereabouts of the ball, is what marks out a true master of the art of goalkeeping – it comes with experience.

Moving for a cross

Once he has adopted the correct position the goalkeeper must delay his decision on whether or not to go for the cross until the ball has been struck. He then has to judge the line, trajectory and pace of the ball and either move to take the ball or, if he is not confident about reaching the cross, adjust his position to defend his goal.

If he decides to take the cross, the timing and the line of his approach are crucial. The key factor in timing is for the goalkeeper to come as late as possible. This gives him more time to assess the trajectory of the ball and the best route to it through what is often a congested area. Coming late also means coming fast, and the body momentum generated helps the goalkeeper to leap into the line of the ball and withstand physical challenges by the attacking players.

If the goalkeeper comes in late and fast for a cross (above right) he will be able to take off on one foot, giving more height to the jump. If he comes too early for a cross, he will have to jump from a standing position, reducing the height of his jump.

The line of approach should be as short as possible, with the aim of taking the ball at the highest possible point in its trajectory. A goalkeeper must make the most of the extra height advantage he has from being able to use his hands.

Taking the ball

Having got to the cross first, the goalkeeper then has to decide whether to catch, punch or deflect (palm away) the ball.

If he decides to catch it, he should do so with the hands to the side and behind the ball.

If the goalkeeper elects to punch, usually because trying to catch the ball would be too risky, he will have to decide whether to use one fist or two.

If the fists are together, as in (a) below, the point of contact is much smaller than if they are slightly apart and angled slightly inwards to fit the shape of the ball, as in (b).

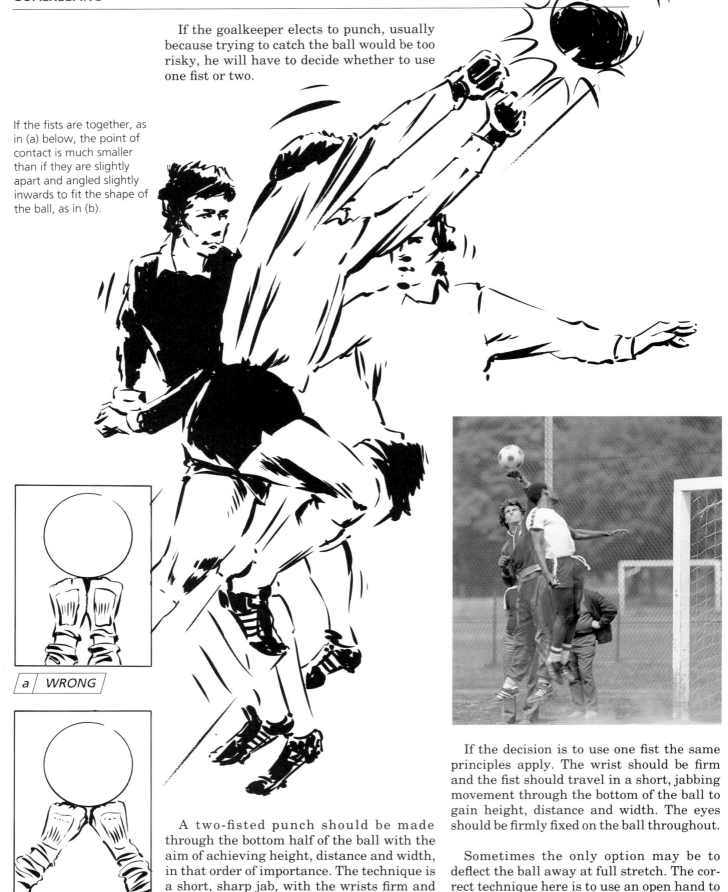

a WRONG

b RIGHT

A two-fisted punch should be made through the bottom half of the ball with the aim of achieving height, distance and width, in that order of importance. The technique is a short, sharp jab, with the wrists firm and slightly apart so that both fists make contact with the ball at the same moment.

If the decision is to use one fist the same principles apply. The wrist should be firm and the fist should travel in a short, jabbing movement through the bottom of the ball to gain height, distance and width. The eyes should be firmly fixed on the ball throughout.

Sometimes the only option may be to deflect the ball away at full stretch. The correct technique here is to use an open hand to deflect the ball as high, as wide and as far away from danger as possible.

COMMUNICATION AND SUPPORT

The goalkeeper is not simply the last line of defence but an integral part of it, communicating with and supporting the other defenders.

Communication

As he almost always has all the play in front of him, the goalkeeper has an important responsibility to let his fellow defenders know what is happening behind them as well as letting them know where he is, whether or not he is coming for the ball or relying on his defenders to clear, and so on.

When calling to his defenders the goalkeeper should observe three principles.

⚽ *He must be **clear.** Confusing information is worse than none at all.*

⚽ *He must be **concise.** There is no time for long-winded explanations.*

⚽ *He must be **calm.** Panic-stricken shouts simply spread alarm.*

Support

The area of support for a goalkeeper is the distance between himself and the rearmost defender. It is the job of the goalkeeper and his defenders to keep this area manageable so they can all do their jobs as effectively as possible. If the distance between them is too great, the attacking team can play the ball forward to exploit the space behind the defenders. If it is too small, the defending players will crowd in on the goalkeeper, hampering his movement.

Correct judgement of the area of support is particularly crucial when defending against attacks from the flanks.

The ball is in a flank position at the edge of the defending third. The outfield defensive players are holding positions on the 18-yard line, while the goalkeeper is at the edge of the six-yard box. The distance between the two, the shaded area in the diagram, is the area of support.

The ball is 20 yards or so from the goal-line and in a wide position. The outfield players are holding positions in line with the penalty spot and the goalkeeper is three yards from goal. With danger more pressing, the area of support is smaller.

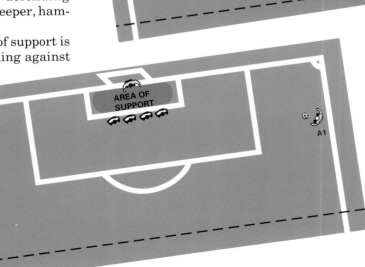

The ball is in a wide position eight or ten yards from the goal-line, and the defenders are now holding a position at the edge of the six-yard box, while the goalkeeper is around a yard from the goal-line. The area of support has shrunk to rather less than six yards deep.

DISTRIBUTION

Once the ball is in his hands the goalkeeper is no longer the last line of defence; his job is to begin the next attack by playing the ball forward with a kick or a throw.

Kicking from hand

The best type of delivery when kicking from hand is one which is high enough to clear all the players in the way but which has a low enough trajectory to reach its destination quickly, allowing the opposing defenders as little recovery time as possible.

The heavy shading shows the target areas to aim for when kicking the ball out from hand. These are difficult areas to mark; either the full backs have to move infield or the central defenders are stretched wider than they would wish. If an attacker can win the ball in one of these areas it is possible to deflect it into the lightly-shaded area behind the defence and away from the central defenders.

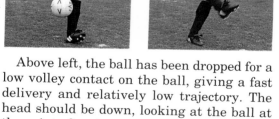

Above left, the ball has been dropped for a low volley contact on the ball, giving a fast delivery and relatively low trajectory. The head should be down, looking at the ball at the point of contact.

Above right, the kick should be followed through in a balanced position. The head remains still and pointing down.

It is normally possible to gain greater distance and an even lower trajectory from kicks taken on the half-volley, just as the ball touches the ground. Care should be taken, though, in using this technique on bumpy or muddy pitches where the bounce is uneven.

Above left, the ball is dropped low for a half-volley clearance. And, above right, contact is made with the ball as it pitches. The eyes should follow the ball throughout.

Throwing the ball

Sometimes it is better to throw the ball out rather than kick it, even though the ball does not travel so far forward. The greater speed and accuracy of a throw can make up for lack of distance.

There are three throwing techniques.

Overarm throws (below) are best for covering long distances.

The body is in line with the direction of the throw and the weight is on the back foot.
The ball is brought forward in a bowling action with the arm straight. The ball is released at the top of the overarm swing as the body weight shifts to the front foot.

Javelin throws, as the name implies, are thrown with a bent arm like a javelin. They can be made quickly and tend to have a flatter trajectory than overarm throws.

The body is in line with the direction of the throw (above) and the ball is released at the top of the swing of the arm, as with a javelin.

Underarm throws are easier for the receiver to control and are best used to play the ball out quickly to an unmarked team-mate in or near the penalty area.

The ball is released (below) from a crouching position with a smooth underarm swing.

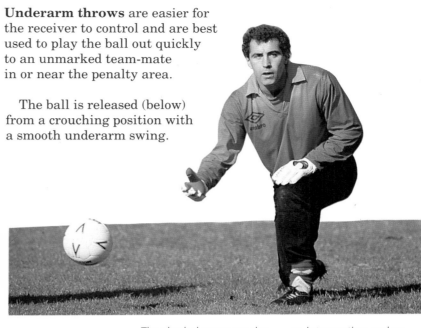

The shaded areas are the best ones to throw to in normal circumstances. The angles and distances are safe from the danger of an interception and an immediate shot into an unguarded goal. Also, the receiver will be at a good angle to receive the ball with a relatively open stance, giving him a good field of vision from which to begin direct play.

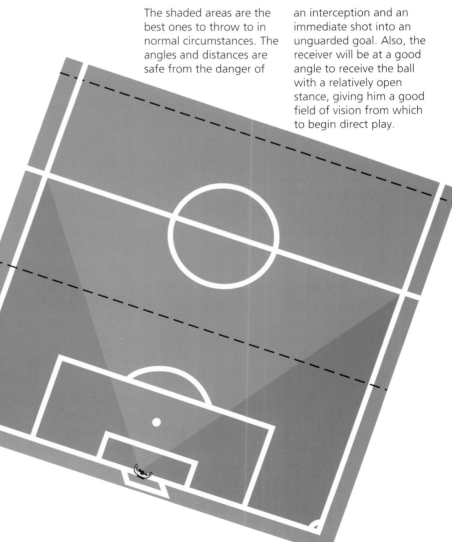

GOAL KICKS

Short goal kicks

Often short kicks are taken so the ball can be played back for the goalkeeper to kick from hand. If, however, the intention is for the outfield player to move the ball forward then it should be played wide of the penalty area where it is safe and where the receiving player can take up a position that allows him to take the ball comfortably and gives him a wide field of forward vision to begin direct play. The target areas are much the same as those aimed for when throwing the ball.

Long goal kicks

If a goal kick is to be played long it should be struck with the instep.

Contact is made through the bottom half of the ball and the non-kicking foot is alongside the ball, six to nine inches away. The head is steady and looking down at the ball. The target areas are the same as those aimed for when kicking from hand.

PENALTIES

Goalkeepers have nothing to lose and everything to gain when facing a penalty kick. They are not expected to save it; if they do, it is regarded as a bonus.

This does not mean that everything should just be left to chance. Goalkeepers should keep a record of the penalty takers in their league, taking note of which foot they prefer, whether they go for accuracy or for power, and which side they prefer to place the ball.

When facing a kicker who prefers to place the ball, pressure can be put on him by standing slightly off-centre, decreasing the space available on the kicker's favoured side. He may try too hard, and put the ball wide, or change his mind and go for the other, less-favoured, side of the goal.

It is important that the goalkeeper should not move before the ball is kicked. Not only is this a law of the game, it also helps the goalkeeper make a save. A goalkeeper has no chance of saving a good penalty, hit with power and accurately placed. However, he does have a chance of saving a poor penalty, **providing he has not moved in anticipation of a good one.**

Far too many poorly-taken penalties score. The main reason for this is that goalkeepers 'sell' themselves by moving too early. Their best hope of saving the penalty is to stay on their feet until the kicker has made contact with the ball.

THE WINNING FORMULA

THE WINNING FORMULA

Association football is often regarded as a game of opinions, some based on experience, some on prejudice, some on pure fantasy. The aim of this book has been to cast the cold light of fact on those opinions and see which, if any of them, stand up to statistical scrutiny.

At the beginning of this book was a simple statement of fact. The number of goals scored per game in the finals of the World Cup tournament – soccer's highest level – has fallen steadily since the 1950s so that the 1986 figure was rather less than half the figure for 1954.

We have to ask ourselves one question. Has winning become so important that teams have adopted strategies which, while making goal-scoring less likely, actually give a team a better chance of winning? The answer to the first part of this is easy. Winning at international level has never been more important than it is at the present time. Whether that is a good or bad thing, or indeed why it should be so, is not the subject of this book. The purpose of this book is to answer the second part of the question, whether what has come to be accepted over the past thirty or so years as the best method of winning football matches is in fact the best. Many teams, certainly most international teams, have adopted possession play as their attacking strategy and retreat as their defensive strategy, and this book demonstrates that these strategies actually decrease the team's chances of scoring goals and winning matches.

This question in turn begs others; is there one method of play which is clearly the best or are there several methods which all bring roughly the same rate of success? Or is it the case, as argued in this book, that there are a number of methods, variations on a theme, which must operate within a well-defined formula in order to achieve success? All our research and analysis has led us to the conclusion that there is indeed a Winning Formula – hence the title of this book – that will not only bring more success, in terms of matches won, but also, in contrast to other modern association football philosophies, will produce more goals.

Previous page: By following the steps of The Winning Formula, players at all levels will more often experience the joy of scoring a goal and the satisfaction of winning a match. Here Bryan Robson celebrates a goal for England and is congratulated by Gary Lineker.

STRATEGIES

Every team must employ two strategies, one for attack – that is, when the team are in possession of the ball – and one for defence – that is, when the opponents are in possession of the ball.

Attacking strategies

There are two basic attacking philosophies, possession football and direct play. Most international teams base their attacking strategy on possession football. The strategy is based on a slow build-up involving a high number of passes (defined in our analysis as six or more passes in one possession). Players patiently probe for an opening to create a shooting opportunity. At the centre of the strategy of possession play is an essentially negative idea; while a side retains possession of the ball, their opponents cannot score a goal.

As a matter of fact, patient possession football does not produce the goals that win matches. Teams which embrace the strategy of possession play in fact score the vast majority of their goals from five consecutive passes or less.

A team like Brazil, one of the main exponents of possession play as an attacking strategy, scored two out of every three of the goals they produced (ten of their matches were included in our analysis) from five consecutive passes or less. In the 1970 World Cup final Brazil beat Italy, another proponent of possession play, by 4-1. Four of the five goals were scored from five passes or less. The fifth goal, Brazil's last, was scored in the dying minutes of the game against a dispirited team from a total of nine passes.

Only one other goal has been scored from more than five passes in a World Cup final in the past 20 years. Argentina scored from six consecutive passes against Holland in 1978. Argentina is the most successful country in World Cup football in recent times, winning the trophy in 1978 and 1986. In 12 of their World Cup matches in our sample, more than nine of every ten goals they scored was from five consecutive passes or less.

In our total sample of 109 matches at the highest levels no less than 87% of goals scored, almost seven out of every eight, came from five consecutive passes or less. It seems absolutely clear that, whatever the preferred strategy of the teams involved, the great majority of goals scored come from direct moves involving five consecutive passes or less. However, it is easy to get carried away by statistics. Could these impressive numbers in fact be less than the whole truth? Was five passes a wholly arbitrary cut-off point? Why not three or four, or six or seven?

Let us look at an analysis that shows the number of goals resulting from moves with varying numbers of consecutive passes.

Number of passes	0	1	2	3	4	5	6	7	8	9	10	11	12
Total goals	53	29	35	26	17	16	7	7	1	5	2	2	2
Percentage	26	14	17	13	8	8	3	3	0	2	1	1	1

These figures show that while there is a drop-off between three and four consecutive passes, the major drop comes after five consecutive passes.

It will be noticed, however, that just over one goal in four was scored from a '0' pass movement; that is, it is scored by a player who has regained possession from an opponent. Could it be that, after movements featuring a high number of consecutive passes, there was a rebound, a partial interception by a defender or a free kick which led to a '0' pass goal being recorded? Each of the 53 '0' pass goals were re-analyzed to count the number of passes in the move immediately before it.

Number of passes	0	1	2	3	4	5	6	7	8	9	10	14
Total goals	12	13	11	5	5	1	2	1	1	1	–	1
Percentage	23	24	21	9	9	2	4	2	2	2	–	2

A similar analysis was done for the 29 one-pass goals in our sample.

Number of passes	0	1	2	3	4	5	6	7	8	9	10
Total goals	11	4	7	1	1	1	2	2	–	–	–
Percentage	38	14	24	3	3	3	7	7	–	–	–

In both cases the proportion of goals following on a movement of five consecutive passes or less is around seven out of eight.

These figures demonstrate that in the hypothetical case of a team making six or more passes every time they are in possession of the ball a team would greatly reduce its chances of winning. Although this is an extreme, hypothetical case it does show that as far as scoring goals is concerned, it is counterproductive to adopt a strategy based on possession football and long, intricate passing movements. Such a strategy flies in the face of the evidence. A goal is **seven times** more likely to come from a move of five consecutive passes or less.

The evidence leads inescapably to one conclusion. If there is a Winning Formula in soccer it must be based on the attacking strategy of direct play, that is on playing the ball forward whenever possible with the aim of achieving a shooting opportunity within five consecutive passes. The strategy of possession play produces fewer shots and goals.

173

Defensive strategies

A team cannot be on the attack all the time. Having lost possession of the ball, a team's defensive strategy must be brought into play. Again, there are two basic schools of thought on what strategy to adopt when the other side are in possession. A team can either retreat, taking up secure defensive positions close to their own goal to thwart their opponents' attacks, or they can 'push up', crowding their opponents and trying to regain the ball in the area in which it was lost.

Sometimes there is no choice. If the defend-ing side is outnumbered, it must retreat. If, however, there is equality of numbers, there is a choice; whether to retreat or to push up is a question of strategy.

Let us look at the facts. Teams win the ball far more often in their defending third of the field or in the middle third than they do in their attacking third. This is to be expected, of course, but it is not the whole story. Our analysis has shown that most goals are scored from positions where possession has been regained in the attacking third of the field.

Total goals	Goals from the attacking third		Goals from the middle third		Goals from the defending third	
	Number	%	Number	%	Number	%
202	106	52	60	30	36	18

The statistics above confirm the value and importance of winning back the ball in the attacking third.

If a team can increase the number of times they regain possession in the attacking third they will score more goals. We can say this with some confidence owing to the evidence of our analysis, and it is confirmed by the ratios of goals to possession regained in each third of the field. The chances of possession being turned into a goal are seven times greater if the ball is won in the attacking third rather than in the defending third.

The best, the most positive defensive stra-tegy, therefore, is to push up on opponents and to pressure them, in order to regain pos-session of the ball as far up the field as pos-sible. In fact, the very opposite of the strategy of retreat.

The first step in creating a Winning Formula is to adopt the best strategies in both defence and attack.

In attack this means going forward as quickly as possible – direct play – and in defence it means attempting to win back the ball as soon as possible and as near as possible to the opponents' goal.

The Defending Third

Goals	Possession	Ratio
36	8,475	1:235

The Middle Third

Goals	Possession	Ratio
60	8,845	1:147

The Attacking Third

Goals	Possession	Ratio
106	3,553	1:34

With the strategic objectives fixed, the next step in creating a Winning Formula is to decide on how they are to be carried out – the team tactics. There are three phases.

TACTICS, PHASE 1 – GETTING INTO THE ATTACKING THIRD

Analysis shows that three times out of every four, the team which most often enters the attacking third of the field will achieve most shots at goal. This makes entering the attacking third one of the most important tactical objectives.

There are five techniques crucial to gaining more entries into the attacking third of the field.

1. Long forward passes to the back of the defence

Effective long forward passes may be played either straight down the field or diagonally across it, but are almost invariably played 30 yards or more into space at the back of the opponents' defence.

The best chance of success comes when this type of pass is hit immediately a side wins possession of the ball. It is at this moment that opponents are at their most vulnerable; space will almost certainly be available at the back of the defence and attacking players may not be tightly marked. It is at this moment that defenders are most likely to lose their concentration.

There has been an orchestrated opposition to long forward passes; teams playing this way have been unfairly pilloried for 'kick and rush' tactics. The fact is, however, that long forward passes are an element in rather more than one goal in every four scored.

Much of this opposition in Britain derives from a defeatist belief that foreign opponents have a tactical superiority based on a short-passing, possession game. This belief can be traced to England's 6-3 defeat by Hungary in 1953, the first time England had been beaten at home by an overseas team. At the time, the general impression was that this famous Hungarian team had achieved their victory with a short-passing game.

In fact, according to an analysis by Stan Cullis, then manager of Wolverhampton Wanderers, one of the top British club sides of the 1950s, Hungary played some 94 long passes, more than 60 of them in the air. Five of their six goals came from two consecutive passes or less: the other from seven consecutive passes.

The figure of 94 long passes is about twice the number of long passes one would expect in a match from a top English club side. There are exceptions of course, the most notable of which is Liverpool; very few teams outscore Liverpool in the number of long forward passes attempted and none outscore them in terms of accuracy.

Accuracy is the essential difference between intelligent use of the long forward pass and kick and rush tactics. Players must learn to make long passes accurately, rather than blindly booting the ball up the field, and develop the judgement to know when to play a long forward pass and when not to do so. At its best it is a great attacking weapon.

Italian sides tend to combine a retreating defence with more direct methods of attack. De Napoli accelerates away from de Agostini in a league match between Juventus and Napoli.

2. Forward runs without the ball

Association football is a forward thinking, forward passing and forward moving game. Forward passes to the back of the defence are pointless unless team-mates are making forward runs to receive the ball. Without forward runs, there would be no-one to exploit the space at the back of defences.

Not all forward running is about the exploitation of space, however. Forward runs are also essential in taking opponents out of key defensive positions in order to create space into which the ball can be played.

Direct play requires all a team's players to 'think forward', whether or not they have the ball. It is about the whole team having a positive attitude, not merely the man with the ball. If the players without the ball do not concentrate on playing in a direct way, the player with the ball will be forced to play in a negative way, passing the ball sideways or backwards for lack of any forward player to pass to.

This sort of negative play is at the heart of possession soccer, based on slow build-ups and long bouts of interpassing. It requires too many players to 'hold' positions behind the ball, and too few players to move into positions in advance of it. If players think in terms of positive movement only once they have inched their way into the attacking third, they are too late.

Forward runs without the ball are an essential part of The Winning Formula, provided they are made intelligently. Just as 'kick and rush' will not produce the desired result, neither will an undisciplined 'cavalry charge' upfield. Runs should always be made with a reason, whether it is to get into position to receive a ball or to take a defender out of position.

Players must learn to recognize situations when it is appropriate to move forward into positions in advance of the ball and when to do so represents an unacceptable risk. However, in every attack it is essential that enough players move forward, ultimately into the penalty area, to give a realistic chance of a goal being scored. Every football spectator has experienced the frustration of seeing the ball rolling harmlessly across the penalty area without an attacking player in sight to apply the finishing touch to a move.

The quick running of England's Gary Lineker not only allows him to be first to the ball but also pulls opposing defenders out of position, creating space for his team-mates to play in and room for them to attack goal.

3. Forward passes to feet, with angled support

The majority of forward passes in a game will inevitably be made to feet rather than into space. The success or failure of such a pass depends not only on the quality of the pass and the technical ability of the receiver but also on the speed and quality of support for the receiver.

The quicker the support arrives, the more likely it is that the supporting player will be able to receive a pass in his turn and to play the ball forward. If support is slow to arrive, then not only might the player in possession be dispossessed, but the defensive team will have had time to mark the support player or at least cut off the routes the player with the ball might use for a forward pass. Once this happens, the team is locked into a pattern of back-passes and square passes, losing the momentum of the attack and their best chance of scoring.

Most teams would benefit from frequent practice in quick support and forward play. This is best done in practice games by allowing players only one touch. All the best teams are capable of high levels of one-touch play, and even the best defenders find it extremely difficult to defend against this. Effective one-touch play depends on good support.

The skill of the Liverpool team in supporting one another was a major factor in making them England's most successful club side of the 1980s. Here Peter Beardsley side-foots the ball forward.

Having received the ball, de Napoli of Italy has turned his marker, Spain's Soler, and laid off a pass to a team-mate.

4. Receiving and turning with the ball

The ability to turn with the ball is an enormous advantage in attacking play. Not only does it disturb defenders and make direct play possible, but it also releases players from supporting positions so that they can move into new, attacking positions in advance of the ball. Not only does turning help create space in advanced positions, but it also helps exploit the space created.

All players should try to master one or two techniques for turning with the ball – the more techniques the better. Most forward passes are played to feet, and most of the time the player receiving the ball will be marked. This means that midfield and attacking players should regard turning with the ball

as an essential technique in their armoury of skills.

Turning with the ball is an element in the scoring of rather more than one goal in five. While some of these turns are in the attacking third of the field, many also take place in the middle third, and it is for this reason that turning with the ball is such an important factor in increasing a team's tally of entries into the attacking third of the field.

5. Forward runs with the ball

Sometimes players pass the ball when they would do better to run with it. Generally, Continental players are better at running with the ball than British players, and they do it more often. One of the reasons for this is that more teams in continental Europe play with a sweeper and as a result often have a numerical advantage in rear positions. If this is so, it makes little tactical sense for the attacking team to continually attempt to pass the ball into an area where they are outnumbered. A much better plan is for a player to run with the ball through the available space in front of the defence while players in more advanced positions try either to free themselves from their markers or take them away from good defensive positions.

However, whatever system the opponents are using, opportunities will arise when running with the ball gives a team an advantage, and all players should learn the technique of running with the ball. It is an element in almost one of every six goals scored, and is certainly an important element in increasing the number of times a team enters the attacking third.

> *Five elements make up the first phase of The Winning Formula. Listing the most important first, they are as follows.*
>
> *1 Long forward passes.*
>
> *2 Forward runs without the ball.*
>
> *3 Forward passes to feet with quick and accurate support.*
>
> *4 Receiving and turning with the ball.*
>
> *5 Forward runs with the ball.*
>
> *Together these five elements bring one result – a tactical advantage through gaining more entries into the attacking third of the field than the opposing team.*

TACTICS, PHASE 2 – MAKING ATTACKS COUNT

Once play has entered the attacking third of the field, one or more of six things will happen; there will be a dribble, a bout of interpassing, a cross, a set play, a shot at goal and/or possession will be lost.

1. Dribbling

Nowhere does the technique for dribbling pay greater dividends than in the attacking third of the field. Not only is it a way of creating shooting opportunities out of nothing, but dribbles are often ended only by the defending team conceding a set play, often a free kick – nearly three of every five free kicks in and around the penalty area are awarded as the result of a dribble. In addition, dribbling is sometimes necessary to create space on the flanks from which the ball can be crossed.

All these factors combine to make dribbling in the attacking third an essential part of The Winning Formula. Players should try to master two or three techniques for dribbling past opponents; remember that failing to beat an opponent is not as bad as failing to **try** to beat him. Being beaten at the expense of a set play is not failure at all, as a set play is an acceptable by-product of a dribble – a second prize, in effect.

2. Interpassing

Direct play requires that interpassing should be kept to a minimum in the attacking third. Its value is likely to be greatest on the flanks, but even here, given the choice between passing or dribbling, players should choose the dribble. Given the choice of shooting or passing, players should *always* choose to shoot.

Many professional teams seem to have a fixation about practising wall-passes (also known as 'one-twos') as a means of beating a defence. Certainly, some goals are scored in this way; such goals are often spectacular and are frequently replayed on television. The fact is that this swift interchange of passes is a factor in only one of every 25 goals scored. The time spent by teams in practising wall-passes is out of all proportion to their effectiveness as an attacking weapon.

The passes in the attacking third that are likely to yield the biggest dividends are those to the back of the defence. As with dribbling, on those occasions where such passes do not produce a shot at goal they often produce an acceptable second prize in the form of a set play. Corners and throw-ins are often conceded by defenders seeking safety when they are forced to run back toward their own goal.

3. Crossing the ball

Just over one goal in four comes from a cross, making crossing the ball a vital part of The Winning Formula. In much the same way that long forward passes should not be confused with kick and rush football, so crossing the ball should not be confused with aimlessly hoisting the ball in the general direction of the opponents' penalty area.

It is important to cross the ball early if possible, preferably into space behind defenders and certainly into the prime target area. More than four of every five goals scored from crosses are scored from the prime target area (see the chapter on *Crosses*). Our analysis also shows that the type of cross that pays the best dividends is one played with pace and below head height.

Not only do good crosses provide good goal-scoring opportunities in themselves, they also often force defenders to make poor clearances – leading to the attacking team regaining possession for a possible scoring chance – or to concede set plays, particularly corners or throw-ins.

4. Set plays

Set plays are the single most important factor in scoring goals and thus in winning football matches. If we add those goals scored when a move from a set play breaks down, but the ball is won back immediately (for example, if a corner kick has been headed away by a defender, only to fall at the feet of an attacker at the edge of the penalty area), then the evidence becomes overwhelming. In our sample of 202 goals from 109 matches, no fewer than 92 goals, nearly half, were scored in this way.

Some people feel that it is unacceptable to win a match through set plays. A manager of the English national side once told me that he would rather not win the World Cup than win it on set plays. The fact, however, is that the last six World Cup finals have produced 27 goals and that no fewer than 18 of these, two out of every three goals, have come from a move that began either with a set play or when the ball was won back immediately following a set play.

Set plays, though valuable, are not an aim in themselves. Rather, they arise out of the natural ebb and flow of the game. Opponents are more likely to concede set plays if they are under pressure – a player under challenge in his defending third may choose to give away a throw, for instance, for the sake of safety, or concede a free-kick with an ill-timed challenge on someone dribbling past him.

Direct play puts pressure on opponents and produces more set plays than possession football. This result is to be expected and is borne out by our analysis. All the set plays awarded in the attacking third of the field (those most likely to result in goals) were analyzed according to how many passes were made in the movement prior to the set play being awarded. The results are shown above.

	Set Plays	%age
Awarded after five consecutive passes or less	1,880	89.0
Awarded after six consecutive passes or more	232	11.0
Total (109 matches)	2,112	100.0

Of course, The Winning Formula is not just about adopting styles of play that will result in more set plays being awarded, but is also concerned with making the best of those set plays. Techniques for doing this are covered in depth in the chapter *Attacking from Set Plays*. Whatever the techniques chosen, they must be practised; set plays represent too good a scoring opportunity to be improvized. Not only the kicker and thrower need to practise. To get the best from a set play the whole team should be involved in the practice, and players should be carefully chosen to do those things they can do best and to take up those positions where they are most effective.

There is one general point that needs to be repeated here. The theory that variety at set plays produces the best results is mistaken. The best policy is one of variations on a successful theme. The best example of this is at corners, where a team will have three times the chance of scoring a goal from an inswinging corner than an outswinging one. Mixing inswinging and outswinging corners does not confuse defenders, it helps them – outswingers are easier to deal with.

5. Shooting

Direct play can and will increase the number of shooting chances a team has. The evidence (below) for the effectiveness of direct play in creating scoring chances is overwhelming.

	Shots	%age
Shots following five or less consecutive passes	1,234	85.2
Shots following six or more consecutive passes	214	14.8
Total (109 matches)	1,448	100.0

Although direct play will increase the number of shooting chances, only the right attitude and the right techniques will turn those chances into goals. The right attitude is a positive one. A positive attitude to shooting means that players recognize and take the chance to shoot whenever it arrives. The main factor in turning shots into goals, however, is accurate shooting.

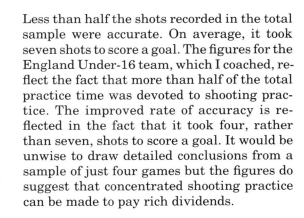

	Total Sample	England Under-16
Matches	109	4
Goals scored	202	15
Total shots	1,448	59
Number of shots to score one goal	7.2	3.9
Total accurate shots	680	37
Percentage of accurate shots	47.0	62.7

Less than half the shots recorded in the total sample were accurate. On average, it took seven shots to score a goal. The figures for the England Under-16 team, which I coached, reflect the fact that more than half of the total practice time was devoted to shooting practice. The improved rate of accuracy is reflected in the fact that it took four, rather than seven, shots to score a goal. It would be unwise to draw detailed conclusions from a sample of just four games but the figures do suggest that concentrated shooting practice can be made to pay rich dividends.

Insufficient time is usually given to shooting practice, and very often the wrong things are practised. Our analysis – see the panel on the right – shows the techniques which most often lead to goals and those which do so more rarely. People planning shooting practices should take note of these figures.

⚽ 71.5% of all goals are scored with one touch; that is, the ball is not brought under control before shooting.

⚽ 22.4% of all goals are scored from the area of the far post (of these, one in three is scored with a header and one in four with a volley).

⚽ 21.5% of all goals are from headers. Two of every three headed goals are headed from below head height.

⚽ 16.8% of all goals are from volleys.

⚽ 15.9% of all goals are scored from outside the penalty area.

⚽ 4.7% of all goals are scored when an attacker is clear of the defence with only the goalkeeper to beat.

Analysis also shows that too many players are one-footed. Two-thirds of all goals scored with volleys and a similar proportion of all goals scored from outside the area are scored with the right foot. This figure suggests either that too many players are ignoring chances to shoot with the left foot or that too many left-footed shots are inaccurate. Players practising their shooting should practise equally with both feet.

Shooting practice

It is important that all players practise shooting, not just those who usually play in attacking positions. Certain situations are more likely to produce goals than others, and some goal-scoring situations occur more often than others. Because of this, more time needs to be spent in practice on some techniques than on others. The priority list, with the most important technique on the top, is as follows.

1 One-touch shots from inside the penalty area from balls served at various angles on the ground.

2 Headed shots from crosses into the prime target area.

3 One-touch volley shots in the penalty area from balls served at varying heights and angles.

4 Shots taken from outside the penalty area while running forward with the ball, from central positions and down both flanks.

5 Two-touch shots from inside the penalty area with the service at varying heights and angles.

6 One-touch shots from outside the penalty area from balls served at various angles on the ground.

7 Dribbling or shooting past the goalkeeper, or lobbing the ball over his head, when clear of the defence.

8 Volleyed shots from outside the penalty area from balls served at various heights and angles.

It will be noted that the priority list does not specifically include shots from the area of the far post, apart from headers inside the prime target area. In a realistic practice, a player should be positioned at the far post to deal with rebounds, deflections and lofted shots.

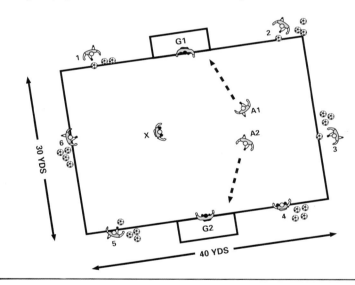

This is a typical realistic practice situation. The area is 40 yards by 30 yards, preferably with two portable goals. There are six servers, numbered 1 to 6, each with a supply of four or five balls. When the coach calls their number they serve the ball for X to shoot. X must shoot alternately at G1 and G2, thus gaining practice in shooting from the left and from the right. A1 and A2 are the support players. When X shoots at the G1 goal, A1 attacks the far post; when he shoots at the G2 goal, A2 attacks that far post.

The players rotate regularly so that each one in turn has concentrated practice in serving, shooting and supporting. The goalkeepers, too, have sustained, concentrated, realistic practice.

In our sample of 109 matches, 202 goals were scored from 680 accurate shots, a figure of one goal for every 3.3 accurate attempts or three goals for every ten accurate shots. The ultimate objective of The Winning Formula is to consistently achieve ten or more shots on target every game. This is not possible without achieving the three points on the right.

Left: A cross from the right into the prime scoring area is met on the volley by John Barnes, scoring one of England's three goals in a World Cup qualifying match against Poland.

1 Sustained direct play to create an increased number of shooting opportunities.

2 Realistic, concentrated shooting practice aimed at improving accuracy and focusing on those elements which are known to produce more goals.

3 A positive attitude to shooting on the part of everyone in the team and the team as a whole. The poor attitude which undoubtedly exists towards shooting today is an extension of the negative attitude displayed toward forward play in general.

6. Lost possession

Of course, not every entry into the attacking third will produce a goal, or a shot at goal. Sometimes the ball will be lost. However, positive thinking should still characterize the attitudes and actions of a team who should all work towards winning the ball back as soon as possible. On average, a team winning possession in its own defending third will have to do so 235 times in order to score one goal. If a team wins the ball back in its attacking third, however, it will get a goal once every 33.5 times. Put another way, a team is seven times more likely to score from a move begun in the attacking third than one beginning in the defending third.

The positive response, then, to losing the ball in the attacking third is to try to win it back as soon as possible in the same area. This will be much easier to do if two things have happened.

1. The team has retained a compact shape, with the players close enough to each other for one of them to quickly challenge for the ball, knowing that support is available.

2. The ball has been lost in an attempt to play it forward. If the ball has been lost by playing it backwards or square, it is likely that players will have been put out of the game, leaving space available for the opponents to attack.

If phase one of The Winning Formula is to outscore the opponents in the number of times entry is gained to the attacking third of the field, then phase two requires that the momentum of the play should be maintained, and if possible increased. Time invariably works in favour of the defending team. The way to maintain attacking momentum is to think positively and apply the principles of direct play.

The formula for success is simple enough.

1 Shoot at every opportunity.

2 Attack opponents by dribbling whenever possible.

3 Look to pass the ball to the back of the defence.

4 Cross the ball in early from the flanks to the back of the defence.

5 Maintain a compact shape.

Following this formula will enable a team to achieve the objective of the second phase of The Winning Formula; once in the attacking third, to do better than the opponents in four areas.

1 Take more shots.

2 Gain more set plays.

3 Put in more crosses, especially to the back of the defence.

4 Win back the ball more often.

Outdoing the opponents in these four areas will usually lead to a team winning a match.

PHASE 3 – WINNING BACK THE BALL

The Winning Formula is not only about attacking, it is also about defending, about getting the ball back. Perhaps the best way to understand how to defend is to ask the question, 'What would I do if I were in the attacker's position?', then to try to force him to do the opposite.

The key to defensive strategy – and therefore a major element in The Winning Formula – is the ability of a team to retain a compact shape. If a team is compact when the ball is lost then it is possible to switch at once into an effective defensive strategy. Players will be in positions where they can challenge for the ball and support one another. If, on the other hand, a team is stretched end to end when they lose the ball, spaces will exist between and behind players and the team will have to retreat in order to recover.

A compact team can lose the ball but keep the initiative; a stretched team invariably surrenders it along with the ball. It is for this reason that physical fitness is so important in soccer; it allows teams to move together as a unit, retaining a compact shape, and they can therefore dictate the strategy of a match.

Good teams, on gaining possession of the ball, will try to get into the attacking third of the field by using one of five techniques: long forward passes to the back of the defence; forward runs without the ball; forward passes to feet with quick support; receiving and turning with the ball; and forward runs with the ball.

If the defending team has kept its compact shape, then a player can quickly challenge for the ball, making passing the ball forward extremely difficult. Forward runs with the ball will be virtually eliminated since there will be no space in which to run. In the same way, forward runs without the ball are unlikely to succeed; defenders will be well positioned to track any such run and even if a player does get free, the man on the ball is under challenge and will be unlikely to be able to pass to him.

It may be possible under challenge to create an angle to squeeze through a forward pass to feet, but the timing and quality of the pass are likely to suffer and it will be difficult to provide effective support to the receiving player. In addition, the receiving player, if challenged by a correctly positioned defender, should find it difficult, and perhaps impossible, to turn with the ball.

In this way, a team which retains its compactness will make it very difficult for their opponents to start an effective attack. However, even teams like Liverpool, Holland or Argentina, who consistently maintain their compactness in every match, are sometimes forced to defend in their defending third.

Defensive strategy in the defending third of the field, whether in open play or at set plays, must provide for the marking of both players and space. There are four things above all that a defender must remember.

1 Be first to the ball.

2 Be positive in clearing the ball, going for height, distance and width.

3 Take particular care to defend the prime scoring area around the far post.

4 Do not get caught in possession in the defending third of the field.

ESSENTIAL TECHNIQUES

Strategy and tactics alone do not win football matches. Each player has to learn and master a range of footballing techniques. Apart from those that are best taught in groups or in practice games, such as supporting in attack and defence, making and tracking forward runs off the ball, or compactness, there are 13 specific individual techniques which are essential to effectively putting The Winning Formula into action.

1 A range of passing techniques, with either foot, covering distances up to 50 yards.

2 Running with the ball.

3 A range of techniques for one-touch control of the ball.

4 At least two different techniques for receiving and turning with the ball.

5 At least two, and preferably more, dribbling techniques.

6 Crossing the ball, especially crossing low and with pace.

7 Shooting from outside the penalty area with either foot.

8 Shooting on the volley with either foot.

9 Shooting first time (one touch) with either foot.

10 Heading for goal, especially diving headers.

11 Defensive heading for height, distance and width.

12 Challenging opponents to stop them passing the ball forward.

13 Challenging opponents to stop them turning with the ball.

Goalkeeping

The goalkeeper is an integral part of The Winning Formula. As an attacking player, he should follow the principles of direct play in selecting passing priorities. In defence, apart from his important role in defending against crosses and at all set plays in the defending third of the field, he can use his unique viewpoint on the game to communicate useful information to the outfield players, helping them to achieve compactness, to track opponents making forward runs, and to challenge and support effectively.

The analysis of our 109-game sample showed that one in every 3.3 shots on target, three in ten, scored. This is a sobering thought for goalkeepers. Of course, the finest goalkeepers in the world can improve on those figures, but to do so they need agility, a good sense of balance and of positioning and, above all, many years of correct practice.

SUMMARY

Attack

The best attacking strategy is based on direct play. The evidence that success is built on moves of five passes or less is overwhelming.

The first objective is to do better than the opponents in gaining entry into the attacking third of the field. Five techniques are important in the attainment of this objective.

1 Long forward passes to the back of the defence.

2 Forward runs without the ball.

3 Forward passes to feet, supported by a player at an angle to receive the ball and pass it forward.

4 Receiving and turning with the ball.

5 Forward runs with the ball.

The second objective is to increase, or at least maintain, the momentum of the attack once the ball is in the attacking third. Five things are important here.

1 Shoot at every opportunity.

2 Attack opponents by dribbling whenever possible.

3 Pass the ball to the back of the defence whenever possible.

4 Cross the ball early from the flanks to the back of the defence.

5 Retain a compact team shape.

If the second objective is achieved, then it will be easier to attain the third objective, which is to outscore the opponents in four important elements of the game.

1 Shooting. Shooting at every opportunity itself provides more shooting opportunities in the form of rebounds and deflections.

2 Being awarded set plays.

3 Crossing the ball.

4 Winning the ball back in the attacking third of the field.

Defence

The best defensive strategy is to win the ball as near to the opponents' goal as possible. This can happen if the team retains a compact shape.

A compact formation makes three important things possible for a defending team.

1 It means the player on the ball can be challenged quickly. This prevents him, or at least delays him, from playing the ball forward.

2 The challenging player immediately has defensive support.

3 Players are available to track opponents making forward runs.

The chances of conceding a goal will be reduced further if players defending in and around their own penalty area can achieve the following four objectives.

1 Being first to the ball.

2 Clearing with height, distance and width.

3 Defending the area of the far post.

4 Not getting caught in possession in the defending third of the field.

SUCCESS AND THE WINNING FORMULA

No formula can guarantee 100% success, but we believe our researches have led to an understanding of the most successful strategy, that of direct play. The application of logic and statistical research have led to a tactical plan with a succession of objectives to achieve. Each objective is made easier to achieve by completing the one before it. The first objective is to get into the attacking third of the field more often than the opponents do, and the final objective is to achieve a minimum of ten shots on target every game. This final objective is easy enough to state, and may appear to some to be a relatively simple task to accomplish, but in fact it is very difficult. In fact, unless the other objectives of The Winning Formula are met first, it is a virtually impossible target.

> *If the strategies we have proposed are adopted and the tactical objectives are achieved, the chances of winning are extremely good – over 85%.*
>
> *The chances of not losing are even better. We have never recorded a match in which a team achieved ten shots on target and lost.*

DIRECT PLAY – THE ANALYSIS

In the research, which was undertaken in preparation for this work, hundreds of matches, at all levels, were analysed. We have extracted 109 games from all those analysed. All the matches, except for the Liverpool matches, are either World Cup or European Cup matches of either Senior, Under 21 of Under 16 level. They also represent all the countries who have either won the World Cup or been runners up in a World Cup Final over the last 20 years.

The six World Cup Final matches, 1966-1986, are included, not only because they represent the absolute pinnacle of world football at four yearly intervals, but also as a spot check and for comparative purposes.

Goal-scoring moves – number of consecutive passes

	No. of Matches	Total Goals	Goals from Five Passes or less No.	%	Goals from Six Passes or more No.	%
Argentina	12	23	21	91	2	9
Brazil	10	25	17	68	8	32
England	29	59	55	93	4	7
England U-21	3	8	7	87	1	13
England U-16	4	15	15	100	0	–
Holland	7	10	10	100	0	–
Italy	12	18	15	83	3	17
West Germany	16	24	19	79	5	21
Liverpool	16	20	17	85	3	15
Total	109	202	176	87	26	13

World Cup Final matches 1966-1986

	No. of Matches	Total Goals	Goals from Five Passes or less No.	%	Goals from Six Passes or more No.	%
Twelve teams	6	27	25	92.5	2	7.4

Set plays in the attacking third – the importance of Direct Play

	No. of Matches	Total Set Plays in A⅓	Set Plays in A⅓ – Five passes or less		Set Plays in A⅓ – Six passes or more	
			No.	%	No.	%
Argentina	12	229	197	86	32	14
Brazil	10	179	145	81	34	19
England	29	554	510	92	44	8
England U-21	3	77	75	97	2	3
England U-16	4	73	73	100	0	–
Holland	7	141	125	89	16	11
Italy	12	205	168	82	37	18
West Germany	16	371	328	88	43	12
Liverpool	16	283	259	92	24	8
Total	109	2,112	1,180	89	232	11

World Cup Final matches 1966-1986

	No. of Matches	Total Set Plays in A⅓	Five passes or less No.	%	Six passes or more No.	%
Twelve teams	6	254	232	91.3	22	8.7

Scoring from set plays – the importance of Direct Play

The following table clearly shows the value of challenging for the ball in the attacking third of the field. More than half the goals scored in our sample came from moves originating in that area.

	No. of Matches	Total Set Play Goals	Set Plays Won after Five passes or less		Set Plays Won after Six passes or more	
			No.	%	No.	%
Argentina	12	10	9	90	1	10
Brazil	10	10	10	100	0	–
England	29	24	20	83	4	17
England U-21	3	4	4	100	0	–
England U-16	4	6	6	100	0	–
Holland	7	6	4	67	2	33
Italy	12	9	8	89	1	11
West Germany	16	15	15	100	0	–
Liverpool	16	8	8	100	0	–
Total	109	92	84	91	8	9

World Cup Final matches 1966-1986

	No. of Matches	Total Set Play Goals	Five passes or less No.	%	Six passes or more No.	%
Twelve teams	6	18	17	94.4	1	5.6

Goal-scoring moves – where the ball was won

In the following table 'Set Play Goals' include both goals scored from moves starting with set plays and those from moves beginning when the ball is lost, then immediately regained, following a set play.

			Third of the field where move began					
	No. of Matches	Total Goals	Attacking ⅓		Middle ⅓		Defending ⅓	
			No.	%	No.	%	No.	%
Argentina	12	23	13	57	6	26	4	17
Brazil	10	25	9	36	9	36	7	28
England	29	59	35	59	15	25	9	15
England U-21	3	8	3	38	4	50	1	13
England U-16	4	15	10	67	3	20	2	13
Holland	7	10	6	60	3	30	1	10
Italy	12	18	8	44	5	28	5	28
West Germany	16	24	12	50	6	25	6	25
Liverpool	16	20	10	50	9	45	1	5
Total	109	202	106	52	60	30	36	18

World Cup Final matches 1966-1986

	No. of Matches	Total Goals	Attacking ⅓ No.	%	Middle ⅓ No.	%	Defending ⅓ No.	%
Twelve teams	6	27	14	51.9	7	25.9	6	22.2

SHOOTING

The importance of accuracy

	Total Matches	Total Goals	Total Shots	Shots on Target No.	Shots on Target %	No. of shots per game	No. of shots per goal
Argentina	12	23	164	74	45	13.7	7.1
Brazil	10	25	186	76	41	18.6	7.4
England	29	59	371	177	48	12.8	6.3
England U-21	3	8	46	24	52	15.3	5.8
England U-16	4	15	59	37	63	14.8	3.9
Holland	7	10	84	33	39	12.0	8.4
Italy	12	18	131	62	47	10.9	7.3
West Germany	16	24	227	109	48	14.2	9.4
Liverpool	16	20	180	88	49	11.3	9.0
Total	109	202	1,448	680	47	13.3	7.2

World Cup Final matches 1966-1986

Twelve teams	6	27	159	77	48.4	13.3	1:5.9

The importance of Direct Play

	Total Matches	Total Shots	Shots from Five passes or less No.	Shots from Five passes or less %	Shots from Six passes or more No.	Shots from Six passes or more %
Argentina	12	164	146	92	20	12
Brazil	10	186	134	72	52	28
England	29	371	315	85	56	15
England U-21	3	46	43	93	3	7
England U-16	4	59	59	100	0	–
Holland	7	84	76	90	8	10
Italy	12	131	118	90	13	10
West Germany	16	227	189	83	38	17
Liverpool	16	180	156	87	24	13
Total	109	1,448	1,234	85	214	15

World Cup Final matches 1966-1986

Twelve teams	6	159	146	91.8	13	8.2

Index

Author's acknowledgements

This book has been written in conjunction with the production of a series of coaching video films of the same title. The video films have been a joint production between The Football Association and CBS/Fox Video Limited.

I wish to place on record, therefore, my grateful thanks to Roy Deverell, the Producer of the series of coaching videos, and David Head, the Editor. I also take this opportunity of thanking Stephen Moore, the Managing Director of CBS/Fox Video Limited.

The production of this book has involved the co-ordinated efforts of a large number of staff associated directly or indirectly with William Collins, the publishers. They have each played an invaluable part and it is with pleasure that I record their names, together with my deep appreciation of their skills: Chris Atkinson, Ron Callow, Alan Gooch, Ray Granger, Michael Johnstone, Michael Kirby, Rick Morris, Tony Palmer, Tony Potter, Mandy Sherliker and Vanessa Wood.

I am also especially grateful to Bob Thomas, who has provided the photographs, some taken specially for the production, others selected from his vast library of photographs.

To Mike Kelly, I record a special note of thanks for his advice and guidance in relation to the chapter on Goalkeeping. Arguably, Mike Kelly is the best coach of goalkeepers in the world.

The book is sponsored by British Aerospace with whom The Football Association is developing a very special partnership. I am grateful to R. H. Evans CBE, the Chief Executive of British Aerospace Defence Companies, for his message of support and to Mike Bonney, the Director of British Aerospace – Sport and Leisure Development, with whom I have worked very closely in helping to forge links between our two companies.

As ever, I am indebted to my wife for her encouragement and her consistent and unselfish support of all my work.

It is appropriate that my final record of appreciation is to Mandy Primus, my Personal Assistant. Her commitment to the whole project has been total and her contribution invaluable. Mandy recorded hundreds of matches in shorthand, assisted with the analysis of the data, helped to select all the match clips, and typed both the commentaries and the book – if only she could coach!! I hope, and believe, that the attitude and work of Mandy Primus is epitomized in these productions – sustained excellence.